Advance Praise for *Suffer and Grow* Strong

Ella Gertrude Clanton Thomas's journals have long been an indispensable source for anyone seeking to understand the nineteenth-century South and Southern white women's experiences. Yet surprisingly, Thomas has never been the subject of a full-length biography. Carolyn Curry's welcome new book carefully documents Thomas's life story and puts her journals into an intriguingly fresh context.

> —Michele Gillespie,
> Presidential Professor of History,
> Wake Forest University

Suffer and Grow Strong is a remarkable biography by Carolyn Curry that is destined to become a classic in women's studies. It tells the story of the redoubtable Ella Gertrude Thomas, who kept a vivid record of her life for forty-one years. Her courage and resilience during and after the Civil War are reminiscent of Scarlett O'Hara. History has been a great silencer of women, but *Suffer and Grow Strong* tells the tale of a white Southern woman who endures the whirlwind of the war and the deprivations of Reconstruction, then fought hard enough for women's rights that my grandmother was eligible to cast her first vote in 1920. This book is a great achievement for Carolyn Curry.

> —Pat Conroy

In her role as unlikely feminist and a leader of the suffrage movement, Ella Gertrude Thomas could be the fictional heroine of a rip-roaring historical novel. Instead, Carolyn Curry brings to life a real woman whose courage and endurance is truly inspirational.

> —Cassandra King,
> *The Sunday Wife*

Suffer and Grow Strong is a fascinating story of a remarkable Southern woman. Carolyn Curry ably brings Gertrude Thomas to life through extensive research and explores Thomas's steel-willed determination to triumph over wartime dislocations and postwar deprivation, her spirited intellect and devotion to her family, and her passionate support of women's rights—important and elegantly written contribution to Southern women's history.

—Kathryn Fuller-Seeley,
Professor, University of Texas, Austin

As enjoyable as it is educational, Carolyn Curry's *Suffer and Grow Strong* utilizes journals and contemporary newspapers to vividly recreate the life of one of Georgia's earliest "feminists." In doing so, she teaches us about a more domestic Civil War, viewed through the experiences of the women left behind.

—Morna Gerrard,
Women and Gender Collections Archivist,
Special Collections, and Archives,
Georgia State University Library

Carolyn Curry's *Suffer and Grow Strong* is a masterfully researched and written story of a remarkable woman, whose journals recorded soul and spirit and engaging insight into the exploding of history that both illuminated and scarred nineteenth-century America. Carolyn Curry has captured the quintessence of both character and period, and the result is a mesmerizing reading experience.

—Terry Kay,
To Dance with the White Dog,
The Book of Marie

Suffer and *Grow* Strong

The Life of Ella Gertrude Clanton Thomas, 1834–1907

Carolyn Newton Curry

Carolyn Curry

April 15, 2015

Mercer University Press

Macon, Georgia

MUP/ H881

Published by Mercer University Press, Macon, Georgia 31207
© 2014 by Mercer University Press
1400 Coleman Avenue
Macon, Georgia 31207

9 8 7 6 5 4 3 2

Books published by Mercer University Press are printed on
acid-free paper that meets the requirements of the American
National Standard for Information Sciences—Permanence of
Paper for Printed Library Materials.

Library of Congress Cataloging-in-Publication Data

Curry, Carolyn Newton.
  Suffer and grow strong : the life of Ella Gertrude Clanton Thomas, 1834-1907 /
Carolyn Newton Curry.
      pages cm
  Includes bibliographical references and index.
  ISBN-13: 978-0-88146-474-0 (hardback : alk. paper)
  ISBN-10: 0-88146-474-0 (hardback : alk. paper)
  1. Thomas, Ella Gertrude Clanton. 2. Women--Georgia--Augusta--Biography.
  3. Women--Georgia--History--19th century. 4. Suffragists--Georgia--Biography.
  5. Augusta (Ga.)--Biography. I. Title.
  F294.A9C94 2014
  975.8'03092--dc23
  [B]
                                        2013045551

For my husband, Bill

With love and gratitude

MERCER
UNIVERSITY PRESS

Endowed by
TOM WATSON BROWN
and
THE WATSON-BROWN FOUNDATION, INC.

Contents

Suffer and *Grow* Strong

Introduction

I have been intrigued with the life of Ella Gertrude Clanton Thomas for more than thirty years. I have researched her life, written her life story for my doctoral dissertation, given speeches about her, and talked about her so often that my children used to tell people "she lives" at our house. It has been a long, fascinating journey that I want to share.

I was in graduate school in the late 1970s and early 1980s—a wife, a mother, and a teacher—looking for a dissertation topic that would hold my interest for several years. Like many women of that era, I was interested in the women's movement. At the time there were no women's studies courses or women's history classes, and in every course I took I found myself asking, "Where are the women?" So often they were simply left out. If a woman was mentioned it was either in connection to her husband—who was the president of the United States—or her name was Pocahontas. I remember there was usually a single line that read "Women were given the vote in 1920." I was very frustrated.

While searching for that all important dissertation topic, I went to hear a lecture by Anne Firor Scott of Duke University about her book, *The Southern Lady: From Pedestal to Politics 1830–1930*.[1] I scribbled notes all over my program and left that night determined to find an interesting Southern woman of the nineteenth century to study. My adviser at Georgia State University, Dr. John Matthews, recommended that I go to Duke and look at the diary of Ella Gertrude Clanton Thomas. He told me she was a Georgia woman who had kept a diary for forty-one years before, during, and after the Civil War, and he thought I might be interested.

I immediately took his advice. At that time, the diary was not particularly well known, and very little had been done with it. In 1973, Professor Mary Elizabeth Massey of Winthrop College in South Carolina had written an article about Gertrude and the diary for the *Journal of Southern History* titled, "The Making of a Feminist."[2] Massey had also arranged for a typist to make a copy of Gertrude's original diary, which was somewhat difficult to read. Housed in the Manuscript Department of the William R. Perkins Library at Duke University, the diary was divided into thirteen volumes and contained 450,000 words. Gertrude simply divided them by dates and the length of the notebooks she happened to be using. She started the diary in 1848 when she was fourteen years of age and kept it off and on until 1889. I was able to secure a copy of that typed manuscript.

One of the librarians at Duke suggested that I look up Gertrude Threlkeld Despeaux, a great-granddaughter of Gertrude, who lived in my hometown of Atlanta. She graciously received me into her home, and we spent many afternoons in the fall of 1985 and the spring of 1986 discussing her great-grandmother and her diary. Fortunately, she had in her possession fifteen scrapbooks that Gertrude had kept in the years after she stopped keeping the diary. They were filled mostly with newspaper clippings that Gertrude had written for the *Augusta Chronicle* and other newspapers. Some contained reports of meetings, others described conventions she had attended, and some were editorial comments. Some of the articles were dated, and the newspaper in which they appeared was evident. Unfortunately, that was not true in all cases. However, after much careful study and weeks of detective work, these scrapbooks became a valuable source of information.

After reading the diary and studying the scrapbooks, I knew
that Ella Gertrude Clanton Thomas was the woman I wanted to
study. She was born in Augusta, Georgia, in 1834, to one of the
wealthiest families in the state. She was an intelligent,
inquisitive girl, who grew up in the antebellum, plantation
aristocracy with all the privileges money could buy, including
clothes, travel, and numerous slaves to take care of her every
need. She graduated from Wesleyan Female College in 1851
and married her Princeton-educated husband in 1852. But with
the coming of the Civil War and its aftermath, her life changed
forever. She experienced loss of wealth, bankruptcy, serious
illness, loved ones dying, and devastating family strife. She
gave birth to ten children and saw four of them die. But,
through it all, she kept pouring her thoughts into her diary. She
examined what was happening and asked questions. She
worked to help her family's dire economic circumstances, by
starting a school in her home and later by running a boarding
house out of the old family mansion. Late in life she moved to
Atlanta and became active in many women's organizations,
finding comfort in her work on behalf of women in the
Women's Christian Temperance Union and the Suffrage
Movement. In 1899, when it was still considered inappropriate
and even radical by many, she was elected president of the
Georgia Woman Suffrage Association the first time they met in
convention. Her life was an amazing story of strength and
survival.

Yet, after reading the diary and studying the scrapbooks, I
knew there was something else I needed to do. I had learned
the general outline of the litigation Gertrude and her husband
faced as they tried to recover from the war, and I realized that I
needed to go to Augusta, Georgia, and spend time looking at
the Minutes of the Superior Court of Richmond County, as well
as other legal documents such as deeds and wills. Again, I was

fortunate to have a close family friend, Sara Brown, who lived in Augusta and who provided lodging, meals, and great enthusiasm for my project.

The court records provided valuable information about Gertrude's family, who had been instrumental in building the city of Augusta before the war. Her father, Turner Clanton, amassed thousands of acres of land and owned numerous city lots containing warehouses to store his cotton. With the labor provided by hundreds of slaves and an excellent mind for business, Turner Clanton worked to ensure the wealth of his family through trust accounts for generations to come. Unfortunately, the war interrupted his plans. The legal and financial history of the rise and fall of Gertrude's family becomes important to the telling of her story.

With these three sources—the diary, the scrapbooks, and the court records—along with interviews with family members and secondary sources about Augusta and the Civil War, I set to work. It took me a couple more years, but I finished my dissertation and graduated in 1987. My life then went in a new direction after my husband's job took our family to another state. I was soon busy working in historical preservation, and, in the last ten years, I have been running a non-profit organization I started for women in Atlanta, Georgia. Even when an early opportunity arose, I did not pursue publication, but my interest in Gertrude's life never waned.

In 1990, another great-granddaughter of Gertrude, Virginia Ingraham Burr, published an abridged, edited version of the diary, *The Secret Eye: The Journal of Ella Gertrude Clanton Thomas, 1848–1889.*[3] The diary then became available to a much wider audience and has been quoted by historians since that date. However, no one has ever written her life story in full. Occasionally, I would think I should get back to work and publish her biography, but something else in my busy life always stopped me. A well-known historian once told me, "Put it on the back burner, and when the time is right, you will come back to it." That time came in September 2011 when I was asked to give a convocation address at Gertrude's alma mater, Wesleyan College in Macon, Georgia—the first college in America established solely for women in 1836. They were celebrating their 175th anniversary. Gertrude had been among the first one hundred or so graduates of the college and described her years there in her diary. On that day there was such interest in Gertrude and her story that I made up my mind to pursue publication.

Now, after all these years, I am again caught up in the story of this amazing woman's life. How many women live through a war with an invading army at their door and leave a written record of it for people to read more than a hundred years later? As one commentator has said, she was a real Scarlett O'Hara. I would add that she had the same grit and determination of the fictional Scarlett, but Gertrude had a true moral compass. In the face of one horrific event after another, she was always looking for that which would give meaning to her life. There is real historic value in her description of the people, events, and changes that occurred in her life. But many of the questions Gertrude asked and issues she pondered are still asked by women today. I know she has made me think about my life. Maybe she does "live at my house." I know she has had an impact on me, and I believe she will have that same impact on other women—and maybe some men, too.

1

Home

"Charming country homes…earnest family groups."
Augusta, Georgia

Ella Gertrude Clanton was born in 1834 in Columbia County outside Augusta, Georgia, a small, yet thriving, community at the head of navigation on the Savannah River, 125 miles from the coast. She lived in and around that city—either in the town home on Greene Street or on one of the family plantations—until 1893, when she moved to Atlanta. Her life and the lives of all her family members were intimately entwined with that Southern city and its history. Her father, Turner Clanton, helped to build Augusta into one of the most prosperous cities in the South while also making himself one of the wealthiest men in the state of Georgia. Before the Civil War, Gertrude's family and the city of Augusta had both risen to great heights on the backs of slave laborers and the plantation system, only to fall into ruin after the loss of the war.

Culturally and economically Augusta shared with its neighboring cities of Charleston and Savannah a rich and colorful heritage. Its history reached back to the very beginning of Georgia when James Oglethorpe realized its advantageous geography, the value of the fur trade, and the friendship of the Indians in the interior of the colony. He asked surveyor Noble Jones to lay out a blueprint for the city similar to the one for Savannah, comprising forty lots of one acre each with a square in the center and with public buildings on each end. In an effort to pay tribute to the future British monarch, who had recently wed in the spring of 1736, Oglethorpe named the new settlement Augusta, in honor of Princess Augusta of Saxe-Gotha, wife of Frederick, the Prince of Wales.[4]

Unlike the rest of Georgia, Augusta prospered from the beginning, enjoying both a lucrative fur trade and fertile soil for farming. Two kinds of settlers, very different in makeup, began to drift into Georgia: unscrupulous, bad-mannered fur traders and the more dignified, Virginia country gentlemen. The rowdy fur traders were called crackers, perhaps because they drove their cattle ahead of them cracking their whips, but for whatever reason, the name was not meant to be complimentary. The more civilizing element was the Virginians, who were better educated and more affluent than the fur traders. They brought their families, slaves, and genteel aspirations. In Virginia they had imitated the code of conduct of upper class Englishmen, seeing themselves as men of honor, benevolent masters, and moderate in all things. Their manners would soon be imitated in Georgia by men who likewise aspired to join the aristocratic, planter class. The Virginians lived as they had at home; they established the plantation system, and they introduced an important new crop—tobacco.

In the eighteenth century Augusta grew less primitive and became the principal market for tobacco and a supply center for the needs of the settlers. The Savannah River gave Augusta such transportation advantages that it was able to maintain its supremacy as a market for tobacco until the end of the century. Because of its strategic location, the area saw considerable fighting during the Revolutionary War. In January 1779 it was captured and occupied by the British for more than a year and recaptured in June 1781 by troops under the command of Major General Nathanael Greene. It was he who masterminded the operation to save the South. In appreciation, Augusta named its most beautiful street in his honor. Greene Street would later be the site of the Clanton Mansion.

During the late eighteenth and early nineteenth centuries an important economic development began that would have a dramatic impact on Augusta and the Clanton family—the cultivation of what would come to be known as King Cotton. The Virginia gentry had already introduced the plantation system, with large tracts of land cultivated by slave labor, and the stage was set for rapid growth. Short-staple cotton was well suited to the loam-covered clay of the lower Piedmont area around Augusta. Rainfall, which gradually increased from the spring to midsummer and then decreased through fall, was just right to leave dry bolls for picking before cold weather. Planters knew they could grow cotton and could sell it, but the process of separating the seeds from the lint was long and tedious. Many of them were looking for a remedy to this problem, when a young visitor from New England, Eli Whitney, came up with a solution—the cotton gin—while on Nathanael Greene's plantation near Savannah.

The results of Whitney's invention were dramatic. Between 1790 and 1800, cotton production in the United States grew from 3,000 to 73,000 bales, and Augusta was one of the trading centers that benefited greatly.[5] Growers from the Georgia Piedmont and South Carolina took their cotton to the factors in Augusta, who sold it on consignment and provided planters with credit and supplies. The section of shops and warehouses nearest the river was frequently choked with wagons loaded with cotton. Reynolds Street was lined with piled bales of cotton awaiting shipment down the river to Savannah or transportation to Charleston to be shipped to Europe and the North. The cotton gin and slave labor had made upland cotton the new staple of the back-country and had relegated tobacco to second place.

Before the development of the cotton gin, there was some sentiment held over from the Revolution that questioned the validity of enslaving other human beings, and the value of slaves had begun to decrease. All of that was to change, however, with the new prosperity that cotton cultivation brought to the South. Augusta's economy thrived on the cotton trade. In 1858, planters in middle and northwest Georgia sent almost 22,000 bales of cotton on the Georgia Railroad to Augusta in February and more than 34,000 bales in March. By the fall of that year cotton was arriving at a rate of 50,000 bales per month.[6] The wealth generated by this cotton trade had ensured the continued dependence on slave labor, and most whites—including Turner Clanton—accepted it without question.

Despite slavery being attacked in the North by abolitionists, the institution would remain strong until the Civil War. It was defended as a "positive good," both for slaves and free men. On 2 July 1859, Alexander Stephens, the popular congressman from Georgia's Eighth District, spoke to a large crowd in City Hall Park in Augusta. He reported that great disputes over slavery had subsided and the South had won. African slavery had not been weakened by the assaults on it but was, on the contrary, "greatly strengthened and fortified." Reinforcing a familiar argument, Stephens pointed out that, true to nature's law and God's law, slavery was "the normal condition of the negro.... If our system is not the best, or cannot be made the best for both races, it is wrong." But Stephens insisted it was the best and the South was "fulfilling a great mission in advancing a new order and a higher type of Christian civilization."[7] Gertrude, her family, and Southern slaveholders in general, were mostly devout, church-going Christians and believed that slavery was condoned by the Bible.

The inhabitants of Augusta and the region prospered as the cotton economy of the Georgia plantation belt matured. Farmers and planters also grew corn and other food products, but cotton maintained its hold because of the prices it would bring in distant markets. The city had benefited from its strategic position on the river to such an extent that it was the second largest inland cotton market in the world.[8]

By the decade before the Civil War, Augusta had become one of the Southern cities that European travelers tried to include in their itineraries. In 1850 the Swedish journalist Fredrika Bremer visited Augusta and noted its hot climate, red clay, and friendly people. She was most impressed with the splendid live-oak trees, with their delicately cut oval leaves, and heard the "hundred-tongued birds" singing in the huge branches. Even though it was "less great, less beautiful and smaller in every way," she compared Augusta very favorably to Savannah. She visited in several "charming country homes and gardens" and enjoyed meeting "earnest family groups." But she was very much bothered by the slave market, where she saw "forty or fifty young persons of both sexes...walking up and down before the house in expectation of purchasers. They were singing; they seemed cheerful and thoughtless....What heathenism in the midst of a Christian land." She did find, however, that many people she met regarded slavery as an evil and believed in gradual emancipation and colonization in Africa. That may or may not have been the majority view, but Augustans were beginning to have to face the issue, as was the rest of the South.[9]

In 1856 the well-known British writer William Makepeace Thackeray was the guest speaker at the Young Men's Library Association of Augusta. He was not as favorably impressed as Fredrika Bremer had been, saying Augusta was a "queer, little, rustic city" with "a happy dirty tranquility generally prevalent." Nevertheless, he also admired the huge oak trees, the charming shops, the wide streets, and the balconied homes. He made special mention of the cows grazing on the commons and, as did most Europeans, he commented on the many slaves he saw walking about on the sidewalks.[10]

By 1860 Augusta had grown to cover fifteen city blocks. Along the riverfront there were a number of wharves for nearby warehouses and the stately private residences on Bay Street. The business section of town, confined primarily to three blocks on Broad Street from Center to Campbell streets, had a charm of its own. The two- and three-story brick and wooden buildings had iron-railed balconies and dormer windows on the roofs. Most of the business establishments faced Broad Street, a wide thoroughfare running the entire length of the city. Trees were planted along the sidewalks, and a few streets, such as Washington and Reynolds, were paved with cobblestones or Belgian blocks. There were even stone walkways across the streets that were especially beneficial to pedestrians during inclement weather.

Many of the older and more affluent residents of Augusta lived on Bay Street on choice lots that faced the river. Others lived on lower Broad, on Telfair, and on Greene Street, which was home to both the splendid City Hall and old wooden City Hospital. It was on historic Greene Street that Gertrude's father, Turner Clanton, built the family mansion.

On her visit to Augusta from South Carolina, to see her beau at the Medical College there, Mary Moragne wrote in her diary of the "most beautiful private houses surrounded by evergreens and gardens tastefully laid off in parterres of flowers." She was impressed by ladies "attired in richest silks or satins with leghorn hats" and described Greene Street by writing that the grass looked "like a verdant carpet over its broad smooth expanse."[11] In fact, Greene Street gained a reputation before the Civil War for being one of the most handsome streets in the country.

The Clanton mansion was a magnificent brick structure built in the Greek Revival style so popular in the antebellum South. Huge Doric columns surrounded the front portico of the three-story, twenty-four room house built with bricks imported from England. To add to its elegance, it had solid-silver hardware and doorknobs, and ornate wrought-iron fencing ran between the lawn and the street. Upon completion, the house—which cost $50,000 to build—was opened for public viewing.[12] This imposing structure befitted Turner Clanton, a planter and businessman, who had reached the pinnacle of his career.

By 1860 Turner Clanton was sixty-two years old and had spent the greater part of his life helping to build Augusta and the surrounding area while amassing his own fortune. By that year, Augusta, with a population of 12,493, was the second largest city in Georgia after Savannah, and the smallest of the 102 urban centers in the United States with a population of over 10,000. It had survived an economic depression by building a canal and railroads, and there were optimistic plans underway for the future. But as one historian stated, "The war hit Augusta's social and economic structure with such force that it shattered the constructive plans for progress and set the city back many years."[13] The families that had risen to success alongside the city would be shattered, too, with one of the most affected being Turner Clanton's. The life of his daughter, Ella Gertrude Clanton, would be changed forever.

2

Family, Wealth, and Privilege

"I think I am like my father."

In 1855 at the age of twenty-one, for the first time Gertrude thought about the death of Turner Clanton: "My father dead! I can scarcely conceive of anything more heart rending. Surely if ever in the heart of a daughter throbbed feelings of the most intense love mingled with feeling of the most intense admiration and pride my feelings must be of the most fervent kind."[14] Her father's brother, Nathaniel Holt Clanton, called Uncle Nat by Gertrude, had just died, and it caused her to think about her own father's death. She was overcome with emotion. Although she came from a large family, Gertrude had always been drawn to her father more than anyone else in her family, and, until this time, had thought very little about how his death would affect her. In fact, she had never had to contemplate many difficulties at all, being born, as she was, into a very large and privileged family—one that had risen rapidly to great wealth and ease.

When Gertrude was born on 4 April 1834, on one of the family plantations in Columbia County near Augusta, there was no indication that her life would be anything but charmed. Her parents were of the planter aristocracy and lived a life very few were privileged to enjoy. Her family roots on both her maternal and paternal sides were in Columbia County, northwest of Richmond County. Columbia County had been cut out of Richmond in 1790 and was twenty-five miles long and twenty miles wide, containing 500 square miles of the best cotton land in the state. Her ancestors had been part of the migration of settlers that had come down from Virginia, North Carolina, and Maryland, through South Carolina and into Columbia County intent on finding suitable land for farming, which they found in abundance.

Gertrude's mother, Mary Margaret Luke, was born in Columbia County in 1812 to Judge James Luke and Elizabeth Read Luke. Judge Luke owned a 700-acre plantation and divided his time between the plantation and judicial responsibilities. He served as a justice of the peace, sheriff, and also judge of the inferior court of the county. Dr. H. R. Casey, a longtime resident of the county, described Judge Luke as being active in the factional politics of the era, "firm in [his] political convictions...not a political aspirant, but made money by planting."[15]

The Lukes had two other children in addition to Mary, a son, William, and a second daughter, Elizabeth. Both William and Elizabeth married and settled in Columbia County. Elizabeth married James Lamkin, whose family had moved from Virginia. He rapidly accumulated property, owning at his death thousands of acres of land and 250 slaves. In 1845, at the age of sixty, he died, leaving Elizabeth a wealthy widow. She lived "on the Jones place on the Petersburg Road, where her husband died and [was] the owner of some 5,000 or 6,000 acres of land."[16] The Lamkins had four children: Robert, James, Emma, and Mary Lizzie. Unlike the Luke daughters, William Luke did not enjoy a long life. Like his father, he was active in politics but made his living from planting, and he died a relatively young man having already acquired large tracts of land. At his death he left two plantations, which were to be divided between his wife Rebecca and his daughter Sara.[17] Thus, all of Mary Clanton's family—her father, brother, and sister—were affluent landowners, well entrenched in the county.

Judge James Luke died 26 August 1841, and was survived by his wife and children. There is no record of his will, but there is one for Elizabeth Luke, who died 24 November 1848. She had joined Kiobee Baptist Church, the oldest Baptist Church in Georgia in April 1820 and remained an "orderly member until her death" at age seventy-seven.[18] She left the 700-acre tract of land on which she lived to her granddaughter Sara Luke, the daughter of the late William Luke. The rest of her estate, "real and personal including the crops of the plantation," was to be divided between Elizabeth Lamkin and Mary Clanton.[19] Just how much Mary Clanton inherited is difficult to say. In the will Turner Clanton wrote in 1861, however, he noted that his wife was "already possessed of a considerable separate estate derived from her mother."[20] One can be sure that Mary Luke Clanton came from a family with position and wealth, and she did not enter her marriage to Turner Clanton "empty-handed."

Whatever her station in life, the most important roles of a woman in the nineteenth century were those of wife and mother. Mary Clanton took those duties seriously and suffered the accompanying hardships. She married Turner Clanton while she was still in her teens and bore him at least eleven children, seven of which survived childhood. Two sons and one daughter were stillborn, and her daughter Victoria lived to the age of four years and ten months.[21] Anne was the oldest surviving daughter, born three years before Gertrude, and was always referred to in the diary as "Sis Anne." Following Gertrude's birth, after an interval of several years, three more daughters were born—Mary, Cora, and Catherine (Kate)—and two sons, James and Nathaniel Holt. Mary must have been a strong woman physically to have survived so many pregnancies in a time when obstetrical care was, at best, limited. Moreover, the frequency of children dying did not diminish the tragedy, and, like most women of her times, she must have suffered considerable mental and emotional anguish.

During Gertrude's adolescent years, her mother was busy with her domestic responsibilities. A plantation mistress, often called a Southern Lady, would be expected to manage the household, attend to illnesses of both family members and slaves, while giving birth frequently and appearing to be a "lady of leisure." Even though her mother was a constant presence in Gertrude's life, she was a quiet presence. Mary took her daughter on frequent visits to family and friends, and on shopping excursions for clothes. She also accompanied Gertrude to church and attempted to pass on to her the expected domestic skills. Gertrude, however, paid no attention to these activities and, in fact, seemed to take her mother and the things she did for granted.

This attitude was demonstrated in 1848, the first year of the diary and a very difficult year for Gertrude's mother. Mary Clanton had four healthy children, but had lost two daughters, one as recently as 1846. Now during the fall of 1848, baby Cora was frequently sick. To add to this anxiety, Mary's mother was seriously ill and died in November. Mary continued all of her regular activities of managing the household, while going out to see her mother in Columbia County as often as she could. During this time, Gertrude did not express any particular concern for her mother or even seem to be aware of the stress she was experiencing. There were no statements of love or affection for her. Some of this may have been adolescent insensitivity; nevertheless, one cannot help but notice the lack of feeling for her mother. Later in her life, Gertrude would be more expressive about her feelings for her mother, but the person she loved and admired most at this early stage—the idol of her childhood—was her father Turner Clanton.

Who was this man often spoken of as one of the wealthiest men in Georgia before the Civil War? How could he be so immensely successful and still have the time and sensitivity to endear his child so strongly to him? What impact did he have on his daughter to shape her thinking in the future? It is a long and interesting examination.

Turner Clanton was born in Mecklenburg County, Virginia, in 1798 to Holt and Catherine Newsome Clanton. That same year, the family moved to Columbia County and bought a farm on the Petersburg Road about eight miles from Augusta. Holt Clanton was a man of "slender means," but had brought with him from Virginia the ideal of the plantation system and the aspiration to establish for his family a genteel way of life. Holt could not afford to give his children more than a limited education, which could be obtained in the "old field schools," but Turner developed traits early in life that marked him as a good businessman. Not only was he intelligent, but he also was impressive in his personal appearance. Dr. Casey wrote, "Physically he was one of the best men in the county, standing six feet, four inches with no surplus flesh, and weighing about 250 pounds. He was one of the best looking men in the county…[with] regular and abstemious habits of living. He did not use tobacco in any form, and I do not think I ever saw him touch the intoxicating bowl." [22] His appearance and personal habits obviously helped to draw people to him.

As early as 1803, records of deeds for Columbia County show Turner's father Holt Clanton had begun systematically acquiring property. In that year he agreed to purchase from one Jephemiah Athey a tract of land on Savage Creek containing 100 acres at a price of $400. [23] In subsequent records, Savage Creek (also spelled Savidge's Creek)—a tributary of the

Savannah River in the southeast portion of the county—was used to designate where he lived. He soon began adding to that land by buying 26.5 acres from George Dent for $172 and 100 acres from Marmaduke Ricketson for $150.[24] Both of these additional parcels of land were in the Savage Creek area.[25] By his death in 1829, Holt Clanton had achieved his goal of amassing large parcels of land suitable for the cultivation of cotton, which had become so profitable in the Piedmont region of Georgia.

In his will, Holt Clanton left all his real and personal possessions to his wife, Catherine. After her death the estate was to be divided among their four daughters and four sons. Turner Clanton's three brothers were Littlebury, who died in 1828 leaving a wife but no children; James, who moved to Louisiana, vanishing from any later family records; and Nathaniel Holt, who before he died in 1855, remained in close touch with Turner and his family.[26] The four daughters were Tabitha, wife of Isaac Anthony; Catherine, wife of Benjamin Paul; Polly, wife of Harmony Lamar; and one unmarried daughter, Elizabeth McKey Clanton. Holt named particular slaves who were to go to his daughters after his wife's death. He also named a group of eleven slaves who were to be divided by his sons. All the land was bequeathed to his sons and was to be divided later; his daughters inherited only some slaves. Turner Clanton, thus, was to inherit land and slaves from his father's estate. Just how many slaves there were at his mother's death or how much land is difficult to determine. Since Littlebury had died and James had left Georgia, relinquishing his share of the land, the remaining two brothers, Holt and Turner, benefited most from their father's property.

Some accounts indicate that Turner Clanton was married earlier to a Miss Clayton, who died childless.[27] It is certain, however, that by 1830, he had married Mary Luke, although they had not yet had children. In this year she would have been eighteen and he would have been thirty-two. Even though they were just setting up their household, the census of 1830 indicates that they already owned fifty-one slaves, some of whom may have come to the marriage with Mary.[28]

By 1830 Turner Clanton had begun buying land in his own name and purchased 720 acres from the estate of John Campbell.[29] His name then appeared regularly on deeds, as he was involved in the buying and selling of land and slaves. The census of 1840 shows him still living in Columbia County, and by 1846 he owned the large sum of 4,959 acres of what was referred to, for tax purposes, as second quality land and 2,509 acres of third quality land. The number of slaves had gradually been increasing until he now owned 197. He also had title to land lots in other counties that he had drawn in the state land lotteries, but his most profitable plantations would always remain in Columbia County.[30]

By the middle of the nineteenth century, Turner Clanton had achieved what his father had envisioned when he moved to Georgia. Clanton was a gentleman-planter enjoying the benefits that came from land ownership and slave labor on a large scale. In 1850 he owned 2,000 acres of improved land on which he produced 1,800 bushels of Indian corn, 1,000 bushels of beans, and 216 bales of cotton weighing 400 pounds each. He had 200 pigs and 238 sheep. By 1860, his improved acreage amounted to 3,200 acres. His corn production was up to 5,200 bushels and his ginned cotton was up to 721 bales. The agricultural census for 1860 lists a number of other items including 21,630 bushels of grass seed and 1,250 pounds of butter. Cotton was his primary product, as it was throughout the area, but he was not tied solely to that one commodity.[31]

Although Turner Clanton had roots in Columbia County and had been very successful there, as early as 1835 he made the decision to extend his real estate interests to Richmond County and the city of Augusta. Since whatever he produced had to be sent to Augusta for shipping, it is likely that he realized the advantage of living in a marketing and transportation center. The first purchase he made in Augusta was a lot on Broad Street in what was to become the business section of town. For this advantageous portion of land he paid John W. Weaver $500. By 1841 he must have decided that he would eventually move his growing family to the city of Augusta because he purchased the future site of the family home on the corner of Greene and Center Streets. The lot had 130 feet on Center and 160 feet on Greene and was bounded on the west by the lot of John Phinizy. It was purchased at public auction from the executors for the estate of the deceased Milton Anthony. Turner Clanton was the highest bidder and got the property for $2,900.[32] It was a considerable sum, but he must have felt it was worth the cost and worthy of his family's new prestige.

The new Clanton home was surely one of the finest—if not the finest—in Augusta at the time. The twenty-four-room, Greek Revival, brick mansion with its massive columns would have taken years to build. There must have been great anticipation when the family finally moved from Columbia County into the city of Augusta, which family tradition says was 1848.[33] The census of 1850, which was the first to list names and ages of family members, confirms that the Clantons were residing in Augusta by that year. Turner Clanton was fifty-one years of age, and his wife Mary was thirty-eight. They listed their children as Anne, nineteen years; Gertrude, sixteen years; Mary, nine years; James, seven years; Cora, four years; and Nathaniel, one year.[34] Also, Gertrude started her diary in 1848, and the family was already living at least part of the year in Augusta and part of the year on a plantation outside the city.

It had taken Turner Clanton years to amass the family fortune, but he was a very good businessman with interests in a wide range of ventures that he hoped would insure his family for years to come. In the census of 1850, Turner Clanton listed himself as a planter and stated that his property in Richmond County, which was only a portion of his holdings, was worth $75,000. His business interests were much broader than simply those of a planter, however, and records show that he kept expanding after 1850. A number of people signed promissory notes for money he was lending them. In 1847 he had leased to Clarke Cook for five years "the store and cellar of the brick building on the corner of Broad and Washington Streets." Cook was to pay rent of $800 in quarterly payments.[35] He also backed Charles Hitchcock and Louis L. Ingalls, who were partners in the firm of Hitchcock and Ingalls, a construction company.[36] One Eliza Robinson was paying house rent on the Newton House and owed him back rent and interest, which came to a total of $4,090 in 1857.[37] When the City Directory of 1859 came out, it listed Turner Clanton having an office at 21 Ellis Street.[38] Other similar arrangements are too numerous to mention, but these few examples illustrate the extent to which he was involved in business dealings in Augusta. He owned a number of buildings in Augusta that he was either using himself or renting out to others for their businesses. He was even venturing into construction with Hitchcock and Ingalls. This diversity would suggest that Turner Clanton's interests would have a better chance of surviving a catastrophe or depression— or even a war—all events that were unseen during this prosperous time.

Unfortunately, the unforeseen event for the Clanton family would be the death of this powerful patriarch in the year 1864 at the relatively young age of sixty-six. It was a traumatic event for Gertrude, and she poured her grief into her diary. She and her entire family loved him very much and would miss his generous spirit. But what they would miss more than anything would be his business acumen and his unifying presence.

Even though the war was still raging at the time of his death, a study of his will shows the large amount of real and personal property he left to his family and the arrangements he was trying to make to secure their futures.[39] It contains an inventory of his property that was made in 1861.The value put on items seems high and indicates that probably they are estimated in inflated Confederate dollars. Despite this possibility, an idea can be gained of the size and extent of his holdings at the end of his life.

In the city of Augusta he listed the family dwelling on Greene Street with an estimated value of $100,000; the Burke House on Broad and Washington valued at $80,000; a warehouse lot on Reynolds valued at $40,000; the Newton House on Washington valued at $45,000; and, four one-half acre lots on the corner of Washington and Taylor valued at $25,000. In addition, he listed a plantation, Rowell Place, seven miles south of Augusta containing 2,209 acres and valued at $176,720. He listed, by name, age and value, thirty slaves attached to the Greene Street house and ninety-two attached to the Rowell Plantation. He also listed in his will a "Pew in the Presbyterian Church in Augusta known by the letter K" valued at $500, bringing his total for property in Augusta to $467,220.

The city property was only the beginning. He also gave an inventory of five additional plantations, four of which were in Columbia County and one in Dougherty County. The first of the Columbia County plantations was the Hicks Plantation, made up of 1,854 acres with land valued at $30 an acre. Along with fifty slaves, animals, and equipment, the estimated value came to $295,944. The second of the plantations was referred to as the Road Place. It was obviously the most undesirable, since its 1,954 acres were valued at only $15 an acre. With twenty-two slaves living on the land, and with various tools and animals, it was valued at $106,729. The Tubman Place on the Savannah River was made up on only 580 acres, but it was occupied by forty-three slaves and was valued at $40 an acre for a total of $166,924. The Cumming Place in the Old Mulberry District was the largest plantation Clanton owned in Columbia County, consisting of 2,350 acres and valued at $30 an acre. With its contingent of seventy-five slaves, and various animals and equipment, its total came to $461,240.

The Dougherty County Plantation was by far the largest and most distant, located in the recently opened southwest part of the state. It consisted of 3,157 acres, valued at $75 an acre, along with eighty-one slaves, animals, and equipment for a total of $742,499. At various times in his life, Turner Clanton had owned land in areas of Georgia located a long distance from Augusta; but, at the time of his death, his Dougherty County property was the only land that remained which was not in Richmond or Columbia Counties.

The fact that Turner Clanton owned 393 slaves is astounding when one considers that by 1860 only some 400,000 Southern white families owned slaves and when they did the number was usually small, with the majority of slaveholders owning five or fewer. Studies show that the number of slaveholding families had decreased from thirty-six percent in 1830, to thirty-one percent in 1850, to twenty-six percent in 1860. A planter family, by definition, owned twenty or more slaves.[40] The extremely large number of slaves owned by Turner Clanton in 1860 would have put him in a category all his own.

His real estate in the city of Augusta and on the six plantations—Rowell Plantation, Hicks Plantation, Road Place, Tubman Place, Cumming Place, and Dougherty Plantation—came to more than 12,000 acres of land and was worth

$2,240,556—a large sum in 1864. This did not include stocks and bonds and various other items he estimated to be worth $54,680. Even if these figures are given in inflated Confederate dollars, it is easy to understand why Turner Clanton was regarded as one of the wealthiest men in Georgia at the beginning of the Civil War.

How he planned to disburse this property to his family and how it was actually broken up and fought over after the war plays a very important role in the life of his daughter Gertrude. In the will, Turner Clanton provided generously for all of his children. The three oldest girls, Gertrude, Anne, and Mary, had already received "property upon trust, to the amount of twenty five thousand dollars" when they had married. He gave each of his three sons-in-law $5,000 "in his own right." The will also specified an additional $15,000 be given to each of the girls, bringing the total to $45,000. Each of the unmarried children was to receive $45,000, which would be held in trust for them.[41]

One of the most important things Turner Clanton did, establishing a trust for Gertrude a little over a year after her marriage to J. Jefferson Thomas on 6 January 1854, was discussed numerous times in the diary. In the trust document Turner Clanton gave Gertrude a total of twenty-three slaves, listed by name, age, and appraised value, which came to $23,290. But he provided that they be given "In Trust...that [the executors] shall hold the said Negro Slaves and the increase of the females, for the sole and separate use of the said Gertrude, during her natural life and that the same shall not be liable for the debts, contracts or liabilities of said Jefferson, or any after taken husband, and that upon the death of said Gertrude the same shall go to trust in the child or children of the said Gertrude..." The men selected by Clanton to administer the trust were Jefferson Thomas, Gertrude's husband; Jefferson's father, Joseph Thomas; Turner's son, James L. Clanton; and Thomas McMillan, all of Richmond County.[42]

It is worth noting that the $5,000 given to Gertrude's husband, J. Jefferson Thomas "in his own right" was made up of one cart, two wagons, two yoke of oxen, six mules, 400 bushels of corn and 4,000 pounds of fodder valued at $1,580, and $3,420 in cash. Obviously, he was trying to help his young son-in-law get started in the planting business. It may also imply that Jefferson did not have the sum himself and was asking for help. Either way, it was generous of Turner Clanton, who was doing what he could to get the young couple off to a good start.

Turner Clanton made a similar arrangement for Gertrude's sister, Mary, when she married Jefferson's brother Pinckney Thomas in 1860. Her inheritance was invested in twenty-nine slaves.[43] However, the trust set up for Anne when she married William Vason in 1859 was different. Family tradition says that because Vason was an attorney instead of a planter and was not a native Georgian, Turner Clanton gave his oldest daughter city lots in Augusta instead of slaves.[44] Since all the slaves were emancipated during the war, her inheritance became the more valuable one in the post-war years.

There are several meaningful implications that follow Turner Clanton's bequests. First, simply the large amount of property, real or personal, to be given each child was significant in 1861. Clanton was obviously attempting to help his offspring establish their homes and live according to the standard he had provided. Second, the male and female children were to be given the same amounts of property, which indicates that any sort of male favoritism was not a part of his thinking. Finally, and very significantly, he was trying to protect property for his daughters, separate from the "debts and liabilities" of their husbands. There is also present perhaps some distrust of his sons-in-laws and their abilities. Unfortunately, he would not live to see the final devastation of the war, nor would he be present to help get the family back on its feet, even if that had been possible.

There was wisdom in Turner Clanton's building separate estates for each of his daughters, but it was not a common practice at the time. The concept of allowing a separate estate to be established for a woman did not even appear on the statute books of Georgia until 1847. There were several ways such an estate might be created: by prenuptial agreement between the husband and wife; by postnuptial settlement, by which property was conveyed to a third person to hold for the wife; or by gift or legacy establishing the wife's sole ownership and disavowing her husband's claim.[45] Turner Clanton chose to make a postnuptial arrangement that did not allow Jefferson Thomas any claim to the property. Despite the fact that Jefferson Thomas was a trustee, he was one of several, and Clanton stated specifically that the trust was not to be liable in any way for his debts.

Under English common law that had been brought to America and taken root in the colonies, married women had virtually no property rights; but, under equity, an alternative system of justice that had developed over the centuries, loopholes emerged. Under equity, a married woman could acquire a separate estate and have control. This was her property over which a husband could not exercise his usual common-law rights. Like most individuals who established separate estates to secure property for women, Clanton was not trying to liberate his daughter or give her more independence. In that troubled economic era, when depressions were common, he was trying to protect her property from disaster at the hands of her husband or her husband's creditors.

It was well known that under common law that when a man became indebted, his creditors had the right to seize the wife's property as payment. However, as studies have shown, even when the separate estate was used in the nineteenth century, there was the potential for problems. Since the estates were used to protect property and not to free women, they were fertile ground for confusion, complications, and expensive litigation.[46] This was certainly the case in the trust deed that Turner Clanton established for Gertrude. It would be brought up repeatedly in court cases as a result of financial difficulties that developed after the Civil War. J. Jefferson Thomas incurred a number of debts he was not able to pay, and his creditors would go after the only thing they could—Gertrude's inheritance. In light of the great financial problems Gertrude's husband encountered, the provisions of Turner Clanton's trust appear wise, and almost prophetic.

It is impossible to know if things would have been better for the Clanton family had Turner Clanton lived longer. Would he have been debilitated the way so many other Confederate men were after the loss of the war? He had supported the war effort and would probably have taken a more active role if he had been a younger man. He received thanks from the Oglethorpe Infantry in Virginia for his generous gifts of food and money. In the diary Gertrude described one occasion when he gave between one and two thousand dollars to aid the soldiers' cause. He had served in the militia in Columbia County as a young man and had served in the House of Representatives in Milledgeville during the 1827 and 1831 terms. But he had eventually chosen business over politics and military service. From the evidence we have, Turner Clanton did not seem to be consumed by rabid hatred against the "Yankees," as was the case with so many Southerners.

When he died, the *Augusta Chronicle* ran a long obituary reciting his accomplishments but also revealing something of a personal nature, "Possessed of shining social qualities and a courteous demeanor, he was well calculated to draw around him troops of friends, to whom, and to his family, his loss is irreparable."[47] Another notice stated, "[S]o gentle and unobtrusive was his charity that the widows, the orphans, and the soldiers' families testify to his acts of kindness."[48]

One person who had nothing but good things to say about him was his daughter Gertrude. At every stage of her life she spoke regularly and fondly of her father. In her carefree youth she noted his comings and goings and reported when "Pa," as she called him, arrived or left, whether early or late. When she was away at school in Macon, she was excited to hear that her father had arrived for a visit. "How perfectly delighted I was! Down stairs I ran, and was welcomed by My Darling father."[49] Years later in 1870, after her father had died and her family was experiencing serious financial difficulties, she wished he were alive. "Pa! Pa! I thought if you were living this would not be so. You would help us with your good judgment, or cheer me with some kind word."[50] Throughout her life, he was the one person she treated with nothing but respect and genuine adoration. She wanted to be like him. She wrote in that same year at age thirty-six, "I think I am like my father in many things, in none more so than in my quiet indomitable pride—that pride which would make me suffer and make no sign."[51]

But, no matter how much she may have wished it not to be so, the truth was her father died and left the family adrift at the end of the war. The difficulties of defeat were multiplied by his absence. Gertrude's life and the lives of other family members were changed forever by the loss of this powerful man.

Fortunately, that long and difficult story can be studied today because, like many other young women of that day, something possessed Gertrude to begin keeping a diary in which she recorded her thoughts and daily activities. In its pages she would keep a running account of her life from 1848 to 1889. Her experience of wealth and leisure did not prepare her for the difficulties that would unfold before her, but she had an inner strength, a resilience, and intelligence that would serve her well.

3

Adolescence and Education

"To what end am I destined?"

Gertrude began the first entry in her journal by writing simply, "Rochester, September 29, 1848...I sent for this paper to form a journal. I will write what happened on Monday Tuesday & Wednesday." Unbeknownst to her, she would write "what happened" in her life off and on for the next forty-one years. At this time, she was only a fourteen-year-old girl living at the Clanton country home outside Augusta. She did not always punctuate or spell correctly, but her writing has a naïve, innocent quality about it that is very engaging. This first journal covers the period between 29 September 1848, and 6 February 1849—a time of transition in her life. At the beginning, she was a bored adolescent waiting for the summer to end; but by its conclusion, she had left her home and family to enter the Wesleyan Female College in Macon, Georgia.

Gertrude immediately revealed something of her literary interest and youthful romanticism by changing the name of their country home, usually known as Piney Woods. She put the new name she had chosen at the top of the page— Rochester.[52] She had just read Charlotte Bronte's novel *Jane Eyre*, published in 1847, and renamed their home after Jane's love interest in the novel, Mr. Rochester. She did not name the home Thornfield, after the grand estate in the novel, but Rochester after the man. She made no explanation, but one sees that the young girl was moved by Jane's great difficulties, her endurance and eventual reunion and marriage with this mysterious man. This brief mention—the very first word in the diary—gives a glance into the mind of this spirited, adolescent girl who loved to read.

The days Gertrude spent at the Columbia County home—Rochester—were happy and carefree. Her family followed the custom of affluent planters who moved their families in the hot summer months away from the city and the possibility of fevers and epidemics. She had no chores to perform, except at times organizing her room, a task she seemed to do by choice rather than necessity. As she described one day, "I can scarcely tell how today has been passed. I have done little or nothing but arrange my room and the contents of my port folio. I had so many things in the latter and they were in such hurly burly and disorder that it took me some time to arrange them."[53] All her needs were taken care of by a number of slaves, whom she referred to by first name in such a fashion that it is sometimes difficult to tell who was family, friend, or slave. Their efforts gave her ample time to pursue her many interests.

She usually began her day late. "This morning I indulged in my old habit of lying in bed late so I did not take breakfast until all the rest had partaken of theirs." In fact, almost every morning she slept late. Her frequent references to relatives and friends indicated there were always a number of people who slept and ate at their home. So many people to feed necessitated first and second sittings for meals. Even then her days were long, and she reported that sometimes she would take "a short nap before dinner which refreshed [her] a good deal."[54]

Gertrude filled her days by writing letters, taking walks and continually searching for things to read. Books and magazines were her consuming interest. When her father left to go into town, she would always ask him to bring back something for her to read. She was also constantly borrowing books and exchanging them with friends and relatives. Even at this early age, she began a habit she would continue throughout her life of listing what she had read and at times discussing it in her diary. Between September and December of 1848, she listed more than fifty books and magazines she had read during that short period of time. She absorbed the popular novels of the day, as well as those less well known, with such enticing titles as *The Breach of Promise, The Nun of St. Ursula* and *The Female Pirate Captain*. She also enjoyed *Godey's* and *Graham's* magazines and referred to particular serials, such as one about a woman named "Catherine Clayton," which ran for several months. In fact, she even included an incident that showed she would rather read than talk. "This evening Ma, Sis Anne and I went to Mrs. Wood's.... I was employed reading some magazines. Mrs. Wood says she intends hiding all her books when I go there to make me talk some."[55]

Gertrude was primarily interested in reading novels but did make an effort at more scholarly works. She studied "Robins out-line of English History" and read "a good deal in Onley's history."[56] Lamenting her likes and dislikes, she said, "I wish that it were possible for me to refrain from reading one [a novel] for six months or a year. I am confident I could study much better." Despite this tendency, she listed Shakespearean plays, some of which she may have read later at Wesleyan, such as *Romeo and Juliet, Anthony and Cleopatra, Macbeth, A Midsummer's Night Dream* and *Much Ado About Nothing*. Years later, when looking over this list, she concluded, "[All] these books I read when I was fourteen years old from the 25 of September to Christmas, I borrowed most of them, eagerly read anything and only regret that my reading had not been directed by someone."[57]

Curious and imaginative, Gertrude would while away the hours daydreaming, a pastime that brought her immense pleasure. After reading one day in October, she confessed, "I was indulging in the habit I have formed of building castles in the air. Oh how delightful it is and the persons that I dream of. Oh it is *very* delightful. But *then* when awakened by the cold realities of life." She was capable of entertaining herself for long periods. "Nothing of importance has occurred today. I have seen no new faces and have been nowhere. I have been in my room all day indulging in some of those delightful reveries." Her writing also became associated with her daydreaming. "I have been busy writing and indulging in my usual *day dreams*. Today they are connected with Josephine [presumably Napoleon's Josephine]." She enjoyed writing in the diary, and it became more and more important to her. "It comes just as natural for me [to] write in this journal as it does for me to eat a meal."[58] Reading, writing, and daydreaming became the things she enjoyed most at this point in her life.

It should not be assumed, however, that Gertrude did not share interests common to other fourteen-year-old girls. Existing portraits from later periods in her life show that she was attractive with dark eyes and brown, wavy hair that she often wore parted in the middle and pulled back from her face. She was concerned about her appearance and wanted to look nice. She very often described her clothes and those of other people. For one outing, she said, "I wore my *eternal tissue silk* and black silk cape." For an ordinary day at home she put on her "pink calico dress and black silk cape and then went down to breakfast." In the evening to go visiting, she wore her "pink muslin dress." Church provided the best opportunity to wear finery. On a Sunday in the fall, she wore her "embroidered dress and black lace cape while Sis Anne wore her black silk dress, Cousin Emily wore white while Cousin Eliza wore her green barashe dress."[59] Of course, there was frequent use of the important kid gloves. Occasionally she mentioned doing some kind of handwork on her clothes, such as sewing the ruffle of a gingham bonnet or putting the whale bones in her embroidered Swiss dress. The domestic art of sewing, however, was never a favorite pastime of hers.

Likewise, as is typical of young girls, she was concerned about her hair and worked at wearing different styles. Her diary records on more than one occasion her buying side combs "to fix the front part of my hair." Since she usually wore it smoothed back from her face, she talked of making "hair greese." Always eager to try something new, she confessed, "I came up and was busy fixing my hair. I first fixed it in the way I saw Virginia Warren wear hers. I did not like it. Took it down and plaited down my back in two plaits, and have worn it so all day but find it very unpleasant. Don't think I will wear it so again soon."[60]

Gertrude's thoughts about her physical appearance were naturally related to her interest in the opposite sex. Even though she was restrained in her comments, she did note the comings and goings of certain young men—particularly a Mr. Merriwether. In a most proper manner, she always referred to men by their last names, preceded by "Mr.," even her husband after they were married. Sometimes on her walks she would meet young men. On one occasion, after encountering Mr. Griffin, Mr. Baker, and Mr. Merriwether, she discussed whether or not they were handsome. She confessed to her diary that when they arrived at church on Sunday, Mr. Merriwether had helped her out of her buggy. On another Sunday, she recounted a visit after church from Mr. Merriwether and Mr. Griffin. She did her "best at entertaining Mr. Merriwether" alone until the other girls entered the parlor. "The gentlemen staid until dark. I was very pleasantly entertained myself."[61] Mr. Merriwether soon had opportunities to call more regularly because they began exchanging books. Late one night she was serenaded by a young gentleman playing the guitar—an event that must have been very exciting to an adolescent girl, even though she never identified the suitor. Although she never confessed to being enamored of anyone in particular, Gertrude carefully noted even chance encounters with young men.

As was typical of elite, young women in the nineteenth century, Gertrude did not have much contact with young men and when she did, it was guarded and chaperoned. Her friendships with females, however, were numerous, and she made a constant effort to keep in touch with them, sending letters and notes into Augusta with her father.[62] Mary Frazier, Martha Phinizy, Isabella Morrison, and Mildred Eve were some of her closest friends in Augusta. Martha Phinizy lived next door and Mildred Eve down the street, and they often took strolls together. There were a number of relatives: Cousin Bee Gardner, Cousin Amanda Lamkin, Cousin Eliza Anthony, and the ever-present Cousin Emily. There was an older woman she particularly liked—Mrs. Berry—who took an interest in Gertrude's love for reading and was always exchanging books with her. Her circle of female friends would broaden later, and she diligently kept up with all of them. In her diary she recorded their marriages, the births of their children, and, in some cases, their deaths.

Gertrude's circle of female friends also included her sisters. At this time, Cora was only a baby whose crying or fretting called her to her sister's attention. There was the occasional mention of her younger sister Mary, also called Mamie, who accompanied Gertrude and her friends on outings to gather walnuts and grapes or some other excursion. Sis Anne, older than Gertrude by three years, was mentioned more than any other sister. Of course, they were not far apart in age and would have been interested in many of the same things. Although it is difficult to know their exact relationship during this period, Gertrude described one incident when Anne was supposed to give her a book. "Sis Anne bought that book for me but will not give it to me as she has got mad with me." On another occasion when they were shopping with their mother, "Ma bought me a very pretty work box and Sis Anne one two. Hers is much the prettiest."[63] One cannot help but detect a degree of sibling rivalry, which is not unusual, but in light of their relationship as adults, one must wonder if these early incidents possess wider implications.

In 1848, even though Gertrude was fourteen and on the verge of becoming a young adult, she still had childlike, playful interests. She included mention of hunting for "muskadine," horseback riding, and staying so long gathering "hickrinuts" that she missed dinner and got a good scolding. One night a cousin brought over something for an experiment—ether. "Cousin Eliza took it and it had affect. Sis Anne took it afterward and so did I but it had no effect and then Sis Anne took it again and it made her cry."[64] Gertrude evidently decided she wanted to try ether again, because her cousin later brought her a bottle. When they were back in Augusta, she reported the circus came to town and she saw the parade, which included an elephant, a spectacle that must have been rare in that Southern town. Pa would later take her and some of her siblings to see the show.

The family moved back to town on 17 November 1848. Gertrude regretted leaving Rochester, that "dear, dear place" and noted that it had been "the scene…of some of my happiest hours. And this summer will be a remarkable epoch in my life." She did not know it then but these summer days were among the most relaxed, carefree days of her life.

The return to Augusta meant enrollment in school again and closer contact with her friends. She attended a school operated for young ladies conducted by the Baptist minister Mr. J. W. Hard who would later be a professor at Mercer University.[65] She entered in her diary a rather long list of subjects included in the curriculum: philosophy, rhetoric, arithmetic, spelling, ciphering, grammar, and geography. Just how devoted she was to her studies at this time is difficult to say, but she appeared to be lax. Oral recitation was required, and she reported, "Yesterday I said the Rhetoric lesson and did not know the Philosophy. Mr. Hard gave me a great deal of good advice which I trust may do some good." Lofty subjects were chosen for compositions, such as "virtue man's highest interest." In arithmetic she spoke of reviewing from "the first to addition [to] fractions."[66] Her training undoubtedly had some gaps in it, but she was fortunate to have as much as she did, since formal education for women was anything but universal in the Old South. Her family's wealth and position in society afforded Gertrude another privilege open to an even smaller number of girls in the first half of the nineteenth century—a college education.

As has been noted, Gertrude had a very special relationship with her father, who by all accounts was a generous man and certainly more sensitive than most fathers of that time to his daughters. He seemed to have taken a particular interest in Gertrude and recognized her intelligence and love of reading and writing. Fortunately for her, at some point he decided to go to Macon, Georgia, and investigate the new college for women that had been started in that Southern city in middle Georgia.

Chartered in 1836 to be the first degree-granting college expressly established for women in America, it was originally called the Georgia Female College and had been started by a group of Macon businessmen and leaders of the Georgia Conference of the Methodist Church. The severe depression of the late 1830s had almost ruined the lofty plans of its founders, but after the trustees announced reductions in tuition and the faculty accepted lower salaries, they had been able to keep the college open and attract students. During this difficult period, the Methodists became more involved in its management, and the name was changed in 1843 to the Wesleyan Female College in honor of the founder of Methodism, John Wesley.

To advocate for women's education in the 1830s was remarkable for the Methodists in Georgia. The majority of people still argued that women should remain silent and invisible outside the public domain and in the domestic sphere raising children and maintaining orderly households. Many ministers were still quoting the Apostle Paul's instructions in the King James Version of the Bible. First Corinthians 14:34–35 was very often repeated: "Let your women keep silence in the churches: but they are commanded to be under obedience, as also saith the law. And if they will learn any thing, let them ask their husbands at home: for it is a shame for women to speak in the church."[67] These and other Bible verses were being broadly interpreted as saying women's minds and emotions were not suited for business, politics, and—unfortunately—education. Even if this new women's college was being operated by ministers and emphasized religious training, it was still a door to a world that these young women had not entered before, and Gertrude was lucky enough to be one of the ones to go forth into the adventure.

From the beginning the founders wanted the school to offer a true collegiate education and for the courses to parallel those of the male Methodist counterpart in the state, Emory College in Oxford, Georgia. Since methods and standards of teaching in the state were so diverse, however, it was difficult for the school's officials to assess the preparation of applicants. Girls who were at least fourteen years old could be admitted to the freshman class, fifteen years of age to the sophomore class, sixteen years of age to the junior class, and seventeen years of age to the senior class. Despite the fact the trustees were forced to reduce the entrance requirements in the beginning, they were determined to keep standards high. Ornamental courses such as drawing, painting, and music were to be provided only when they did not interfere with the more serious work.[68]

The high moral tone of the first commencement address given by the first president, George Foster Pierce, on 16 July 1840, left no doubt as to what was expected of the new female graduates. Their education was to remove "scholastic restraints" and give "redemption from irksome duties and an introduction to social life," but there would be "sterner demands and more onerous duties." Their ambition ought to be "[high] and holy" and "...indefatigable and earnest your efforts for good..."[69] On this high note, the first women's college in America conferred degrees on its first graduates.

When Gertrude went to Macon in February of 1849 to enter the sophomore class, she was one of a very select group. Including the eleven graduates of 1840, a total of one hundred women had received diplomas. The average graduating class size was eleven, the largest class having had twenty and the smallest class having had six.[70] The college had always been plagued with criticism that the cost of tuition and board was prohibitive to many. At its inception the trustees had set the cost for a year at $250, which included tuition of $100. Parents had to furnish the dormitory rooms assigned to their daughters. In 1838 when the trustees began to advertise for students, they were forced to reduce the tuition first by $25 and then $50 and the cost of room and board from $150 to $120.[71] Furnishing one's own room became an option in 1850–51. Then the catalogue stated, "Heavy furniture supplied in the Institution if it be desired; but in every instance the young ladies must furnish their own napkins, bed linen etc. and the light and more perishable articles of furniture."[72] Laundry wood (or fuel) and candles (or lights) were listed as separate expenses. Of course, none of these expenses would have been a problem for Gertrude's father.

In January 1849, Gertrude gave a vivid account of her first trip to Macon on the train. Her father, who had found the college suitable for his daughter and had arranged for her to go, accompanied her. Gertrude's older sister Anne was also with them, but there was no explanation of why Anne was not entering the college. Perhaps she felt too old or did not have the same interest Gertrude did. For whatever reason, Gertrude was entering alone, and she was apprehensive. With mixed emotions, she recounted, "I was crying a good deal but the excitement of the ride on the cars soon engaged my attention." It was the first time she had been on the train since a trip to Charleston when she was a baby. She and Sis Anne were the only two women on the train for much of the way. Traveling in the night through Union Point, Greensborough, and Decatur, they had breakfast in Atlanta, changed trains, and left there about eleven o'clock in the morning. When they left Atlanta, Gertrude noted that it was snowing, an unusual occurrence for that city, which would have added to the excitement of the day. They stopped in Griffin and had their midday meal at Mr. Huson's Hotel and then went on to Macon, arriving late in the evening. By the time they arrived at Mr. Floyd's Hotel, she was too tired even to go downstairs for dinner, but went to bed anxious and excited about her first visit to the college the next day.[73]

As was her habit when she was very busy, Gertrude did not write in the diary for the first three weeks. But, when she resumed, she reported that at first she was unhappy. "I disliked the place, found the girls unsociable." It did not take long for her to have a complete change of heart, however, for by February 1, she wrote, "Oh how happy I am now... I believe I love *all* the girls. Oh my heart is much changed."[74] Part of this transformation resulted from her getting over a natural homesickness and becoming accustomed to a new place and new people. But she attributed part of her new attitude to her religious conversion, which occurred soon after her arrival.

Gertrude mentioned repeatedly how she arose early to attend prayers, and went to regular prayer meetings and services conducted by the professors, who were mostly Methodist ministers. After she had been at the school a few weeks, she reported, "On Monday evening downstairs in the chapel I was co[n]verted and made to feel how good God is. We have had prayer meeting every night since. Many of the girls have been converted... There has been a great out pouring of the spirit of God."[75] The evangelical movement was strong in early nineteenth-century Georgia, as was the interest in the expansion of Methodism among its clergy.[76]

This does not lessen the genuineness with which Gertrude and many of her friends embraced Christianity. She reiterated in April 1851, in her senior year at Wesleyan. "Yesterday I felt that although I had repented of my sins I was still unpardoned. In fact, I did not feel certain with reference to the state of my feelings. I doubted. Now Thank Heaven I feel certain of my acceptance with God. How delightful is the thought. How transporting! How rapturous. How divine what a change. Can I ever doubt the goodness of my God, of My Savior?"[77] Even though there would be later times in her life when she would question her faith, it was always of greatest importance to her, and she would look back to her days at Wesleyan as the time of her conversion to Methodism and true Christianity. Her faith would be an ongoing theme in her life, affecting many of her decisions and her attitude toward life.

After describing her arrival at Wesleyan and her conversion experience, Gertrude made only a few brief entries in her first volume, the last of which was dated 6 February 1849. Her second volume begins in April 1851 when she was in her last year of college. She spoke of a "journal I commenced the last day of [my] fifteenth year which I continued for some time."[78] That journal must have been lost, because at the beginning of her second volume, she was seventeen years old. It was in this second volume that she left a record of her days at Wesleyan.

Gertrude never gave an hour-by-hour description of a full day, but another student, Octavia Rush Andrew, who graduated in the class of 1852, left a vivid picture. She said the rules were rigid with the bell ringing at 6:00 a.m., which required the girls to be in chapel by 6:30 for morning roll call and prayers at 7:00. They had breakfast at 8:00 with recitation, as she called the classes, scheduled throughout the day at 9:00, 11:00, 2:00, and 4:00. They were not dismissed until after evening prayers at 5:00. After their evening meal, at 7:00 the bell rang and they were expected to study in their room until 10:00 with lights out at 10:30.[79]

Gertrude's diary confirms this rigorous routine of rising early, going to appointed classes and retiring early. The form of learning in vogue was recitation, whereby a young woman would learn her lesson and go to class prepared to present the material orally. "I attended Mr. Stone's recitation at two o'clock…. He has since Christmas been giving us 'Lectures on Natural Philosophy.' Now we study the book. He did not call on me." On another day, "I went to Dr. Ellison's recitation in astronomy and recited."[80] The regimen seems to indicate how serious the college was about the need for structure and discipline.

When one considers the disagreement among educators about what was proper for women to study, the subjects listed in the curriculum were very ambitious. In her study of the inception of Wesleyan, the historian Elizabeth P. Young stated, "The president and trustees of the institution took up the task of arranging a curriculum at a time when it was considered by some a profanation of the word college to connect with it the education of women."[81] As recently as 1835, the code of laws for Franklin College, later to become the University of Georgia, did not even allow women to be on the campus. The trustees of a school such as Wesleyan had to consider the diverse backgrounds of students who would be coming from church schools, home schools, or academies with no unified standards. They wanted to broaden and elevate the level of women's education and bring it as close as they could to that of men's colleges.

The earliest outline of the curriculum can be found in a pamphlet, "Circular of the Georgia Female College for the Session of 1842–43." Since very few changes were made in the forties, it would have been the curriculum in use when Gertrude was at Wesleyan. It listed in great detail what was to be undertaken each year, including arithmetic, grammar, geography, composition, algebra, history, biology, rhetoric, chemistry, and, of course, religion. Those courses traditionally associated with female education—music, languages, drawing, and painting—were only to be taught if the parent requested them.[82]

Throughout their years at Wesleyan, the girls worked very closely with their instructors and often developed lasting relationships with them and their families. In fact, faculty members lived in the dormitories with the students to ensure their security and supervise their progress. For astronomy, Gertrude had Dr. William H. Ellison, who served as president of the college from 1840 to 1851. He had been the first man elected to a professorship at the college and had replaced the first president of the college, George Foster Pierce. Ellison, a Methodist minister originally from Charleston, South Carolina, headed the mathematics department. He was a favorite of Gertrude's. Eleven years after she graduated, she met his niece and told her "that with the exception of my husband who was then in Richmond [serving with Confederate troops] that I would rather see him than any other man in the Southern Confederacy."[83] Fifteen years after graduation, when she finally did see him again, her eyes filled with tears when she remembered how kind he had been to her. She was delighted to hear him speak and told him she had come all the way to Macon "expressly to see him."[84]

If Dr. Ellison was the teacher she liked the best, Mr. Stone, her natural philosophy professor, was the one she liked the least. One Wednesday evening she said she "received the harshest reproof I ever did receive from Mr. Stone…. My opinion of Mr. Stone has greatly…changed. I no longer either consider him a Christian or a gentleman."[85] Remembering this episode years later, Gertrude said, "There was one professor at college whom I did not like and whom I do not think I would like very much if I were thrown in contact with him now. *Mr. Stone.*" She recalled that he had scolded her for talking during recitation. It was the fact that he used a passage of scripture to reprimand that gave her such astonishment. Revealing her sensitivity to criticism and her somewhat defiant nature, she stated, "It has been more than eleven years since then but I have not yet forgotten the look I gave him."[86]

She had kinder things to say about other professors. One that she liked was her music teacher, Mr. Guttenberger, who, she was sad to hear, went blind in his later years. Her teacher for mental philosophy was Osborne Smith, who served as president of the college late in the 1850s. No one commanded more respect from her than Mr. Thomas, a professor she had for two years, who possessed a "calm profound dignity" and later became president of Emory College at Oxford, Georgia.

Living with a building full of excitable, young girls was not always easy for the professors, evidenced by an incident Gertrude included in her diary. It occurred in relation to the girls' newfound religious enthusiasm and involved Edward Myers, who taught history and served as president of the college from 1851 to 1854 and again from 1871 to 1874. "The girls all appeared very much excited. All were shouting and praying and making a good deal of noise when someone said *Mr. Myers* was coming up. Laura Chew commenced blessing him when he very *politely* requested us all to come to our rooms. I never saw a sett of girls scatter so in all my life. They all stopped shouting immediately and left the room."[87] Dr. Myers was no doubt annoyed by the noise. The president and his family lived on the second floor of the main building of the college and the girls lived on the third and fourth floors.

The incident must have amused Gertrude for she found she could not abide the air of dignity Mr. Myers attempted. "I had no love for Mr. Myers while I was in college on the contrary it always afforded me pleasure to see him annoyed by the girls." Part of her reaction to him was as a capricious schoolgirl, but part of it was a feeling of dishonesty on his part. "He was constantly reminding us that we were young ladies yet never appeared to be impressed with that knowledge himself or if he was it never gained us any additional respect. I do not mean that he was disrespectful—quite the contrary—but it was the *most perfect* indiference imaginable and it was this very indiference which was so annoying."[88]

The variety of emotions that Gertrude felt toward her professors was probably a good reflection of how they felt toward their students. Some of them were undoubtedly genuinely interested in teaching females and showed them kindness and concern. Others may have had a prejudice against the girls and doubted their ability to learn. At any rate, Gertrude's instructors made vivid impressions on her young mind because incidents that occurred during those years in Macon were recalled years later in the diary.

Life at Wesleyan was not all work and no play, however. Gertrude developed many close friends, among them her first roommates, Ann Lizz Persons, Mary Quigley, and Lou Warner. In her senior year, she remarked, "How I love my roommates *Joe* [Jo] *Freeman* and Lou Howard! Of *course* I love cousin *Emma very dearly.*"[89] One of her closest friends, who would often spend the night in her room, was Ella Pierce, daughter of the first president of the college. Other friends were Mat Oliver and Fannie Floyd, who later was an attendant in her wedding. Gertrude enjoyed her walks into town to attend church and sitting on the steps talking with these and other girls. They consumed numerous treats together, such as molasses candy, saucers of strawberries, and ice cream. There was an ice cream shop in Macon they frequented and even an ice cream wagon that came up to the college. There were fireplaces in each room, and they enjoyed making a fire, talking, and "cooking cheese." Also, very often, they would play a game called Gaces. On the lawn, they engaged in a game called simply "base and thirdman," presumably something like baseball or perhaps even hide and seek.[90]

From this camaraderie at Wesleyan, the first women's sororities developed. Gertrude was approached to join the first one formed. "When I returned from Mr. Stone's recitation *Eugenia Tucker* came in with a note for me. I found it was from the 'Adelphian Society' as they style themselves unanimously soliciting I should join them. I returned a note *respectfully declining.*" Her good friend, Ella Pierce, was one of the six founding members. The Constitution of the Society had as its object "the mental, moral, social and domestic improvement of its members." Gertrude later reported, "The Adelphian Society came out with very pretty badges. The design is quite pretty. Two hands clasped, and the words 'We live for each other.'"[91] From the beginning the organization was successful and developed into the first Greek sorority for women. In 1905, it became a national organization, and, in 1914, the name was changed to Alpha Delta Pi. Wesleyan was also home for the second Greek sorority, the Philomathean Society, which was formed in 1852 and became Phi Mu in 1900.

Getting into the spirit of the times, Gertrude and some of her friends attempted to form their own society that they called "The Laconic Club." Her friend Camilla Boston was to be president and Gertrude was to serve as treasurer or secretary. But they soon changed their minds. "The Laconic Club I thin[k] is a project which will scarcely succeed. Our president is scarcely energetic enough. I have lost all interest in it. The fact is both *Camilla* and myself are thinking about something of much more importance, *our souls salvation.*"[92] By now, Gertrude was trying to read regularly the Bible and spend her time on things she considered to be more important than mere social activities. Although she declined to join the sorority, the fact she had been "unanimously" invited was very important to her, and she remembered it years later in her diary.

It was customary to have an oral examination at graduation and to present a composition, and Gertrude frequently mentioned consulting various professors about her topic. In April she compiled a list for Dr. Myers. "What subject should a young girl lady write on when she graduates? 'Adversity favorable to the development of Genius' or 'The source of all great thoughts is sadness'.... 'The Keystone of thy mind, to give thy thoughts solidity—to bind them as in rock…is to learn from the word of the Lord, to drink from the fountain of his wisdom.' The latter I think I shall take."[93] She considered other topics after mention of the above, but the Commencement Day program for 11 July 1851, lists Composition #19 as that of Miss Ella G. Clanton titled, " Learn from the Book of the Lord; drink from the well of his wisdom."[94] Forced to sort out some of their values and to organize them in a composition, the young women were beginning to become aware of the more complex issues of life.

Her sensitive treatment of the death of an infant demonstrates this development. "Mrs. Ellison's babe was not expected to live. I went in to see Ella Pierce after supper and then went in to look at the child." The next morning "[I]t was dead…. I asked Dick Holmes to go with me to see the corpse of Mrs. Ellisons baby. It was lying in the parlour with two white rose buds on each side of its little head. While in there I took up a volume of Dr. Bascomb's sermons and became very much interested in a sermon on 'The Judgement.'"[95] It seems as though Gertrude was trying to formulate an answer to one of the devastating problems for women of her era—infant mortality, an event she would face numerous times in her life, just as her mother had.

In the second volume, Gertrude's life is briefly foreshadowed when she casually mentioned the man who would become her husband. Girls at Wesleyan did not have much contact with young men, but she would occasionally refer to the men who came over from Emory College at Oxford or to relatives of some of the girls who visited Wesleyan. But, on 9 May 1851, she reported, "Several of us received invitations to attend the Ball given in July in Princeton New Jersey. Jeff Thomas sent them I think."[96] J. Jefferson Thomas would go on to graduate from Princeton that same year and return to Augusta and marry Gertrude in 1852.

As would be the case at other times in her life, when Gertrude became too busy, she did not write in her diary and did not leave a description of her graduation. She did have time to note that she finished her graduation composition on Tuesday night, May 20, saying she was "heartily glad." A Princeton-educated minister, Samuel Kennedy Talmadge, the president of all-male Oglethorpe College in Atlanta, gave the graduates a solemn admonition in their commencement address. In his oration, which reflected widely held opinions of the day, Talmadge left no doubt about how he felt about young women and their education. He gave a somewhat limited endorsement of female education, but he stressed that it should always be based on religion. For, after all, "Her physical frailty, her dependence on others, her exposure to more ills than the rougher sex, her ruin if she strays, her sensibilities...all demand that the help and consolation of Christianity should be hers." He reminded the audience, "An infidel man is a monster; an infidel woman is more than a monster." He encouraged the young women to cultivate honesty, refinement, and sensibility because they were their "ornament and protection." He emphasized, "The times are out of joint," because some of "your own sex, whose reputation is respectable, are securing an unenviable notoriety." His summation was, "Your theatre is the domestic and social circle, and not public display. It is to go down to the fountain of action, and to influence brothers, fathers, husbands, sons, to noble deeds."[97] At the end of his speech, the young graduates must have felt overwhelmed and somewhat demeaned rather than encouraged.

That education should be utilitarian and Christian was a widely held view at this time in the nineteenth century. Those who wanted to establish academies and colleges for women used the argument that if women were educated, they would be better mothers to their sons and wives to their husbands. It was not argued necessarily that the women would be fulfilled or happier in their own right. But nevertheless, this was the widely used argument, and these young Wesleyan graduates probably understood it.

But Wesleyan had begun to try to take women's education out of the purely "domestic and social" sphere. Elizabeth Young came to that conclusion in her study of the formative years of the college. "Although the general design of the College was to prepare for a radical change, the change contemplated, if it may be judged by the faculty appointed, was in the direction of broadening and elevating the general education given this sex, rather than of completely rerouting it."[98] Given the limitations of the applicants and the emphasis on religion, Wesleyan was still charting a new direction for female education and a modest challenge to the circumscribed rules of women in the antebellum South. The way Gertrude regarded her education and valued her experiences at Wesleyan later in life would strengthen the argument that Wesleyan achieved far more than it originally intended.

In 1861 Gertrude evaluated female education and concluded one problem was the young age of the students. "I am inclined to think that we are wrong so far as the education of our women is concerned. It is apt to be two superfic[i]al and our young girls leave school *two* soon. The mind should be trained, disciplined for after all it is only laying the foundation."[99] She had only been seventeen years old when she finished Wesleyan and felt she had learned far more since that time. But she was very thankful for her own education, and it gave her a sense of well-being. In 1864, when she was anticipating the approach of Northern troops and possible destruction of her and her husband's property, she wrote, "Poverty is not the worse evil which can befall us. I now realize what I have always thought that Dr. Franklin was right when he said 'If a man (or woman) empties his purse into his head, no man can take it away from him. An investment of knowledge pays the best interest.' The enemy can take all else—Thank God they cannot deprive me of education."[100] When she and her husband later faced poverty, it would be her degree from Wesleyan that would make it possible for her to open a school in her home.

That she loved Wesleyan College there can be no doubt. During her life she would take many sentimental journeys back. She described returning to the commencement ceremony in 1862, a trip her father made available to her hoping it would cheer her up during the war. When she went back to a meeting of the Alumnae Association in 1866, she had the honor of being elected second vice president. She recorded that she got a unanimous vote and was pleased to be elected. "I am realy interested in the progress of the school and hope to be present at many meetings of the alumni. I am realy and truly interested in the success of the school and hope that it may prosper and continue to improve."[101]

The girls graduating from Wesleyan in the mid-nineteenth century were undoubtedly too immature to benefit fully from all they were being taught, but the seeds were being planted. Females were beginning to read and to think new ideas that were not confined to the "women's sphere." Once they had started to think on a wider range of topics, some of them would never stop; Gertrude was one of those who would begin to question the role that women were expected to fulfill.

In April 1851, during her senior year, Gertrude was in a pensive mood and began to look back over the past few years. It made her sad to think how rapidly the time had flown. Now that she was seventeen, she wondered, "How will all this end. To what end am I destined. Surely for something else than to waste the precious moments of existence...."[102] She was beginning to measure her years by what she had accomplished. Gone were the days when she would while away the hours reading, writing, and daydreaming. She now wanted her life to have meaning and purpose.

4

Marriage

"I have selected my destiny and I am content with it."

"To be married is to be blessed" was the often-repeated conviction of virtually all young women in the nineteenth century, and Gertrude was no exception. She had had several suitors in Augusta and Macon, but when Gertrude graduated from Wesleyan Female College in 1851, she did not have any immediate plans for marriage. She soon resumed the carefree life she had known in her youth and "spent a most delightful summer...at Indian Springs and Catoosa Springs," favorite resorts of wealthy planters and their families. Looking back a few years later, she remembered, "The next winter made my debut in society and although I did not dance [because of religious convictions] and was thus incapacitated from entering into all the excesses of gayety yet I spent a delightful winter as a gay girl of fashion." During that winter her diary is full of references to Jeff Thomas, the handsome brother of a girlfriend at Wesleyan, Jule Thomas. In Gertrude's words, "During this time I regularly kept up my Journal and in that I see many allusions to Mr. Thomas and can there read how unconsciously to myself he was quietly laying siege to (as I [conceived] my impregnable) heart."[103]

James Jefferson Thomas was one of the five sons of General Joseph D. and Louisa K. Thomas of Burke County, Georgia, which was just south of Richmond County and Augusta. The other four sons were Joseph, Jonathan Pinckney, John Robert and Andrew Jackson. Julia, or Jule, as Gertrude referred to her, was the only girl. Pinckney Thomas would later marry Gertrude's younger sister, Mary, and was often mentioned in the diary. Jule Thomas, who married E. B. Scales, remained a close friend of Gertrude's and was also frequently mentioned in the diary.

General Joseph Thomas had represented Burke County in the Georgia legislature. He owned several plantations and enough slaves to be considered part of the planter aristocracy. At his death in 1858, an inventory listed the Shrival Place with forty-five slaves, the Millwille Place with thirty-two slaves, the Rosemary Place with thirty slaves, and the Baldee Place with seventeen slaves. Along with the property he owned in Richmond County, the valuation of his estate came to $212,500. Although his wealth did not equal Turner Clanton's, General Thomas was able to provide his family with a way of living comparable to that of other affluent planters.[104]

In keeping with the tradition of many Southern gentlemen of the time, Joseph Thomas sent his son J. Jefferson north to Princeton University in New Jersey. J. Jefferson had gone to the University of Georgia prior to 1850, then entered Princeton and graduated in the class of 1851. His intention at that time was to be a doctor, and, during the winter of 1852, he was attending medical lectures in Augusta at the Medical College.

The romance between Jeff and Gertrude got more serious in January of 1852 when she was invited out to the Thomas home in Burke County, ostensibly to visit her friend from college Jule Thomas. Gertrude recorded a pleasure-filled weekend of games—cards, backgammon, Old Maid, Smoot, and "Magic Music." During the day, they would take long rides on horseback through the woods, and, in the evenings, they dressed for formal dinners. Even though Gertrude's religious convictions did not allow her to dance, there was no taboo associated with smoking. On this, as well as other occasions, she casually referred to smoking "cigarettas." On one night, they "all smoked a cigar after dinner in the parlour."[105] Gertrude obviously enjoyed very much being with Jeff Thomas—and he enjoyed being with her.

Their courtship continued that winter in Augusta. He would come to tea in the afternoon, escort her to church services, and take her to concerts at the Masonic Hall. He was also present at a large party given for Gertrude that winter, presumably her "debut party," when three hundred invitations were sent. Gertrude wore a white satin dress and reported, "I enjoyed myself very much that night. It is scarely worth while writing any thing concerning the party as the occurences (some of them at least are two indelibly impressed upon memory ever to be effaced)—I went into the supper table with Mr. Thomas. How *very* pleasant and agreeable he is! I did not retire until after four oclock Friday morning."[106]

During the spring and summer, the romance blossomed. That summer the Clanton family took the "cars", as Gertrude called the train, to Athens, Georgia, and then to Madison Springs, another popular summer resort. Many of her friends from Augusta were there such as the Phinizys and the Lamkins. She met new people, among them the son of Governor James Henry Hammond of South Carolina. But the person Gertrude was most interested in was Jeff Thomas. They went to an elaborate costume ball, took afternoon tea together, and dined in the evenings. She went to the bathhouse several times, but reported she "only bathed" once. One activity they seemed to enjoy was bowling or "ten pins". She even reported her progress. "We play a good deal at ten pins. The largest no I have played has been 129. This morning I played two games— one 112—the other 104."[107] By the end of the summer, she knew she was in love and was sad when Jeff left Madison Springs before she did. Aware of maintaining proper decorum, however, she had a "farewell kiss for Jule and cordial grasp of the hand for Jeff. I did not hear a word he was saying when he bade me farewell. I was endeavoring to look calm for I knew I was observed."[108]

By this time there had already been talk of marriage. Gertrude was eighteen years old, and she felt she was ready to take the momentous step. Jeff Thomas was her choice. However, Turner Clanton was somewhat reluctant to agree to the match. After a conversation Gertrude had with her father on the "all important subject," she reported that it ended only "*rather* satisfactorily."[109] Although no explanation was given, as the historian Mary Elizabeth Massey said, "[S]ubsequent events would seem to show that the wise father may have seen the handwriting on the wall."[110] After they were married, Gertrude confessed in her journal, "I loved calmly and was undisturbed by fear till he called for Pa's permission…I had a short conversation with Pa just before he went into the room and then commenced my agonized feelings. Hurrying to my own room I…burst into tears and prayers…. Although not a direct consent Pa's answer was satisfactory. I did not write this in my journal *then* for I dared not." After that visit with her father, Jeff then "persuaded" Gertrude "to consent to marriage the next fall."[111]

Just why Turner Clanton was less than enthusiastic is impossible to know definitely, but several things may have contributed to his feelings. Turner Clanton was said to abstain from intoxicating drink and, whether he could have known anything this early about Jeff's use of alcohol, is not known. Also, it was around this time that Jeff abandoned his plans for studying medicine, a decision he and Gertrude would later regret. There may have also been financial concerns, even at this early stage. As has already been discussed, Turner Clanton made a sizable gift to Gertrude at the time of her marriage. A study of Joseph Thomas's will reveals that he specified that his whole estate, "lands and negroes and stock of all kinds be kept together and kept up in a farming condition" until his sons became of age and then be given to them as the "law directs."[112] The will was drawn up in 1856, and he died in 1858. A writ of partition was filed in 1859 by J. Jefferson Thomas, his brother, Joseph A. Thomas, and his sister, Julia Scales. Thus, Jeff Thomas did not receive any of his inheritance until seven years after he married Gertrude. He received a total of twenty two slaves, seven mules, three horses, and produce in corn and fodder, in addition to 143 acres valued at $12 3/8 each. The total came to $35,370, including cash in the amount of $12, 435, which had been advanced prior to his father's death.[113]

Despite the fact the inheritance was sizable, it was smaller than Gertrude's, especially with the $12,435 subtracted. Jeff and Gertrude also lived on land given to them by Turner Clanton that was about one mile from the Rowell Plantation. As has been mentioned, Turner Clanton gave Jeff "$5,000.00 in his own right" made up of goods and cash when they married. It would appear that upon Gertrude's marriage, her family was more or less "footing the bill." Although none of this was explained in the journal, Turner Clanton was a wise businessman and would have certainly realized that these circumstances did not bode well for the couple's financial success. Since Gertrude was the first of his daughters to marry, and he and Gertrude had a special relationship, he would have naturally been cautious.

However, once it became apparent to Turner Clanton that the marriage was indeed inevitable, he got into his usual generous mood. Gertrude acquired much of her trousseau from New York. "I sent on a letter to Mrs. Holt who is there now requesting her to select some portion of my bridal paraphanalia. My bridal dress—second day dress—bonnet and velvet cloak." She remarked that, "Pa gave me permission and with his usual kindness is quite liberal." Gertrude was also pleased when, in October, Jeff presented her with her engagement ring, "a beautiful ring with a cluster of nine large diamonds."[114] The marriage was originally set for November but had to be delayed because Jeff became very ill. The cause of the illness was never made clear. When he was fully recovered and plans could be finalized, the young couple wed on 16 December 1852. The Methodist minister and former Wesleyan professor Mr. Myers officiated with some of Gertrude's Wesleyan friends and sisters as bridesmaids.

Gertrude gave no more description of her wedding in the diary. True to a pattern she had begun around her college graduation, when she was very happy, content, and busy, she did not write in it. She was describing plans for her wedding in her 18 October 1852 entry, which concluded volume five, and did not take up her diary again until 8 April 1855. At that time she reviewed what had happened in her life during the intervening years. She had just turned twenty-one. She recalled how during the summer after their marriage her family, including "Pa, Ma, Sis Anne [cousin] Jimmie Lamkin, Mr. Thomas and I...went North" for a trip to New York and Saratoga. She also reported that her father had bought the Rowell Plantation, south of Augusta, which would become the Clantons's new summer home. But the most significant thing that had happened in her life since her wedding was the birth of her first child, a boy, in December of 1853. It was only natural that she would name her "darling little boy...Turner Clanton Thomas for Pa."[115]

Gertrude admitted that she had not been keeping her diary since she had started "housekeeping," but she intended to persevere in the future. "I am writing for my dear little boy and for my children should I have others and in this book they will read, hurriedly recorded a statement of events unimportant in themselves yet they make up the sum of my life as 'Trifles make up the sum of human ills.'" She said the diary would show that heretofore her life had "glided on smoothly." Her happiness and contentment radiate. "[A]m I not twenty one? I do not feel old. My feelings are still as gay and as buoyant as at seventeen. I am much happier now than then. I have selected my destiny and am content with it."[116] She was thankful she was more fortunate than other people and wondered why God had so blessed her. Indeed, she was probably as happy and fulfilled as she would ever be. Up until this point, her life had read like a storybook, but during the mid to late 1850s, one begins to see shadows of discontent and forebodings of things to come.

Nothing in Gertrude's experience had prepared her for the domestic sphere in which she now found herself. Having always loved to read and to write, Gertrude had resisted her mother's efforts to interest her in needlework, and could not cook and sew, as she was now supposed to do. Although slaves took care of much of the work, she was expected to supervise and participate in the labor. She reported on her first effort at sponge cake and her first attempt to make boiled custard. Of course, she had a cook, named Tamah, and only seemed interested in joining in to make a single dish—usually a dessert.

Sewing, which was a huge responsibility, she found "troublesome," because she was so inexperienced. She had been able to avoid it successfully in her youth, but in the spring of 1855, she had decided, "I am endeavouring to cultivate a taste for sewing, for which at present I have rather an aversion." But by the fall of the year, she had made no progress. "I have no seamstress and knowing so little, and disliking so much the use of the needle. I am often troubled in having my sewing done. Ma however is very kind in having the greater portion done for me."[117] As he always did during his lifetime, Turner Clanton tried to rescue his daughter from her dilemma by offering $1,000 to his sister Aunt Paul for a slave named Mary, who was very skilled in sewing. Gertrude said he had intended making the slave a present to her, but Aunt Paul refused to sell. Therefore, the problem of sewing and mending for herself, her son, her husband, and growing number of slaves went unsolved.

The inability to pay to have her sewing done or to purchase a slave skilled in that area was the first indication Gertrude gave of financial difficulty developing. In the spring of 1855 she said, "I am endeavouring to be economical." Later in September that same year, she observed, "Mr. Thomas having had a short crop last year and also having to contend with the disadvantage arising from a new beginning, it behooves us to practice an economy, which is hardly consonant with my nature. Yet to know my husband was in debt would be even less to my taste." In March 1856, she wrote, "As it is I endeavor to economize in some degree and assist Mr. Thomas in disengaging himself from his embarrasments."[118]

For the first time in her life, Gertrude was giving up things she wanted—that is, unless Turner Clanton would provide. In August of 1856 her father learned of her long cherished wish to have a piazza, or porch, built onto their house. He remarked to Jeff, "[A]s *Gertrude wishes to have a Piazzi in front of the house if you will see Goodrich I will pay for it* ."[119] The underlining added by Gertrude stressed the importance it had for her. Turner Clanton paid $500, and it was built in four weeks.

The hard economic times did force Gertrude to change a way of life to which she had been accustomed. By the winter of 1857, which has been referred to as the Panic of 1857, she had to admit, "Occasionally when I am in town I think I would be extremely pleased to spend the winters in town, but then it appears extravagant for us to have two homes and plant in Burke besides." She was hearing of families and businesses losing large amounts of money. "I am the more reconciled to a slower but more sure mode of progress when I hear of the failures which are constantly occurring."[120]

Having given up plans to practice medicine, J. Jefferson Thomas had chosen the most acceptable profession for a gentleman in the Old South. He had decided to become a planter. From the beginning, however, he did not seem to have the managerial skills or knowledge to be successful. When crops were bad and prices for produce were in a state of flux, one with less than great resources and good fortune could lose large sums. At this time, there was no indication from Gertrude's diary that Jeff had tried his luck in any other business ventures, but men did not think it was necessary or appropriate to discuss business with women. Gertrude had very little insight into what was going on in her husband's affairs. Even though the Civil War was still several years away, J. Jefferson Thomas was already experiencing serious financial difficulties about which Gertrude knew very little.

Not only did Gertrude begin to know financial uncertainty for the first time in her life, but she also began to exercise the single most important responsibility of a woman in the nineteenth century, along with its attendant joys and sorrows—childbirth. She had been fortunate when her first child Turner was born in 1853. "I was confined with a sickness which did not last very long and the advent of the birth of a son was hailed with a degree of rapture mingled with silent yet fervent thanks to God, the giver of all good things." She had reason to be thankful because she knew the dangers of childbirth, as did all women of her time, because she had seen her mother's frequent pregnancies and her sorrow when infants died. Gertrude recorded in her diary the accounts told to her of women's difficulties relating to childbirth. For instance, she heard of the death of Mrs. William Turpin, a young lady she had known at Madison Springs. "She has only been married a few years. Had had several abortions [miscarriages] and Dropsy [edema] ensued from the last confinement."[121] She also knew she could look forward to childbearing for the rest of her adult years. In 1855, when Gertrude was twenty-one, she had a child eighteen months old, and her mother, who was forty-three, had a child two months old. However, Gertrude accepted without question that this would be her destiny.

She greeted her second pregnancy with mixed emotions, writing in June of 1855, "I have had a great deal of sick stomach and headache and find I am again destined to be a mother. Turner Clanton is now eighteen months old. The knowledge causes no exhilarating feelings neither do I regret it. Yet suffering almost constantly with sick stomach as I am I can not *yet* view the idea with a great deal of interest or pleasure." This baby was two months early, and its premature birth caused Gertrude great anxiety. Alarmed about unexpected pain, she sent for Dr. Eve and her mother, both of whom were in Augusta, and neither arrived before the baby was born. Jeff and his sister, Jule, were with Gertrude, along with Tamah, her cook. "Neither of them knew anything—Mr. Thomas was already fully frightened…Such a time I am in hopes I will never experience again." Unfortunately, the baby lived only three weeks, and Gertrude grieved when he died. "Now I do indeed begin to know what are the trials of life." She tried to reconcile her suffering to her Christian beliefs. "'The Lord giveth and the Lord taketh away. Blessed be the name of the Lord.' But oh it is hard. Nature rebels and turns shudderingly away from the thought that tonight my poor little darling will sleep its first sleep in its grave."[122]

Seven months later, Gertrude was pregnant again. As with her second pregnancy, she was less than elated. "Again, I have prospects of becoming a mother, and the idea (aside from the fear of accident and the natural shrinking from pain) causes pleasurable emotions." She admitted that she did not want an only child but would not object to *"long intervals"* between pregnancies. Only two months later, she had a miscarriage, or "abortion" as she called it. "I was not very much frightened and have suffered more from extreme dibility than any thing else."[123] She said she had been sick two weeks but felt as if it had been two months. The losses were beginning to take their toll on her.

The new year of 1857 began with Gertrude expecting yet another child. Feeling she had been unfortunate in her last two pregnancies, "being in a similar state I naturally fear a similar accident." However, by September she was rejoicing. "[M]y little daughter, my darling 'Anna Lou' is born and now I have an additional cause for continuing my journal." She was pleased to have a daughter who could "best appreciate a mother's feeling." Her joy was short lived, however, for on December 28 she wrote, "Our precious little Anna Lou is dead. Today one week ago she breathed her last." Gertrude was reduced to "uncontrollable weeping." She poured out her emotion into her diary. "My child Oh my child how I miss your sweet smile, your little twining fingers as they clasped mine, even your feeble moan of pain expressive of so much suffering—Would to God, he had blessed you with life and health and you were still here to cheer our hearts." As happened so often, she never really knew what was wrong with the babies. The treatment probably made them worse. Gertrude took the infant to Dr. Eve. "He attended on her, applied various remedys—had her blistered and on the Sunday following she appeared to be dying."[124] The infant seemed to have had a cold, was congested, and had trouble breathing. The child who died earlier had similar symptoms.

It is not at all surprising, then, that in April 1858 when Gertrude found she was pregnant, her response was not enthusiastic. "I have been feeling very unwell all this morning—Indisposed for exertion of any kind. Suffering from a sickness with which in the course of my short married life I have become strikingly familiar."[125] It is easy to understand why women in the nineteenth century very often referred to pregnancy as "sickness." Gertrude was only twenty-four years old. She was "with child" for the fifth time, having had one healthy child, one premature child die, one pregnancy end in miscarriage, and one child, born at full term, also die. It was certainly reasonable that she should be preparing herself for the next disappointment.

When she recorded the birth of her daughter in November of 1858, she was closely guarded in her comments and apprehensive about her survival. "I hope I am grateful to a kind Providence for his many mercys—Again has he blessed me with a little babe and to make that blessing doubly dear—she is a girl…" She was compelled to pray, "Father in Heaven I pray thee that thou wilt preserve her in life and health, and enable us fully to appreciate the immortal soul thou hast given in our charge."[126] The baby, whom they called Mary Belle, did survive and brought Gertrude great joy, but the price had been high. Gertrude would have other healthy children later and she would also have another child die; but when she made her last entry in this diary on 14 March 1859, her state of mind was somber. Pregnancies, suffering, and dying children had changed her from the gay, young girl she had been when she married.

During this period of her life, Gertrude's attitude toward other things—particularly slavery—also began to change. She worked closely on a daily basis with a number of slave women; Tamah, her cook, Amanda, a house servant, Lurany, Amanda's mother, and others were constant companions. They worked cleaning the house, doing laundry, tending children, and gardening, and while they worked they talked. She attended church services with them and went to their baptisms and weddings.

Gertrude was especially interested in going to hear one of the well-known black preachers, Sam Drayton. "I find it very delightful to go down and hear Sam Drayton preach. He is a negro of extraordinary talent and cultivation and well repays one for listening to his sermon." On another occasion, "In the afternoon went over to see Tamah married and heard Sam Drayton preach. He is one of the most intelligent Negroes I have ever met with, and has a decidedly fine command of language." After one sermon by Drayton, Gertrude described how

> Aunt Pink [a slave]...swaying to and fro fell perfectly flat upon the floor. Several women rushed to her assistance when she rose and commenced shouting. This had such an effect upon Amanda that she went up to the altar. I believe in her for she is not one to act from impulse as much as settled conviction. When she went up I noticed Lurany (her mother).... I was unexpressibly touched by her manner, for her maternal affection is the most strongly developed feeling she has.[127]

Gertrude's close association with the slave women, and their shared suffering during pregnancy, soon caused her to take their side in a discussion with Jeff. At the time she was again pregnant herself and not feeling well. She and Jeff got into an "exciting conversation with regard to women, plantation and etc...." Two slaves, Judy and Maria, were expecting to be confined in a month or two, and she felt that in that condition "all women ought to [be] favored." Her husband was obviously not as sympathetic and wanted to keep them working, presumably in the fields, closer to the time of their delivery. Gertrude concluded, "I know that had I the sole management of a plantation, pregnant women should be highly favored. A woman myself, I can sympathize with my sex, whether white or black."[128]

Gertrude was not blind to miscegenation and was actually hostile when she considered the ways in which black women were abused by white men. She was upset when Lurany brought in her baby "as white as any white child." It was a great concern to her. "How can she reconcile her great profession of religion with the sin of having children constantly without a husband?" Then Gertrude answered her own question. "Ah after all, there is the great point for an abolitionist to argue upon.... They are subject to be bought by men with natures but one degree removed from the brute creation and with no more control over their passions—subjected to such a lot are they [the slave women] not to be pitied." She did not blame the slave women—she blamed the white men.

Gertrude never speculated in the diary about who might have been the father of Lurany's children. If her suspicions turned to Mr. Thomas or another relative, they do not appear in the journal as it currently exists. At any rate, Mary Boykin Chesnut's comments in her well-known diary would seem to apply here. "Like the patriarchs of old our men live all in one house with their wives and their concubines, and the mulattoes one sees in every family exactly resemble the white children—and every lady tells you who is the father of all the mulatto children in everybody's house hold, but those in her own she seems to think drop from the clouds, or pretends so to think."[129] Gertrude was well aware that the subject was supposed to be "off limits" for women. "I know that this is a view of the subject that it is thought best for women to ignore but when we see so many cases of mulattoes commanding higher prices, advertised as 'Fancy girls,' oh it is not enough to make us shudder for the standard of morality in our southern homes?"[130]

There were instances when miscegenation came out into the open and caused slave owners and their families to become the topic of gossip and scandal. Gertrude was mystified by a "most striking illustration of general feeling on the subject," when George Eve, member of a prominent Augusta family and friend of the Clantons and Thomases, carried a mulatto slave north with him under the "name of wife." Although it was known that he lived constantly with her, nothing was thought of it. "*Public opinion* was outraged by the report that the ceremony of marriage had been passed between them—then his father was terribly mortified and has since attempted to prove that he is a lunatic.... He preferred having him living in a constant state of sin—to having him pass the boundary of Caste." Gertrude was enough of a product of her times to understand how Eve's father did not want to have negro blood "mingle in the veins of his descendants," but could not understand his indifference to having the same "blood flowing through the veins of a race of descendants held in perpetual slavery."[131]

Gertrude abhorred the idea that a white man could sire a child by a slave woman and then sell the child for payment of debt. She had once had a conversation with her mother's nurse, Susan, who was speaking of her reputed father in a most contemptuous manner. "Laughing I said to her, Why Susan, was not he your father? What if he was, she said. I don't care any thing for him and he don't for me. If he had, he would have bought me when I was sold. Instead of that he was the auctioner when I was sold for 75 dollars—She was sold for debt, separated from her mother and has lived in the yard ever since she was three years old." Gertrude responded to this story by agreeing with the Swedish journalist, Frederika Bremer. "What a moral! It speaks for itself—and these white children of slavery as Miss Bremer calls them lower the tone of the South." Gertrude did not blame the mulatto offspring. "Oh No! They know no incentive for doing well and often if they wished they could not."[132] The blame was placed on white men who took advantage of slave women.

In January 1858 Gertrude concluded her thinking on the subject with the observation that the destruction being done to the "Happiness of homes" was a "mystery" she could not solve. She did feel, however, that other Southern women held her viewpoint. "There is an unborn earnestness in woman's nature to teach her to do right...." With strong feeling Gertrude concluded, "Southern women are I believe all at heart abolitionists but then I expect I have made a very broad assertion but I *will stand* to the opinion that the institution of slavery degrades the white man more than the Negro and oh exerts a most deleterious effect upon our children." Gertrude realized how contrary this view was to Southern popular opinion. "But this is the dark side of the picture, written with a Mrs. Stowe's feeling...." What she saw every day caused her to think the way she did. "[W]hen I look upon so many young creatures growing up belonging to Pa's estate as well as others—I wonder upon whom shall the accountability of their future state depend."[133] It was Gertrude's "earnestness" about a woman's nature and her sensitivity born out of identifying with black women that had brought her to this emphatic conclusion on slavery. Her views vary at times, as she tries to unravel the problem, but her attitude regarding slave women and their plight does not change. At this point, Gertrude was not advocating emancipation, but she was becoming more vocal about her dislike of the system.

Not only did Gertrude have strong feelings about female slaves, but she also was concerned about the status of white women and felt they were being abused by the standards of the day. The fact that she discussed incidents in the diary, sometimes on more than one occasion, shows how much they were bothering her. She described how one Mary Culbreath had visited in the home of one Matt Higgie and how, while his wife was away, he had taken advantage of Mary. The incident had caused great "excitement" in the area. Mary's brothers had pursued Higgie when he fled and tried to kill him. However, Higgie was caught and brought to trial. Gertrude followed the trial and was angry when the jury ruled in Higgie's favor. "The testimony is conflicting, but my opinion is in favour of her innocence *very* decidedly and oh it does indeed speak little in favour of a woman having a defender for insulted virtue in chivalrous man when such men as Matt Higgie, are permitted to go free, to desolate the life of some other woman. I would sooner trust myself with a wild beast than with a man so totally devoid of all that is noble in man."[134]

Gertrude realized that part of the problem was rooted in the double standard of what was considered permissible behavior for men and women. Great improvement was needed in the code of ethics, which sanctioned many wrongs. "But I mount my hobby when I commence on the subject of woman and her wrongs. I am no 'Womans Right Woman', in the northern sense of the term, but so far as a womans being forever 'Ananthema Maranatha' in society for the *same offense* which in a man, *very* slightly lowers, and in the estimation of some of his *own sex* rather elevates him. In this, I say there appears to be a *very very* great injustice."[135] She was now convinced that some of the responsibility for personal morality should belong to men as well as to women—a progressive realization in the antebellum South, where it was taken for granted that women were the moral guardians of society.

Gertrude placed some of the blame on her "own sex." She deplored the holier-than-thou attitude women showed toward those who had erred and felt they should at least be pitied instead of scorned. "Oh how many of those women are more sinned against than sinning." Gertrude decided it was time to change ways of thinking and acting. "It is a shame that what is considered a venial thing in man should in a worldly point of view *damn* a woman and shut her out from every avenue of employment."[136]

Some of Gertrude's attitudes may have been shaped by what she was reading at this time, as on several occasions she mentioned the women's rights movement that had begun in the North. She became interested in Laura Curtis Bullard's novel, *Christine: or, Woman's Trials and Triumphs*, which she described as a "very decided woman's rights book advocateing...[woman's] perfect equality with the other sex." She discussed how she agreed with some of the author's points and was confused by others. Some of Bullard's arguments were "very good indeed," but she could not understand why the heroine of the book could be an outspoken advocate of divorce and then say after her marriage that she was "glad the *tie* of marriage is so strong that it cannot be broken."[137] Gertrude shared this latter viewpoint, however, and said, "I look upon a separation of a married couple, very nearly equivalent to a disgrace."[138] Her attitude toward divorce would never change.

Gertrude did hold some conventional opinions with regard to women, however, which she would later abandon. Once in 1855, during a church service she attended, a woman rose to say a few words to the congregation after the minister had encouraged those who felt the "spirit" to respond. Gertrude was bothered because of what the Apostle Paul said in the New Testament, "Let not your women speak in public and this aside from their natural diffidence would cause a female to remain silent upon such an occasion."[139] Later in her life Gertrude would address large groups of people frequently and derive great satisfaction from it.

One of Gertrude's strengths, however, was that she was not afraid to read and think about issues that were proscribed or considered inappropriate for Southerners, especially for women. She read and was impressed by Harriet Beecher Stowe's *Uncle Tom's Cabin* and Mary Hayden Pike's *Caste*, which she recognized as very "abolitionist." Some of the work written by women she considered "licentious literature" and thought George Sand "[a] libel upon womanhood...The only redeeming trait is her refusing to sign the name given her by *her mother* to her infamous productions." When she read *Light and Darkness* by Lissie Petite, she was bothered that any *"unmarried* woman should write so freely and express herself, on *certain* subjects so independently."[140] But whether she agreed or disagreed, she was still reading a wide range of literature. During this period she commenced reading Thomas Babington Macaulay's history of England in four large volumes and was half way through it. She never abandoned reading the Bible and searching the scriptures for comfort and answers during these difficult times.

The period of time from 1852 to 1859 was one of dramatic change in Gertrude's life, and the transition can be seen in the way she wrote about her marriage, her relationship with her husband, and her role as a wife and mother. In April of 1855, after her marriage and the birth of her first child, Gertrude was very contented and somewhat naïve about what the next years would bring. "I thank thee oh Heavenly father for thy many mercys, but for none do I so sincerely thank thee as for *my husband.*" At this point, she accepted it was her destiny to be married and enter that domestic sphere appropriate to the weaker vessel. She felt Jeff combined "such moral qualities, such an affectionate heart, with just such a master will as suits my womans nature, for true to my sex, I delight *in looking up* and love to feel my womans weakness protected by mans superior strength...." But even then there was a hint of loneliness, for in the same entry, she referred to her journal as "friend for a lonely hour." She was thankful to have it to confide in for with "their [men's] thoughts filled with busy care, men are not always ready to enter into all those silver threads of feeling, which make up the poetry of life."[141]

During the next few years, there were times when Gertrude's feelings were hurt and she and Jeff had disagreements. Although she was convinced her husband would never read her diary because he showed no interest in it, she was, nevertheless, guarded in what she said about him, primarily because she believed her children would read the diary someday. In February of 1857, when she discussed the "charm of married life," she had reached the conclusion that after the first bloom of romance had faded, the birth of children would bind a husband and wife together, enabling them to overlook the faults they now saw in each other.

By New Year's Day 1859 there was a decided change in her mood and outlook. Having undergone the rigors of childbirth, the care and responsibility of home and family, and become aware of the injustices around her, she was no longer the gay, young girl of her youth. "I sometimes think were I to die tomorrow—or any day soon how little *I* would be missed...." Making an effort not to appear too pessimistic, however, she said, "I have no morbid feelings on the subject and mine is not a disposition to picture for myself a gloomy future. Life is very dear to me—I have many ties to bind me to earth, and to the loved ones in my family circle—I wish my children to *remember me*—and for my girl or girls should I have others, these pages are penned...."[142]

Remembering that she was writing for her girls, Gertrude then seemed to catch herself and become more positive. She wanted them to know what "[a] glorious thing it [was] to be a *woman* in the *proper sense*. A woman made 'to suffer and be strong.'" She wrote that as a child she had heard that to be a woman meant to be *"of course* unhappy," but she did not believe it was necessarily so. "Yet I do think that a woman is so constituted as to be very easily affected—'Trifles light as air' can excite or depress—Make happy or the contrary and happy are those who are blest with a kind husband, dear children, Father, Mother, Sisters and Brothers, together with friends and relations...."[143] She thanked God that she enjoyed these blessings, but, at the same time, there was a tone of melancholy in her words. She was constantly asking questions and struggling to understand what it meant to be female in this time and place in her life, and her words were particularly poignant when one considers the implications of impending events.

The next time she picked up her pen to write in her diary, it would be 1861 and the Civil War would be under way. As she had never before in her life, Gertrude would have "to suffer and be strong"; her husband would leave to go and fight, perhaps never to return. Beloved family members would die, and economic hardship would beset her family. At times she would have to cope alone and continue to sort out the meaning to her ever-changing life. What had happened in the past seven years had made Gertrude stronger, and she would survive—and eventually thrive.

5

The Civil War

"Trusting to the God of Battles, I shall see my husband go."

"Events transcending in importance anything that has ever happened within the recollection of any living person in *our* country have occurred since I have written last in my journal.... Since then *war* has been declared."[144] On 15 July 1861 Gertrude opened a new volume of her diary with these solemn words. She described the "intense excitement" which had consumed the city of Augusta. Her father had rushed to Charleston to view the bombardment of Fort Sumter from the roof of the Charleston Hotel. She had seen thousands of troops pass through Augusta on their way to Richmond, Virginia, and other Northern cities. Richmond County and Augusta had already sent ten companies of troops and could boast of one cavalry unit—the Richmond Hussars—that had already been instructed to hold itself in readiness to leave. It was to this proud company that J. Jefferson Thomas belonged, holding the rank of first lieutenant.

Even though Gertrude was naturally concerned about her husband's safety, "When Duty and Honour call him it would be strange if I would influence him to remain 'in the lap of unglorious ease' when so much is at stake." Along with Jeff, Gertrude's brother Jimmie Clanton and Jeff's brother Jack would serve in the Hussars. Gertrude was proud "to see them exhibit the noble, manly spirit which prompts them to do." She said she could write without one wish for her husband to remain with her. "Trusting to the God of Battles, I shall see my husband go, feeling that if one word of mine could keep him at home I would not utter it."[145]

Gertrude believed in the justice of the Southern cause and could articulate it well. "'He is thrice armed who hath his quarrel just' and surely ours is a just cause—we are only asking for self government and freedom to decide our own destinys." In her opinion, the South wanted *"to be let alone,"* and the North should have been more understanding since America's independence had been won by secession and rebellion. She believed the war had been forced on the South, and despite preferring a peaceful solution, Gertrude did not think the South should submit to "vassalage." In her mind the Confederacy would eventually be victorious. "I have faith to believe that we will conquer—sooner or later, *it must be so."*[146]

Even though Gertrude believed Jeff should fight, she dreaded seeing him leave. However, she was soon busy organizing the clothes he would take, getting shirts made, and taking care of other responsibilities that needed to be dealt with prior to his departure. "The uniform of the Hussars is an army blue shirt trimmed with yellow. Mr. Thomas has one of those, two very nice coloured flannels and three plaid worsted ones." Like many other Southern gentlemen headed to war, Jeff was taking a slave—Daniel—with him to attend to his personal needs.

Gertrude was very proud of Jeff and how handsome he looked. He was an outstanding rider, and his horse, Stanley, was the best in the company. When she went to watch the Hussars train, she was pleased to hear the exclamations from people standing near her. "Mr. Thomas is a fine rider," or "What a beautiful horse," they said as Jeff took his leaps with polished style. Finally, on 18 August 1861, all preparation was complete, and Jeff left for Richmond. Fully convinced that he was leaving home for many months or, even perhaps forever, Gertrude was distraught.[147]

That, however, was not the case. By October 12 Jeff was home on business connected with his troops, "selling Confederate bonds, purchasing winter clothing etc." Gertrude was delighted to see him and to know that he was safe. The leave actually lasted longer than the allotted twenty days because Jeff's mother was very sick and he also came down with an "attack of jaundice." He left again on November 12 to return to Virginia. By the end of February 1862, however, he was home again, this time recruiting for the Richmond Hussars. During his stay at home, Gertrude accompanied him to Atlanta when he went on business for his company. The time went by rapidly, and, when Jeff left in April, Gertrude was utterly depressed. She felt a great "void" in her life and cried uncontrollably, praying that God would spare her husband so that she would see him again.

At this time, all seemed to be going well for Jeff. Upon his return, he was elected Captain of Company B and was serving under Colonel Thomas R. R. Cobb, a member of a prominent Georgia family whom Gertrude greatly admired. Thomas Cobb's older brother Howell Cobb was a Democratic congressman for six terms, Governor of Georgia, and Secretary of the Treasury under President James Buchanan. In 1841 Thomas Cobb had graduated from Franklin College, later the University of Georgia, and helped start the law school there. He was widely known for being an ardent secessionist and writer of an 1858 proslavery study titled, *An Inquiry into the Law of Negro Slavery*. He was also on the committee that wrote the Confederacy's constitution.[148] So when Thomas Cobb organized Cobb's Legion, or the Georgia Legion as it was sometimes called, Gertrude was proud that Jeff was an officer in such a prestigious unit. At the beginning of the war when she met Cobb, it gave her great pleasure, and she said his name was the "synonym for everything that is upright and noble."[149]

By 27 June 1862, however, things had begun to change, and Jeff was unhappy. "Col Cobbs order of rank which he has established has caused Mr. Thomas a great deal of dissatisfaction as he is placed as the 6th cap when he think[s] he ought to have been 1st or 2nd."[150] By September, conditions had not improved for Jeff, and he resigned his commission and returned home. Gertrude wrote in her diary that while Jeff had been contented with "camp life and soldiers fare I never should have been the woman to have urged him to come home...but when Col Tom Cobb by the promotion of several others over him did him great injustice and he wrote me that a due sense of self respect demanded his resignation I wrote him 'to come.'" Jeff procured a man from Maryland to serve as his substitute and felt "fortunate that he succeeded in obtaining him as soon as he did as the law on that subject is becoming more and more stringent." Even though Gertrude was relieved and enjoyed having him home, she had mixed emotions and seemed to regret that she had told him to return home. She admitted, "I would not have recalled him from the service."[151]

When the Civil War started, there had been great enthusiasm, and men—both rich and poor—rushed to volunteer, believing their side was destined to win. But by 1862 things had begun to change, and buying "substitutes" (as stand-in soldiers) was widely practiced by wealthy men in both the North and the South. It was legal and could be done for as little as $300, which was appealing to a poor man in the nineteenth century. The practice prompted many to call the Civil War the rich man's battle but the poor man's war. The war was now deadly business, and lives were being lost in huge numbers. It should be noted that Cobb's Legion was assigned to the Northern Virginia campaign and took heavy losses. Cobb's men fought at the Battle of Antietam on 17 September 1862, one of the bloodiest days of the war, when approximately 23,000 soldiers were either killed, wounded, or reported missing. Cobb was promoted to Brigadier General in November 1862, but his career at that level was short as he died from wounds received at the Battle of Fredericksburg on 13 December 1862.

By September, Jeff was already safe at home and would have felt that he had got out just in time. The official record for Cobb's Legion stated that Jeff resigned "due to physical and mental debility," and that he received a medical discharge "due to chronic gastritis."[152] He was only thirty-one at the time, and one would think he could have recovered enough to stay in the service. Was there cowardice or fear involved? There is no other comment in the diary to suggest that Jeff resigned for any other reason than that he had been passed over for promotion. He had enjoyed camp life and later in his life preferred sleeping in tents and living in the outdoors. He was an expert horseman and skilled marksman; these talents would be passed down to his sons. Late in life he would take great pride in the fact he had served in the army of the Confederacy, but his resignation seemed to have gradually been forgotten— at least, by Jeff.

Gertrude was guarded in her comments about Jeff's resignation, but what she does write in her diary gives some indication about how she really felt. When Jeff joined a local militia called the Wheeler Dragoons and became first lieutenant, Gertrude was not impressed. "The fact is I cannot get up any very great degree of interest in companys which remain about town. This company has been entered for the defense of Augusta for the war and is thought to be the safest to join to prevent being sent off." By 1863 buying substitutes was no longer legal. When men who had purchased them were recalled to the field, Jeff was unapologetic about his decision to use a substitute. He had been a "member of [the Wheeler Dragoons] for some time and thinks the repeal of the substitute law *perfectly right.*" Gertrude's underscoring of words always indicated some strong feeling on her part. This was written on the last night of 1863.

By the fall of 1864, when Augusta was preparing for a possible attack by General Sherman and his Union troops, Gertrude was irritated that the local militia was receiving "indiscriminate praise" from the press. "The idea of praising militia and local troops in the same eulogistic strain as the volunteer organization! It wars with my ideas of justice—for certainly this was not their *first* call and they went because they were compelled to." She said she was glad Jeff had "so comparatively comfortable a position," but she was still very proud of the time he was in "active service."[153]

Jeff was on active duty for barely over a year. He was away from home only nine months in a war that continued for three years after his resignation. Gertrude had very strong feelings about the justice of the South's position and would spend time later in her life celebrating the memory of the war. She would work to get monuments built and would be a member of the Daughters of the Confederacy. From the comments she made in the journal, one can conclude that she was somewhat ashamed that Jeff had returned to the security of home.

Throughout the war, Gertrude worked to serve the war effort in the only ways women could. Considering how much she disliked sewing, it must have been a true act of dedication when she joined the Ladies Sewing Society. At one point early in the war, she was lining blankets for the Hussars, and, on another occasion, was making a coat for a man in the Walker Light Infantry. The women would gather once a month for meetings and be assigned various tasks to perform. Gertrude was also a "Directrise of the Soldiers Aid Society," a loosely formed organization that did whatever was needed. "Yesterday in accordance with a call from Col Rains the ladies met at the City Hall for the purpose of making Cartridges for the Army—I found it pleasant agreeable work and brought home a number to make."[154] Feminine enthusiasm for "the cause" paid off in a number of practical ways and made women like Gertrude feel good about making a contribution.

Gertrude was also a participant in one of the most beneficial projects performed by the women of Augusta—The Augusta Ladies Lunch Association. The troop trains coming through the city had no meal service, so the women set up tables and benches on the cotton platforms and served food to the hungry and tired soldiers. "On Tuesday I sent to the bakers and bought six loaves of bread at one dollar a loaf and buttering the slices we started with this and a nice lunch of Ma's and milk which Mamie had bought to the Georgia Depot to give the soldiers there something to refresh them." On another occasion, she enlisted the help of servants and children. "At dinner taking Cate and Turner with me with Susan and Palmer I carried the same men a tureen of chicken soup. Chicken and bread—all of them appeared glad to receive it."[155] The combined volunteer work of the women of the city had quite an impact, and it was something of which they were proud. The captain of the Ringgold Rangers wrote in the Griffin newspaper, "It is due to the noble ladies of Augusta, Georgia, to say they have fed every company that has passed through the city. Such deeds of patriotism should be recorded in the history of the Confederacy."[156]

The real horror of the war came alive for Gertrude through her work at the Third Georgia Hospital, where she also prepared meals for the sick men. Arriving there one hot July day in 1864, she and her sister Mary found "a state of destitution such as I had read of but never imagined before." Men, wounded in every conceivable way were lying on the floor on beds hastily filled with straw, "some with their arms and legs cut off, others with their flesh wounds, two men in a dying state, another poor fellow with the ever present thought of home mingling in his delirium as he sits up and gathering his coarse shoes proceeds to put them on saying I am going home, I have a furlough to go home." Moved by this pathetic man, Gertrude "Soothingly...spoke to him and smoothing his coat his only pillow I persuaded him to lay down." She talked to the soldiers, wrote letters for them, and did whatever she could to ease their suffering. One of the greatest problems was the "horrible ...accumulation of dirt." She found that what the men needed after something to eat was "good washing and clean clothes" more than anything else. After spending the day in the hospital tending these men who aroused such sympathy in her, she would spend "all night...dreaming of wounded soldiers."[157]

These experiences in the hospital, along with the news that her brother had been wounded and some of her friends had been killed, brought the horror of the war home to Gertrude and kindled her interest in politics. More and more, she was becoming interested in the world outside her own domestic sphere. In her diary she had made occasional comments in the past about various political leaders. She had gone to the memorial service when Henry Clay died, and, upon Daniel Webster's death, wondered who would fill the void. She had gone to her first political rally back in 1855 and heard Alexander Stephens speak. Stephens was representing the eighth district of Georgia in the House of Representatives at that time, but would later be vice president of the Confederacy as well as Governor of Georgia. Hesitant to go because she feared she would be the only woman present, Gertrude enjoyed his "speech of two hours length." Stephens weighed only about one hundred pounds, and she was shocked at his diminutive size and person, bearing the stamp of a real "Piney Woods Cracker." She said, "Never having attended a meeting of the kind I was quite pleased."[158]

Once the war started, she would go to political rallies, report on troop movements, record the outcome of important battles, and discuss various issues in dispute between the North and the South, all in the pages of her journal. She kept herself well informed by reading the *Chronicle* and the *Constitutionalist*, Augusta's two newspapers, and even though she was often frustrated by the lack of books, she satisfied her passion by re-reading ones she had read earlier. She was fearful that other people, and probably many women, were not as aware as she and did not realize what was happening. "Indeed we are now in the midst of what all of us have read of—thought of—and dreamed of before, but never realized—a revolution."[159]

Gertrude was so caught up in the monumental events in the outside world that she sometimes failed to write about important personal events. Upon realizing this, she wrote, "In my last entry in this book I was so much interested in the political events of the past few months that I did not allude to a domestic event of much greater personal interest to me, the birth of my little Jefferson."[160] Perhaps her absent-mindedness was a manifestation of her growing resentment toward pregnancy. Of course, once her children were born she became the loving mother. The baby had been born on the 27 April 1861 and named after his father, even though Gertrude said she did not like the name, but, since Jeff was about to leave, she had chosen the name in honor of him.

After Jeff resigned his commission and returned home in September 1862, it soon followed that Gertrude was once again pregnant. By December, she wrote, "I am suffering terribly from nausea and lack of energy—for the last six weeks I have been I cannot say blessed with the prospect of again becoming a mother—I am two sick and irritable to regard this circumstance as a blessing *yet awhile.*" Gertrude seemed to be even worse off than she had been in previous pregnancies. Whether it was the war or Jeff's resignation is difficult to say, but she was angry and depressed. "The fact is my nervous organization is so completely disorganized that I require perfect quiet." She felt she did not have enough energy to raise her head, and the children annoyed her terribly. "I think my intellectual as well as spiritual nature sympathies with this depression of the body. I do not feel the same aspirations—the same clearness of view—the quickening of thought of ordinary times."[161] She hoped that she would have more strength and energy in a month or two.

By June 10 she was "expecting to be sick," as she referred to delivering a baby, and the prospect made her anxious. In light of her former difficulties with childbirth, this was perfectly understandable. The baby, however, did not come until June 23, and this time Dr. Eve was with her. An important new drug was used that she had not had prior to this delivery. "I took chloroform for the first time and was pleased with the result at the same time not altogether satisfied as to its safety." She described how, after a long inhalation, everything became "indistinct." "I appeared to see Dr. Eve who was just before me as tho in a dream. Everything seemed dim and distant. I appeared to be floating off."[162] Fortunately, this birth went well. A girl, Cora Lou, was healthy and Gertrude had survived again.

Giving birth left Gertrude in a weakened state, and she now became more dependent on her female slaves for the survival of her babies. When young Jeff was born, he had been frail and sick, and Gertrude had not had sufficient milk for him. She tried cow's milk and then goat's milk but finally decided it would be best to use a wet nurse. She first called on the slave woman Georgiana, who had a baby almost a year old, and Jeff began to gain weight and do much better. When Georgiana began to run out of milk, Pa had arranged for America to come from his plantation. She had just lost an infant who would have been three weeks old. Gertrude was grateful as Jeff continued to grow and do well with America nursing him.

Frustrated after Cora Lou's birth, Gertrude said, "I sometimes lose patience and think that people who do not have nourishment enough for their children ought not to have them...."[163] To her relief, a wet nurse, Nancy was feeding her baby at that time, and the milk seemed to agree with the infant. She had already lined up America's sister Emmeline, in case Nancy's milk failed. There is no doubt that Gertrude wanted to nurse her own children, and there are other accounts in the diary of her doing so. But, when she could not, there was no stigma in Southern society to having a slave nurse her children. There are no comments in the diary about concern for disease or danger, only gratitude that her children were healthier.

This shared intimacy and concern for the survival of children was another example of Gertrude's link with slave women. She was very upset when Georgiana's son died. In a depressed mood, she wrote, "Poor *little George is dead.* Since he has been sick I have had him in the house and have nursed him until he had become an object of great interest to me. Dr. Eve was to see him and yesterday I called for more medicine for him. When I reached home tonight I found that he was just dead."[164] Gertrude understood Georgiana's grief and sympathized with her feeling of loss. After all, Georgiana had been nursing her baby George at the same time she had been nursing Gertrude's baby Jeff.

Black and white women relied on each other for assistance and comfort when a child's life was in danger. Even though doctors and husbands might be consulted, it was other women who gave real support and understanding. Despite the fact there are no comments in the diary about how the slave women felt about nursing the white babies, they did seek help from the mistress when their own babies were sick. The life-threatening moments surrounding breast feeding and infant care described in Gertrude's diary are good examples of female bonding between the races in the antebellum South.[165]

Because of her pregnancies, Gertrude was not as emotionally and physically strong as she was early in the war. But toward the end in April of 1864, a significant event occurred in her personal life to depress her even more—the death of her father. It caused what she called "wild tumultuous grief to be succeeded by a quiet approaching to apathy." She regarded it as the "saddest event which ever occurred in my history." She had loved and adored Turner Clanton more than any other person; he was the only person who never disappointed her. It was difficult for her to accept the fact that his "bright mind, the vigorous intellect" and his "strong will" would not be with them any longer.[166]

Gertrude wrote more about the death of her father than she did about any other single event. Covering twelve modern, typed pages, she wrote of how he had been sick all winter, suffering from what one doctor had thought was dysentery. He had been in great pain and discomfort but had never complained. She described the last days and hours in minute detail. Calling all of his family and faithful servants around him, he had said "good-by" and given instructions for the future. He warned his son, whom he called Buddy, against "gambling" and "drinking" and blessed each of his children, including Gertrude, separately. Turner Clanton, even in his

death, seemed to sense some of the hardships that were ahead
for his family. He told his son and Jeff "that he did not think he
would live [,] that his will was written, that they must both
look after his interest." To Sis Anne's husband, Col. William
Vason, he said, "I leave a large interest here sir, which I expect
you to be interested in. I wish you all to live in peace and
harmony."[167] Unfortunately for the family, that would not be
the case, and Turner Clanton's shrewd sense of business and
calming influence would be sorely missed.

Her father's death left a void in Gertrude's life that no one
else could fill. She went into a deep and intense depression for
several months. Bad dreams, nervousness, and irritability were
recorded in the pages of her diary. After Pa's death, more than
ever, she sought answers to religious questions. Where was
Pa's soul? Could one communicate with departed loved ones?
In the nineteenth century there was widespread interest in
spiritualism, a belief that spirits of the dead could
communicate with the living, and Gertrude mentioned it more
than once. She confessed to her journal, "If I could commune
with my Father's spirit I would willingly do so."[168]

Gertrude was grieving and needed an understanding
person to just listen, but "Mr. Thomas is not much given to
expressing himself freely upon religious subjects...."[169] On
several occasions she even thought of the appeal of religious
confessions. "There are thoughts, doubts, suggestions which
present themselves to my mind If I could only *talk of them*.... I
find my thoughts recurring to the Catholic confessional (that
great repository of secrets) with a longing checked by the idea
that these priests are *men*." At times, thoughts of "spiritualism"
and "rank papistry" annoyed her but "to whom shall I go for
assistance." She tried to pray but was not comforted. On one
occasion, after attempting to explain her problems to Jeff, she
found that he listened but did not respond. She concluded, "I

don't think Mr. Thomas understands or is interested in my struggles and trials."[170] Since Gertrude could not communicate with her husband and, since she had no spiritual or religious advisers, she finally decided she needed female friends and advisers. "I wish to read some healthy, strong, sensible, womans writings—Nothing sentimental or romantic—no strange dream of fiction. Why the silent struggles of each heart, the nervous depression of a womans nature, the responsibilitys resting upon her—make of her a heroine. I know women who have lived a life of silent martyrdom which ought alone to secure for them a crown of glory." She wanted to be under the influence of a "pious" woman, perhaps "some sensible, practical woman, who has 'suffered and grown strong.'"[171]

Adding to her depression was the lengthening of the war. By July of 1864 Gertrude was "heartily tired of the war and wish[ed] for peace oh so sincerely—but not upon humiliating terms, oh no!" The situation, however, was not improving. By September Gen. William Tecumseh Sherman had taken Atlanta, and Augusta was preparing for a possible attack. Jeff and the Wheeler Dragoons had been called to active duty. Gertrude was packing up to leave their plantation Belmont, where she had spent her time during the war, and move into the city. "Oh these are troublous times. I leave Belmont not knowing what an hour may bring. I carry all the children with me… In case of a nearer approach of the Yankees I will remain in town. I wish to carry something in with me and don't know what to take. I will carry the Confederate Bonds and silver spoons and forks." Jeff had invested $15,000 in 8 percent Confederate bonds, telling her they were a protection from "the Yankees" in case they came.[172] But by this time in the war, Gertrude seemed to have little faith in anything or anyone.

She made her last entry in this volume of her diary on 17 September 1864. How different it was from her first entry more than three years before when she was sure the Southern cause was just and that the South would be triumphant. Now, the "very heart of our state is invaded and the whole state threatened with being overrun." The anxiety and fear she felt were revealed. She felt she could not breath, everything was closing in on her, and she was "utterly impotent to avert the impending doom." She imagined "men clad in Yankee uniform rudely violating the privacy of my home. I imagine the booming of Yankee cannon and the clash of Yankee sabres and I ask myself how soon shall this thing be?"[173] She was completely disillusioned, and, whatever was to come, she wanted the uncertainty to end.

The circumstances of the war, her father's death, her suffering in childbirth, her disappointment in her husband—all of these things were weighing on her. They combined to make Gertrude question and doubt things she had always held sacred. Not only did she question her religious beliefs, but, she questioned more than ever that sacred Southern institution— slavery. She confessed, "I have some times doubted on the subject of slavery." She saw many of its evils, but "chiefly…the terribly demoralizing influence upon our men and boys." Making an effort to also think of the slaves themselves instead of their masters, she said, "[O]f late I have become convinced the Negro *as a race* is better off with us as he has been than if he were made free." But, she went on to add that she was not sure that "we would not gain by his having his freedom given him." Unable to solve the complex problem, she concluded, "I grant that I am not so philanthropic as to be willing voluntarily to give all we own for the sake of the principle, but I do think that if we had the same invested in something else as a means of support I would willingly, nay gladly, have the responsibility of them taken off my shoulders."[174] Here, she is speaking more than ever as a woman, because it was the women who supervised making clothes for the slaves, taking care of the sick, and interceding with the master when they had problems. Also, she spoke as a woman when she again brought up the "evil influence" on men and boys, namely those who were fathers of mulatto children. In the pages of her diary, she could honestly confess her doubts about slavery and echo earlier sentiments that Southern women were all abolitionists at heart.

The last few lines of this volume of her diary well describe where she was in her thinking. Gertrude wondered what the next year would hold and "how I would feel exiled from my home as the citizens of Atlanta have been, and compelled to realize the...curse of earning my own livelihood." Sherman would burn down parts of their plantations, but, although he would not come to Augusta and violate her home, she did not know it at this time. She did sense, however, the impending economic hardships.

There was also a real sense of isolation in her life. Jeff did not try to understand her, and her father, whom she had loved and respected so much, was gone. She sought friendship and communication with other women, who understood what she felt. At this point in her life, her mother and sisters seem to have been companions only, not sensing Gertrude's deeper needs, and there is no mention of her trying to talk to them about anything other than day-to-day activities. More than anyone or anything else, her journal was her friend and confidant. She certainly saw her journal as something very important and more than just a record of her life. "Dear old journal. I realy dislike to give you up—to lay you aside and form a friendship with a new one. I have shown more of my real self to you than to any of your predecessors, and a weak vascillating creature I have proven myself...." In its pages she wrote of issues inappropriate for women to discuss and confessed doubts she probably did not utter to another living soul. She may not have realized it at that time, but writing was very therapeutic and helped her in ways she did not understand. During these dismal days, she did not feel good about herself or her life. She wanted very much for her life to have more meaning, but she seemed never to attain her own "idea of excellence."[175]

6

Adjustment to Defeat

"Today I am a matured woman."

"It has always been a source of great comfort to me to express my thoughts in language. Indeed this has often times proven a source of subsequent regret for sometimes to express the idea in homely phrase 'I talk two much' and yet I can but think in some cases it is better to talk than to brood over troubles."[176] With these words Gertrude started her new journal on 22 September 1864. She had waited only five days to begin writing again. Previously, there had been long gaps between some of the volumes, but that was not the case this time; her diary was now a great consolation to her, and she made frequent and lengthy entries. She would keep this volume until October of 1866, and in it she recorded the last months of the war and the beginning of her family's adjustment to defeat.

The war had continued too long for her. "Shall I dare hope that this new journal which I am commencing will record *Peace*, an independent Southern Confederacy?" She had not completely given up hope, but the prospects were not good. Worry about the approach of the enemy had gone on so long that now Augustans had become accustomed to the idea. "Truly the skies are gloomy—and the heavy storm appears ready to discharge its thunders in our very midst—and yet how calm, how indifferent we are—we laugh—we talk, we jest just as tho no enemy were at our door."

As had become her habit, Gertrude reported on what was going on in the war effort or, at least, what she thought was happening. General Sherman's capture of Atlanta had sent shock waves through the Confederacy. "The deep gloom which hung over us just after the fall of Atlanta has been lifted from our midst and the movement of Gen. [John Bell] Hood has brightened both the army and the people, but we are kept in as complete ignorance of the movement of Hoods army as if they were in the Crimea, instead of the upper portion of Georgia."[177] As she had learned from experience, if news were good, the people would hear quickly; but if it were bad, it would be slower in arriving.

She reported the meeting of the governors of six Southern states—Virginia, the Carolinas, Alabama, Mississippi, and Georgia—who gathered in Augusta in late October and were determined to continue the war in spite of their disagreements. She happened to run into Georgia's governor, Joseph E. Brown, downtown at Long's Store. "I walked up to the upper end of the store and pretending to examine a piece of goods, I tried to get a good view of him…. I did not see him as well as I could have wished but he is entirely diferent from what I had imagined Gov Brown to be—I had supposed that he was jolly and plump, stout, red face—rather on the Hoosier order, of course I had imagined him to be smart but he has the *appearance* of a scholar—he is rather thin, tho as Mr. Thomas remarked 'almost all the talented men in Georgia are stout.'"[178]

Gertrude was also very disappointed that she did not get to see the president of the Confederate States, Jefferson Davis, when he made a speech at the Waynesboro Depot in September. She had arrived just as a large crowd was dispersing, having heard the president speak. "I was within ten steps of him, which made the disappointment of not seeing greater than it would have been." A Mr. Fargo remarked to

Gertrude that the "President was much more infirm—more decrepid than he had expected to see him, yet when he spoke there was a great deal of fire and vigour about him."[179] President Davis received heavy criticism for his "autocratic manner" from the *Charleston Mercury* and Gertrude admitted that, although she had always been an "advocate of the President," she did not approve of some of his remarks. Davis was under fire for removing General Joseph E. Johnston from the command of the Army of Tennessee. Johnston had inflicted heavier casualties than he had received, but nonetheless, Davis was replacing him with General John Bell Hood of Kentucky for the defense of Atlanta.

Gertrude was further upset by President Davis's plan to enlist slaves to fight. By promising them "their freedom" if they fought, "He so clearly betrays the weakness of our force that I candidly confess I am disheartened." Gertrude took, as she called it, a "woman's view" of the subject and concluded it was "inconsistent" to offer the "priceless reward of freedom to aid us in keeping in bondage a large portion of his breth[r]en when by joining the Yankees he will instantly gain the very reward which Mr. Davis offers to him after a certain amount of labor rendered and danger incurred." Gertrude concluded, "I fear I grow toryish in my sentiments."[180]

The military leader most on Gertrude's mind in the fall of 1864—indeed, on the minds of all Georgians—was the Union General William Tecumseh Sherman. Sherman had been born in Ohio and named after the Shawnee Indian leader Tecumseh. Sherman's father had admired Tecumseh for his great skills as a warrior. His father had died when Sherman was a young boy, and he was raised by a neighbor, Thomas Ewing, who would later serve as senator from Ohio. Ewing had three boys and a girl, named Eleanor, but called Ellen, whom Sherman would later marry. Sherman had graduated sixth in his class from

West Point in 1840 but had left the military and tried, and failed, in several different professions. When the Civil War started he was running a military school in Louisiana, Louisiana State Seminary and Military Academy, which would later become Louisiana State University. He had many friends in the Confederacy and was not morally opposed to slavery, but he did think any attempt to dissolve the union was wrong. After entering the war on the Union side, Sherman went through several disappointing assignments as well as a very difficult time of serious depression. His wife Ellen had gone to powerful allies and family members in Washington to get Lincoln to reassign him. Eventually he would end up in a very advantageous relationship with Ulysses S. Grant and become Grant's most trusted ally and friend. Thus, when Lincoln promoted Grant to lead the entire Union effort, Grant promoted Sherman to take his old job and command the West. Sherman was then in command of the forces that would invade and burn Atlanta.[181]

After coming down from Tennessee in the summer of 1864 to face difficult fighting in Georgia and around Atlanta, Sherman's troops had finally occupied Atlanta on September 2 and ordered all civilians to evacuate the city. Sherman's motive was to demoralize the Confederacy and show the South they could not protect their homes or their supplies. Sherman supposedly ordered that only buildings of some military importance were to be burned, but obviously, his soldiers were careless with their torches and many other buildings went up in flames. He had captured and burned Atlanta, and now everyone in the state was wondering where he would strike next.

On October 21, Gertrude turned to her journal. "Again Mr. Thomas is ordered from home…Last night Cap Kirkpatrick brought an order…commanding all the local companys with the Wheeler Dragoons included to meet today—prepared with sixty rounds of ammunition, rations for two days, blankets, canteens and…prepared to go to Macon." By the next morning Gertrude had decided they were actually bound for Atlanta in an attempt to recapture the city. The confusion was typical of the fear and uncertainty that gripped everyone. Three weeks later, on November 17, Gertrude wept with joy when she received a telegram from Macon saying, "Wheeler Dragoons and self—all well."[182] Gertrude did not realize it at the time, but Sherman had begun his "march to the sea" with five thousand cavalrymen and fifty-seven thousand infantrymen. The only opposition was a number of scattered militia units and the three thousand Confederate cavalrymen under the command of Joseph Wheeler.[183] Jeff Thomas was one of those few who, in most instances, could only retreat in the face of superior force.

Gertrude was greatly relieved when the Wheeler Dragoons were ordered back to Augusta as she knew that the Confederates could not stop the advancing forces. "This may appear strange but I was not as much frightened when I supposed they were coming towards Augusta as I was when I supposed them marching for Macon where Mr. Thomas was. I have never been afraid of the Yankees—and their taking *property* is so small a consideration compared with my husband's life that I scarely regard it." Gertrude kept saying she was "perfectly calm," but, when she got a note from her sister Mamie on November 22 saying, "For the first time in my life I have to confess to having *nerves* and they are a good deal shaken this morning," one can be sure Gertrude was beginning to feel much the same way.

She began to pack up cherished mementoes of her childhood, letters from Jeff and her journal, "faithful record of my life since I was fourteen." Feeling that she was putting away a portion of her life, she began to lose courage and cry, praying that his bitter blow might be spared her. She finally resolved, "I could risk leaving silver but those journals, those letters, those treasured locks of [Pa's] hair I *could not* let them go and I have packed them to be sent off instead of the silver." She said she did not know what to do. She would laugh awhile and cry awhile. While she was packing, she received a note from her mother saying, "The reflection is awful as I begin to realize poverty and starvation staring me in the face."[184] Mary Clanton was speaking for all the women in the family.

Finally, in late November, Gertrude wrote, "'[T]he Philistines are upon us.' The enemy are near us."[185] After leaving Atlanta, Sherman's troops had originally split into two large forces, one going toward Madison and the other toward Macon. They had rejoined forces near Sandersville, having entered the undefended capital of Milledgeville on November 22. The troops then fanned out and cut a forty-to-sixty-mile swath through the state. It was one of these scouting or foraging parties that destroyed the Thomas plantations in Burke County.

Gertrude wrote a vivid, detailed description of the damage in her diary. *"Sherman's men visited our plantation Monday Nov 28th* at the time they burned Waynesboro Depot. Henry one of our Negroes left the plantation Sunday night joined the Yankees and the next morning conducted them to Cotton Town and showed the place in which Uncle Sykes (our Negro driver) had concealed the horses and mules." The Union soldiers stole the horses and mules they wanted, put Henry in a Union uniform and then mounted him on one of the most valuable horses named Melnott. They set the gin house on fire and broke into the overseer's house. They then left headed toward Jeff's brother Pinck's plantation pursued by Wheeler's militiamen. The one Union soldier who was left to make sure the gin house was burned completely down was killed by the militia. Gertrude wrote, "When our Negroes were tempted by the Yankees to go with them they refused with the exception of Henry and proved most faithful—but Mr. Thomas writes me that John Boss who drove us for five or six years after we were married has since left."[186] She went on to describe how the Yankees spent the night at their other plantation in Burke and burned the rest of their cotton and the corncribs. She admitted she had *"been frightened."* As she looked back on that Sunday night filled with fear and anxiety, she could compare it to only one other night in her life—the night she received the summons to go to her father who was near death.

Having completed their long march, the Union soldiers entered Savannah on December 21. Sherman sent his famous Christmas telegram to President Abraham Lincoln, "I beg to present you as a Christmas gift the city of Savannah, with one hundred and fifty heavy guns and plenty of ammunition, also about twenty-five thousand bales of cotton."[187] The Confederate troops in Savannah retreated, and the city surrendered—in the opinion of some, all too easily. Gertrude felt the loss but concluded, "Since Savannah surrendered—Savannah the pri[d]e of Georgia—Georgians have felt the disgrace was keen but I have wondered if under the circumstances Augusta would not have acted in a similar manner."[188]

Gertrude was nervous and depressed during Christmas, thinking of her father's death and feeling anger at the Yankees. As did many other Southerners, she focused her hostility on Sherman. On 3 January 1865, in her frustration after Sherman's men passed through Burke, she sat down and wrote Sherman's wife, Ellen, a letter that she had planned to have published under "Personal" in one of the Richmond papers. Of course, she did not know Sherman's wife's name, nor was it really "personal." She never mailed it and, after hearing about the recent death of Sherman's six-month-old baby, she was glad she had not sent it. But Gertrude wrote, "I know that amongst the jubilee attendant upon her husbands 'Christmas present' to Lincoln I could send Mrs. Sherman 'A New Years gift' which would dim and make hollow and empty the mirth by which she is surrounded." Gertrude said she felt very, very sorry for Mrs. Sherman and would "not send this letter if I could." However, Gertrude did preserve a copy of it in her diary.

"Mrs. Gen Sherman—A few days since I read your husbands telegram to you dated Atlanta. Will you believe it? *for a moment* I felt sorry for you...." She went on to say that as a "rebel lady" she was giving her some information about her husband's movements. "Last week your husbands army found me in the possession of wealth. Tonight our plantations are a scene of ruin and desolation." She asked if she thought it was a "gallant deed, ...[a] brave act to frighten women and children! Desolate homes, violate the sanctity of firesides and cause the 'widow and orphan to curse the Sherman for the cause' and this you did for what? to elevate the Negro race." Mrs. Sherman should be satisfied because the mission had been accomplished. "Enquire of Gen Sherman when next you see him who has been elevated to fill your place?" She asked, "Did he tell you of the Mulatto girl...spoken of by the Negroes whom you are willing to trust so implicitly as 'Shermans wife'?" She said Mrs. Sherman should tell her Northern sisters: "Your husbands are amongst a coloured race whose reputation for morality has never been of the highest order—and these gallant cavaliers are most of them provided with 'a companion du voyage.'" She then ended her vengeful letter, "I will only add that intensely Southern woman as I am *I pity you.*[189]

In September 1866 Gertrude was reminded of the letter she thought of sending Mrs. Sherman. "Reading that now I can see how my nervous system was completely unstrung—for now that sober reason has resumed her sway without alleviating my bitterness for the Yankee nation I should never think of visiting upon Mrs. Sherman retaliation for the enormous crimes committed by her husband...."[190] Gertrude was somewhat embarrassed to think of what she might have done; she had lashed out in anger.

Sherman rested his troops for the month of January, then, on 1 February 1865 they started their march north toward Augusta and the Carolinas. Gertrude was again thrown into a state of anxiety. One can understand the fear she felt when, on February 12, she rode into the city of Augusta. Passing by the deserted camps of the militia, she entered Broad Street and was "met by every indication of excitement." She saw companies of soldiers grouped in the middle of the street with "guns, muskets, haversacks and other military accoutrements... stacked ready for the march." All down the street at various intervals two to three hundred bales of cotton were "packed to burn at a moments notice." Men, women, and children were gathered in doorways and standing on the street discussing the latest rumors. What really bothered Gertrude was that children and servants were helping themselves to sacks of cotton "unmolested" by the guards. "The militia refusing to go over into South Carolina were detailed to roll cotton (I spelt cotton with a small c I wonder if it is because poor old King Cotton is dethroned)." All of this combined to make Gertrude "feel that the dreaded hour had come."

Their own cotton had been stacked on a vacant lot with the order to burn it if the enemy approached. But there was great fear among many residents that the city was going to catch on fire. Some people had made ladders and attached bags onto poles to dip into water to wet the sides of houses. Others had buckets of water in their attic ready if needed. Gertrude was worried they had done nothing: "I believe the burning of the cotton is more dreaded than the approach of the Yankees. One thing is quite sure. If it is fired and the wind is high the greater portions of the city will be burnt."[191]

Fortunately for Augusta, the main body of the Union troops did not invade the city, and it was spared the horror of going up in flames. But the fear of the nearby army, combined with other circumstances, made the second week in February one of the worst Gertrude had ever experienced. "The expected approach of the Yankees—aided by the coldest weather I ever felt combined to place me in a truly uncomfortable mood." But what upset her the most was the knowledge she was again pregnant. "Unfortunately I have a prospect of again adding to the little members of my household—of again becoming a mother. Happening as it does in these troublous times I am sincerely sorry for it." She confided that she usually felt bad when she was pregnant, but with "so much to depress [and] so much to unnerve I am totally deprived of energy." She could muster no courage to face the coming events as she had earlier. "How differently I feel from what I did in Nov. when the Yankees were expected…Now I shrink appalled."

Gertrude went through extreme mental anguish during this pregnancy late in the war. By March she could make no plans for the future, and since their planting interests in Burke County had been destroyed, she saw nothing but poverty "staring [her] in the face." Looking back to that horrible week in February, she admitted her nervous condition was bad. "I was made realy sick by the combined prospect of Shermans visit and the burning cotton. That was a terrible, never to [be] forgotten week." She grew so sad and low-spirited that she began to think of dying when the "hour of trial" came. "Mr. Thomas says I 'always say I expect to die'—but I don't think so. I know I have thought of it this time more than usual and if I do die I hope that my baby will die with me."[192] So genuinely concerned was she at this point that she began to write instructions to the future stepmother of her children and describe their personalities and temperaments to her.

In July Gertrude came dangerously close to fulfilling her prophesies. She abruptly stopped keeping her diary and did not take up her pen again until mid-October. She then recounted her ordeal. Confined to bed for *"three months* lacking one week," she would always remember the experience. "On Tuesday July the 25th I gave birth to an infant son whose birth was premature, caused I know by the constant strain upon my nervous system. I gave to him the name of Charley and sighed to think it was all I had to give him." Since her slaves had begun to leave by this time, she had no wet nurse and could not provide what "Gods poorest creatures" could supply "a mothers nourishment." When the baby died the next night she thanked God. "Little Baby! little darling if I could have you back again I would not."

Gertrude took chloroform when the baby was born, and whether an improper dosage contributed to the baby's death and her illness cannot be known. Certainly the fact that wet nurses had helped her babies to survive before and were not available for this child was a factor. Perhaps Gertrude was correct that her weakened state of health and nervous instability could have caused the death of the child. For whatever reason, she came down with a severe cold and came "nearer the valley and shadow of death than...ever before."[193] She had numerous relapses and a very slow recovery.

Not only was Gertrude debilitated physically, but she was also facing the reality of how drastically her life had been changed by the end of the war. By May 1865, on a day she had been feeling weak and light-headed, she admitted, "It will require all my energy to meet the emergencies of the time ahead of us. The fact is our Negroes are to be made free and a

change, a very change will be affected in our mode of living."
Jeff advised their slaves that they were to be freed and that he
was going to have to hire workers. He asked them to wait
"quietly and see what would be done." At first their slaves
accepted his offer and worked with a "more cheerful spirit than
ever," but soon they began to leave one by one.[194]

Gertrude and Jeff felt that they had been benevolent masters
to their slaves. Their reaction to their slaves' leaving was
similar to many other slave masters who were disappointed
and chagrined that their slaves chose to depart rather than
stay.[195] Gertrude had displayed, in her words, the "kindest
possible feeling" toward their servants. But when the war
ended, the slaves would leave without letting the Thomases
know, almost as if it were too awkward to say anything. Jeff
and Gertrude would be hurt and sometimes concerned for
them but would not let these emotions be known. Daniel, Jeff's
personal slave for many years who had accompanied him to
Virginia during the war, "Took off all of his clothes during the
night and left without saying anything to anyone." One day
when Gertrude was busily occupied, "Betsy...went for the
Chronicle as she was in the habit of doing every day and did not
return again. I was realy annoyed about it." One Sunday
morning they discovered that their cook Tamah had left during
the night. "If any expression of surprise or sorrow was
expected by the servants they were disappointed for none was
made by Mr. Thomas or I." Soon Milly, the nurse for little Cora
Lou, had slipped away, too.[196]

Very close relationships had developed with some of the
female slaves. Gertrude and her mother were both indebted to
one woman in particular, "Susan, Kate's nurse, Ma's most
trusty servant, her advisor, right hand woman and best liked
house servant has left her. I am under two many obligations to
Susan to have harsh feelings towards her. During six

confinements Susan has been with me, the best of servants, rendering the most efficient help. To Ma she has always been invaluable and in case of sickness there was not one like Susan."[197] By now it seemed that Gertrude could feel appreciation, and even affection, for some of her slaves, but she was still not able to understand their longing for freedom and independent lives.

Of course, it was impossible to replace most of these people, and new hardships were placed on the masters and their way of life. In late May Gertrude went to Dublin, a section of Augusta where many Irish immigrants lived, looking for a white woman to be her cook. Having never learned to cook herself, she had made up her mind to try to do so a few months before Tamah left, but found making bread very difficult:"[M]y back ached when I was through and I have seen things I liked to do better. Yet I intend hereafter to do more cooking—make up bread and etc—Once before I had a similar idea and tried to help Tamah in drawing some fish and it was about as hard work as I ever did."[198]

By late May she had hired a woman to wash clothes for her and agreed to pay her thirty cents a day. She admitted she "had no idea what was considered a task in washing." With the number of children Gertrude had, washing would certainly have been no small "task." Having hired a cook to replace Tamah, Gertrude "assisted her in wiping the breakfast dishes a thing I never remember to have done more than once or twice in my life." Such comments show just how pampered and unsustainable her lifestyle had been—those days were gone forever. On Monday, May 29, she wrote, "Out of all our old house servants not one remains except Patsy and a little boy Frank. We have one of our servants Uncle Jim to take Daniels place as driver."[199] This child and two servants were a vast difference from the large staff of personal slaves to whom the Thomases had been accustomed before the war.

In October of 1865, reflecting on the great changes that had occurred in their standard of living, Gertrude wrote, "We owned more than 90 Negroes with a prospect of inheriting many more from Pa's estate—By the surrender of the Southern army slavery became a thing of the past and we were reduced from a state of affluence to comparative poverty...." It seemed that the reality of the situation was beginning to dawn on her: "[T]he thirty thousand dollars Pa gave me when I was married was invested in Negroes alone."

Through the years Gertrude had vacillated in her attitude toward slavery. She had read books and articles that attacked the institution and some that defended it. But not until the end of the war, when all was lost, did she know "how intimately my faith in revolution and faith in the institution of slavery had been woven together." Like many other Southerners, she had believed that slavery was condoned by Christianity. She saw some of the evils of it, "but if the Bible was right then slavery *must be*—Slavery was done away with and my faith in Gods Holy Book was terribly shaken. For a time I doubted God. The truth of revelation all—everything—I no longer took interest in the service of the church." Gertrude had always read the Bible regularly and now, when she opened its pages, the "numerous allusions to slavery mocked" her. Gertrude's faith was not permanently destroyed, but hers was an honest and searching reaction. In addition to the scriptural sanction for slavery, she believed many good people in the South had supported the institution. She finally admitted, "I was bewildered—I felt all this and *could not* see God's hand."[200]

Despite the advantages of having slaves, there were definitely some things that had bothered Gertrude for years. She wrote that she "breathed a sigh of relief that I had no

Negro clothes to cut out.... Oh what a burden like that of Sinbad the Sailor was the thought of 'the Negro clothes to be cut out.'" She had often questioned the morality of slavery and summarized her feelings in her last entry on New Year's Eve 1865. "Slavery had its evils and great ones and for some years I have doubted wether slavery *was* right and now I sometimes feel glad that they have been freed and yet I think that it came two suddenly upon them. As it is we live in troublous times."[201]

Despite her confusion and mixed feelings about slavery, after the war Gertrude was glad that the slaves had been freed. This was one point about which she and Jeff consistently disagreed. He was so desperate to find a labor supply to work his plantations that he was never able to see anything advantageous about the emancipation of the slaves, nor was he able to admit that slavery might have been morally wrong.

The former owners and the ex-slaves both suffered after emancipation. Jeff had offered to hire some of them to work for wages but was short of money at the end of the war. When Jeff did not pay them on time, many former slaves left. They were then encouraged to sue for back wages by one Captain Bryan, an officer of the Freedmen's Bureau. On 22 July 1865 Jeff received a notice from the "Yankees Cap Bryan in Augusta summoning Mr. Thomas to appear before him to answer to the demand of these Negroes for wages." Jeff and Gertrude were annoyed and upset. They felt these ex-slaves from their plantations in Burke County had caused them a lot of trouble. By January of the following year, Jeff had worked out a compromise with all but one of them that led to their being hired to work for wages. The Freedmen's Bureau had been set up to work out these arrangements between ex-slaves and their former owners, but the Thomases did not appreciate it. Like many other Southerners, Gertrude was hostile and saw the incident as an intrusion by an outsider and a Yankee. "*Cap*

Bryan of the Freedmans Bureau aided as much as was possible in sowing broadcast the seeds of dissention between the former master and slave and caused what might have continued to be a kind interest to become in many cases a bitter enmity."[202]

There is evidence to support the idea that Gertrude and Jeff had a "kind interest" in their former slaves. Gertrude could not feel any hostility toward Susan, who had been with her when her children were born. When Daniel sought employment with Dr. Cumming and wished to obtain a recommendation, Gertrude confessed she had "always liked Daniel and spoke kindly with regard to him." The first time she saw Daniel, "He stopped outside of the gate and spoke to me then turning came up to the steps with his hat off and what I knew so well to be a pleased, gratified expression of countenance that I extended my hand and shook hands with him, a mark of favor I bestowed upon him." When Jeff saw one of his Burke County slaves who had tried to sue, Jeff told him that he "took more interest in him than anyone else, and etc—to all of which Willis appeared to agree. Coming home and commenting upon it Mr. Thomas said, 'Poor fellow he looked badly'."[203] It took a while, but Jeff and Gertrude came to be somewhat reconciled to the emancipation of their slaves and realized they would have to make whatever adjustments were necessary.

After the war, one of the issues that really bothered Gertrude was the treatment of the Confederate leaders by the North. She was particularly upset with their handling of Confederate President Jefferson Davis. Any feelings of disagreement or hostility toward Davis had vanished instantly in the spring of 1865 when he was captured by the Union troops. He was caught on his way to Florida, near Irwinville, deep in south Georgia and was carried through Augusta as a prisoner. Gertrude was outraged. It was "the crowning point, the climax of our down fall. I buried my face on the pillow and wept bitterly." Gertrude saw great crowds of people rushing down Greene Street to see the procession as Davis was brought from the train. She stopped at Dr. Eve's and waited for the crowd to pass while the former Confederate president was driven down Reynolds Street to the Sand Bar Ferry. She was convinced that they were making a great mistake having Davis carried through the Southern states in such a way. "It will prove a triumphal procession to him for even those persons at the South who were becoming disaffected towards him will have their sympathys aroused and manly emotion of regret for him will be experienced."

This sympathy for Davis was certainly true in her own family. A few nights later Jeff proposed that they add Davis to the name of their own son feeling, "[I]t is all that we can do in honor of Davis." Even though she had chosen to name young Jeff after his father, Gertrude agreed and only joked that it might "hereafter retard his political progress."[204] She sincerely hoped the United States would not make a martyr of President Davis by executing him as some people were suggesting. She did not know it at the time, but she would meet and talk with Jefferson Davis later in her life.

As early as May of 1865, delighted that the war was over, Gertrude was beginning to rebound and feel better. Her spirits were high. "Our negroes will be freed our lands confiscated and imagination cannot tell what is in store for us but thank God I have an increased degree of faith—a faith which causes me to feel that all this will be for our good." The Thomases had suffered great financial loss, but Gertrude had regained her health and energy. Even though the emancipation of the slaves had brought the loss of so much property, she confided, "[I]n my utmost soul I cannot regret it." Only gold and silver were being accepted in payment for goods. Gertrude confessed, "I have 25 cents and one 5 cents in silver—and yet strange to say I feel bright and somewhat hopeful—The war is over and I am glad of it."[205]

Now she would have more time to spend doing what she loved best—reading and writing. Material had been so scarce during the war that she had been reduced to rereading old copies of *Harper's Magazine*. She had gone through Charles Dickens's *David Copperfield* for the third or fourth time. Drawn, as Gertrude had said, to some sensible woman's writing, she had read Mrs. Gaskell's biography of Charlotte Brontë. Gertrude concluded, "I do not think that to have been the author of *Jane Eyre* would I have been willing to have suffered the torments of ill health, extreme nervous excitably [sic] and sensitive shrinking from mankind which she endured." By contrast, after reading the autobiography of the actress Anna Cora Mowatt, Gertrude was impressed with the "cheerful genial womanly spirit of the book, essentially feminine." She was moved by the poetry of Elizabeth Browning, who she believed captured a woman's anguish. After reading a poem about death and war, Gertrude confessed, "I don't think among all the pieces of poetry I ever read I know of any thing more touchingly sad and characteristic of womans yearning, tender nature...."[206] Obviously Gertrude's reading helped her to identify with other women's suffering, and, in many ways, it was a great comfort to her.

It was around this time, soon after the war, that Jeff decided to try his luck in the business world. Gertrude's first mention of his business was on 12 October 1866 when she was discussing their move into Augusta. They had rented the Twiggs house for $1,200 in gold, "a very high rent" for a house they had always wanted to buy. She was anticipating a very nice winter, Turner and Mary Belle were going to school, and "Mr. Thomas will be at his store."[207]

The Augusta city directory for 1865–66 still listed J. Jefferson Thomas as a planter with an address of 189 Greene Street.[208] By 1867 he was listed as partner in Mosher, Thomas, and Schaub with a business address at 244 Broad Street. The company was described in the business directory as "manufactures, importers and dealers in china, porcelain and glassware."[209] It received a good rating from the R. G. Dun representative, who filed a report on 30 July 30 1866, saying, "The firm is solvent and all its members are monied men. 'Thomas' is a clever business man and Schaub also." Despite the report saying Mosher was "the only member that lacks business char[acter] he is unreliable," the company seemed to be doing well.[210] Gertrude not saying anything about the company might be an indication of how little it interested or concerned her. After all, that was not her sphere. Jeff probably did not discuss it with her, and she did not ask him questions. It would become a topic later in the diary only when it was a major financial concern.

By now Gertrude was occupied thinking about things of more interest to her. In July of 1866 an episode occurred in Gertrude's life that was a confidence-building experience for her. She had enjoyed going back to Wesleyan College during the war when her father had arranged it to cheer her up; now she was going to Macon again to attend the Alumnae Meeting and Commencement. It gave her a chance to reflect on her life—where she had been and where she was headed. In a positive mood, she wrote, "My life has been a happy one— truly the lines have fallen to me in pleasant places. I have experienced much love to support me in all trials. In having married the husband I have and in having been the happy mother of children, I feel that I have filled the mission for which Providence intended me."

But Gertrude had begun to move beyond simply fulfilling her mission of being a wife and mother. She felt that her nature had expanded, her life had been ennobled, and she was a more intelligent woman, capable of thought and appreciation of things that she could not have conceived of earlier. In the past fifteen years she had gone from being a young girl to a more mature woman. "I read and read books which then would have bored me terribly—I think and think boldly, I act—and act boldly as for example my going to Macon without a gentleman to escort us." The simple act of going to Macon with her sister Cora without a male escort was the first step in Gertrude's public career.[211]

As has been stated, Gertrude grew up in a time when women were taught to be silent and not speak up in public. A couple of seemingly small incidents occurred that demonstrated her new boldness and willingness to speak her mind where, earlier in her youth, she would have remained silent. They were significant enough to her that she described them in detail. During her visit to Macon, she was seated by a Mr. Fleming when the Wesleyan students were reading their compositions. When he picked up a newspaper and began to read, she felt it was very rude. "Mr. Fleming if *your* wife were here I don't think she would permit you to read that paper." When he smiled and continued to read, Gertrude was annoyed but also persistent. "And I am quite sure if *my* husband were here *he* would never think of doing so." He smiled again but in a few moments the paper was laid aside. Despite the fact she used the example of her husband and not her own wishes, Gertrude had found her voice and won a small victory.

Gertrude also won a small debate at the meeting of the Alumnae Association. As the gathering was called to order, she realized that no men were present and that the women were conducting their own meeting—something that was novel in itself. Gertrude reported that a question had been raised as to whether juniors should be allowed to join the association as alumnae. "To this there was no reply but a good deal of animated whispering. No one else replying and feeling I know as much [and am as] interested as any other member, I remarked 'that I thought that this was not usual custom to colleges.' 'This' Mrs. Dr. Graffenried replied was 'the mooted point.' 'Would it not be establishing a bad precedent' said I.'"[212] Gertrude went on to argue that if juniors were allowed to join, sophomores and freshmen could claim an equal privilege. When the vote was taken, the alumnae agreed with Gertrude. She had obviously received the attention of some of the women in attendance, because later in the meeting she was unanimously elected second vice president of the association. She was very pleased.

Indeed, Gertrude was beginning to say things and act on ideas in ways she never would have done before the war. She had grown stronger during the hardships, and now she was looking ahead. After their crops had been destroyed and their slaves freed, Gertrude recalled, "[E]ven then I nerved myself and was prepared to do *something* if I could—I believe it was the sitting still and doing nothing which unnerved me more than any thing else—I looked forward and asked myself what can I do? Nothing, except teach school."[213] She undertook the study of French, something she had always wanted to do, but now she thought it would help her in her plan to earn some money—by teaching.

The loss of the war and the emancipation of their slaves were devastating to both men and women in the planter aristocracy. Their world was turned upside down. In the beginning there was widespread anger and depression, but, over time, men and women responded very differently. In the past twenty to thirty years there have been numerous studies that have argued this point.[214] Jeff and Gertrude Thomas are excellent examples of this dichotomy, with Jeff having been seemingly destroyed by the war and its aftermath while Gertrude gets stronger and is able to change and, ultimately, move on with her life. Everything that appears in the diary at this time pertaining to Jeff would support this premise. Like every "*true man* and *soldier*," Gertrude reported on 1 May 1865, "Mr. Thomas is particularly sensitive upon the subject, expects *no good times* and in some degree tonight impressed me with his gloomy views." When he knew the slaves were to be free and he was to lose so much, "Mr. T appeared cast down, utterly spirit broken yesterday when the news first reached him and when I would hint at a brighter sky would mock at such anticipations." By September 1866, his attitude had not improved. He had not been well during the summer months and had been "worried in mind as well as body." He had decided to continue to plant in Burke County, but "[t]he unsettled state of the times, *the price of cotton* and the freedman have all conspired to annoy him." He was pessimistic, "utterly depressed," and refused to look on the good side of anything that had happened. Gertrude said there was nothing she could do to lift his spirits.[215]

With Gertrude, however, the opposite was true. On Sunday afternoon, 14 October 1866, she sat down on a bench in the back yard to make her last entry in this volume of the diary. It was another "charmingly delightful day" as she began to think of the great changes that had occurred since she had commenced that journal two years earlier. "Since then what? Country lost—property lost—Just then I looked up and conscience whispered—'Shame'—My head bows in humiliation, my heart responds. 'All is not lost, honor is still thine own. I have husband, home, children, dear loved ones and a bright sky overhead—Dear God I thank thee.'"[216] She believed the worst was over. Thankful to have home and family, Gertrude had no way of knowing what stood in store for them. She had survived another childbirth, serious illness, loss of property, fits of nerves, and destruction by an invading army. But through it all, she had become stronger and more intelligent—"a matured woman." She would need all the strength she could muster to face the future hardships— hardships that would be worse for her than the war had been.

7

Bankruptcy

"Infinitely worse than Sherman"

"Tuesday will be the day for the Presidential election and the South feels instinctively that she is standing upon the mouth of a volcano, expecting every moment an eruption, and if it takes place then—what then? Widespread desolation in the moral world which will exceed anything ever exhibited in the convulsions of nature."[217] On Sunday, 1 November 1868, on the eve of the first presidential election after the war, Gertrude sat down to describe this tense and fearful time. Ulysses S. Grant, the hero of the Union army, was the Republican candidate, and Horatio Seymour, former governor of New York, was the Democratic candidate. Grant was backed by members of the Republican Party who wanted to punish the South for secession and make it difficult for them to re-enter the Union. Seymour and his followers were in favor of the more lenient policy that had been first described by Lincoln before his assassination. Like many other Southerners on the eve of the election, Gertrude did not know what to expect.

Mistrust and fear were being fueled by rumors of what might happen now that the former slaves had been made citizens by the Fourteenth Amendment to the Constitution, which had been adopted in July of that year. The Republicans expected them to support the radical ticket, as their party was being called. The white Southerners wanted them to vote for the Democrats or Conservatives, as they were sometimes labeled. For Gertrude, it appeared that agitators were stirring up excitement. "[T]he present unsettled state of affairs among the Negroes and white people" was on everyone's mind and the topic of all conversation. The situation had reached a tipping point such that on the night Gertrude was writing, it was "reported that all of the houses in the neighborhood are to be burnt up."

For a reason she could not explain, Gertrude felt calm. Jeff and her oldest son Turner had been sleeping downstairs with guns to guard their property. She planned to carry a gun upstairs with her, but confessed she would not know how to use it if she needed to do so. They were living at their plantation Belmont outside of Augusta, and she refused to move into town as many women were doing. "If I were a man I cannot imagine myself a coward and as a woman I dislike to show that I am afraid to remain at home. Indeed I think the women of the country are *very wrong* in showing this exhibition of fear." She felt that such action by women encouraged the "evil passions" in the Negroes and left personal property unprotected. "True the coloured people are not now as they were during the war but we trusted ourselves to them then. Why not now?"[218]

Gertrude recorded a conversation she had with a fourteen-year-old black male named Ned. He was telling her many of the things that were being said by other blacks, particularly Isaiah and Mac, who were "farming with Mr. Thomas on shares." The ex-slaves had been meeting at a church and decided that "they was all gwine to meet at the creek tomorrow night to march to town the next day with uncle Isaiah as captain—and that uncle Mac said 'if he had a son who was willing to be a Democrat he would cut his throat.'" He also added that, "these men said 'that all the white folks was scared of the niggers.'" He told her that Dr. Eve's family was moving into to town that day. Ned told her, "[U]ncle Mac said, 'that things wasn't like they used to be, that they weren't afraid of white folks like they used to be and that they was gwine to have fine times, and burn up every house along the road.'" After these remarks, Gertrude concluded simply, "I listened to Ned without being in the slightest degree alarmed."[219]

Gertrude had frequent, open conversations with the freedmen similar to this one. She even overheard the cook chiding Ned for "telling the white folks everything what is said in the kitchen." But when the "state of excitement" reached a fever pitch, some of the servants in Gertrude's house were afraid that it was going to be burned. "I took a seat and talked with them awhile, told them that the white people were anxious to avoid a difficulty but that if forced to it they would fight and fight well—that I did not feel uneasy...." To this statement, one Bob was moved to say, "Why Miss Trudy would be a good soldier herself."[220] Gertrude did not know if she would be a good soldier, but she knew for sure she was not a coward. Gertrude was correct in this particular situation. There was far more talk and threat of violence than ever materialized.

Despite the fact Jeff had been elected president of the local Democratic Club, Gertrude demonstrated a more mature and open-minded attitude toward the Republicans than did many of her friends. She believed that Ulysses S. Grant was probably going to be president and that his election would not make much difference in the South. She did not blame the ex-slaves for voting the radical ticket; it would have been against her conscience to try to persuade them to do otherwise. "Think of it, the right to vote, that right which they have seen their old masters exercise with so much pride, and their young masters look forward to with so much pleasure is within their *very grasp*." She went on to say, "They secure a right for themselves, which it is true they may not understand, but they have children whom they expect to educate. Shall they secure this right for them or sell the right away?" Now that it was within their grasp, she asked, "Who can guarantee that they will ever have it extended to them again?"

Her sympathy toward the freedmen and their voting was another example of Gertrude's independent thinking. She had never fit into the conventional mode as far as slavery was concerned and had often expressed sentiment that ran counter to the strict Southern position. Her many remarks regarding slave women and their plight testified to her concern. This was not an isolated expression and was evidence of her more liberal views. Empathizing with the blacks and foreshadowing her future interest in the vote for women, Gertrude confessed, "If the women of the North once secured to me the right to vote whilst it might be an honor thrust upon me, I think I should think twice before I voted to have it taken from me." She was well aware that her thinking was out of line with popular sentiment and "smack[ed] two much of radicalism to promulgate" outside her family.[221]

Early in this volume Gertrude was caught up in the political issues surrounding the election. She even discussed in great detail two speeches that John Quincy Adams made in South Carolina in which she saw "no good to be gained." She did not attend in person, but she scrutinized the newspapers carefully. His attitude was that the Southerners had to be punished, had "to *deserve* and then to obtain the confidence of our Northern communities" in order to be restored to constitutional rights. But in Gertrude's opinion, "the South had made sufficient concessions. Let us resolve to do our duty—We need no Northern man to teach us that." She added, "with most of us the present duty—the duty of the hour is to provide sustenance for our familys and *avoid politics*. The South has a glorious record. Let us not dim her glory by senseless humiliation."[222]

After the election was over and the racial unrest began to subside, it was this duty of "providing sustenance" for her family that obsessed Gertrude's thinking. In fact, it became the central topic of this volume and the next. The economic times were bad after the war, and Gertrude's husband was especially hard hit. Jeff was still planting on their two plantations in Burke County, but with many attendant problems. A labor force remained one of his biggest concerns. He was trying to hire reliable help—black or white—but could not keep them working. He was also borrowing large sums of money to purchase supplies and to make the repairs for damages inflicted on the plantations by Northern troops. In addition, Jeff and Gertrude had both been accustomed to having large numbers of servants, traveling where they pleased, and buying whatever they wanted. They were trying to learn to do without luxuries, but it was difficult. Their problems seemed to result from a combination of hard economic times, Jeff's lack of managerial skills, and their inability to live within their means.

Gertrude began to write about not being able to repay lenders. Jeff decided during these years to approach various family members for money; he borrowed from his brother Pinckney, putting up part of the Burke County property for the collateral. He also mortgaged some of his other Burke County property to his sister, Julia Scales, and her family. Gertrude's sisters, Anne Vason and Cora Snead, were also approached. Cousin Polly Watson lent them money, and one relative, Gertrude's brother James Clanton (called Buddy), became very involved in the Thomases's economic affairs by signing on a number of notes with Jeff. Unfortunately, when Jeff did not have any money to repay them, these debts led to a number of family controversies and complicated litigation.

Aside from the two plantations in Burke County, Jeff and Gertrude owned several other pieces of property. They were living on their ninety-acre plantation in Richmond County named "Belmont." Gertrude had always enjoyed naming property after something or someone meaningful to her. In this case, she had named their plantation for "the Residence of Portia in the *Merchant of Venice* and like her home, it is approached by three avenues." The three avenues she named for well-known Confederate generals, "one named...Lee [for Robert E. Lee] the upper one, Jackson [for Thomas Jonathan Jackson, known as Stonewall Jackson] and the other which commands a view of the church and mill has a winding path is called Beauregard [for Pierre Gustave Toutant Beauregard, known as P. G. T. Beauregard]."[223] Gertrude loved her home with its flower gardens and quiet tranquility. She often spoke in her diary of the pleasure she derived from sitting on the porch watching the cows and horses grazing in the beautiful, green pastures. However, their ownership of all this wonderful property was in a fragile state. Like so many other plantation owners after the war, they owned land but had little money to maintain it.

In the city of Augusta they also owned a house at 189 Greene Street where they would go in the winter. Of course, Jeff had his porcelain and china business, Mosher, Thomas, and Schaub, on Broad Street in the commercial district of downtown. In connection with his company, Jeff had invested in stocks of kaolin, white clay used in the manufacture of ceramics. There were deposits in South Carolina and parts of Georgia. No specifics were given in the diary, but on one occasion Gertrude referred to the kaolin works, while telling her children that their father "had owned many shares in the stock, operations had been unsuccessful and that he had lost money."[224]

This was not the only phase of the business, however, that was not doing well. By November 1868, Jeff and his partners were in serious trouble. Gertrude had alluded to his financial problems in the past, but now she had become aware of their severity. She confessed her anxiety to her diary, "Old friend! dark days are gathering around me, heavy clouds obscure my future. Tears gather, it is only with an effort that I prevent them from rolling down upon your pages." She went on to say, "Mr. Thomas' affairs are so complicated, and he is so depressed 'run to death' as he expresses it." She had known about his "pecuniary embarrasments" for a long time, but now, "With in the last two or three days a man who is the agent for a New York company has been in Augusta and it is in his power to fall the firm into bankruptcy."[225] Jeff's "complicated affairs" were an entanglement of overlapping loans. He had borrowed money from every conceivable source, signing numerous notes, and now he could not come up with sufficient cash to repay his obligations.

The dreaded agent of a New York company was the representative of the R. G. Dun Company that was doing credit ratings, and one can trace the demise of the business in his brief notations. On 30 July 1866, the representative had reported that the "firm is solvent and all its members are monied men," and on a later visit he recorded, "Mosher, Thomas and Shaub keep the largest stock of crockery in town and are agents for kaolin works...collectively [worth] $50,000, good businessmen." On 19 February 1868, he briefly noted, "cr[edit] good and d[oin]g a fair Bus[iness]," and in May, 1868, "no change." But, on 30 October 1868, the company was "not worth over 5,000$," and "they are not paying their debts." The agent recommended the company should be required to "pay cash." Finally, in May 1869, he wrote simply, "Dead broke and the U.S. Marshall is now selling out their stock: dissolved."[226]

The bankruptcy to which the agent alluded so glibly was devastating for Gertrude. The crisis—the crash—had come at last. "Mr. Thomas has had a sheriff to take possession of his store and on the eleventh of this month his goods will be sold at public auction. Ah me, ah me!... For two years I have watched a death struggle, have heard every sigh, every groan, have seen the anquished brow, and convulsed lip—have seen the *mask* off...." She had known that her husband's affairs were terribly complicated and that they had been living beyond their means, but she had felt "utterly powerless to avert the blow which [she] knew was coming." She concluded that it would have been better if it had happened earlier. "The debt which now hangs like an avalanche above us would not have reached such magnitude."

Gertrude was mortified. She could not bear to read the advertisements for the sale in the newspaper. Embarrassment kept her from going into town. She said it would have been absolute torture to have walked up Broad Street the week the sale was being conducted. She asked, "Oh my God! I have been so proud a woman. What have I done that I should be so punished?" Then with a somewhat ambivalent mixture of pity and disdain, she answered her own question. "My life, my glory, my honor has been so intimately blended with that of my husband and now to see him broken in fortune, health and spirits."

Gertrude still professed concern and felt compassion for what Jeff was enduring, but she also resented him and, at times, was angered. One of the major reasons for her anger was the way Jeff had involved her family members. She was particularly sensitive about her younger brother, James "Buddy" Clanton. "Poor dear Buddy. His generous act of endorsing for Mr. Thomas will involve him in trouble. Ma blames him that he did not require collateral or security from

Mr. Thomas, but I blame Mr. Thomas more." The fact that Buddy was going to be hurt only added to her frustration. "I think I could have borne the loss of property and cheered my husband and toiled by his side but the knowledge that Buddy will lose so much by him paralyses me."[227]

The family disagreements went far beyond the problem involving her brother. In fact, the relationship with Buddy seemed to be one of the better ones. The most serious differences appear to have been with Gertrude's sister, Anne, and her husband, Judge William Vason. Sis Anne was her older sister, with whom Gertrude had some sibling rivalry early in life. Despite the fact that Gertrude was younger than Anne, she had married before Anne and received special favors from Turner Clanton. Evidence that this favoritism caused trouble surfaced in a remark Gertrude made in 1858 before Anne married. "Pa made me a present of twenty dollars yesterday and the same to Sis Anne. She does not like my receiving the same she does—It is quite natural. I wish Pa would give her a sett of diamonds and Negroes and houses to hire and rent out so that she could feel more independent." Gertrude was married with children and had received her home and slaves from her father while Anne was still living with her parents. Evidently Anne was somewhat resentful and jealous at this time.[228]

Anne had married William Vason from New Orleans in 1859 and had received her inheritance from her father, which had consisted of city lots instead of slaves. Turner Clanton undoubtedly conveyed town property to Anne because William Vason was an attorney and not a planter. No specific details are given, but Vason and Jefferson Thomas did not have much in common, and they did not get along well. By late 1868, when Turner Clanton's estate was yet unsettled, there was clear evidence that family members were squabbling. On

November 29 Gertrude wrote, "During the past few weeks Pa's estate has been in the hands of arbitrators for settlement and from the length of time they occupy I think they can arrive at no determination. Col Vason and Mr. Thomas are at deadly enmity with each other..." Gertrude was definitely on her husband's side in this dispute. "I scarely know which to do most [,] condemn or pity Col Vason for the vindictive spirit he has shown." Gertrude's youngest brother, Holt, also testified to the family's feuding. He was leaving for Paris in 1869, and Gertrude noted the humorous remark he made: "'If I am lost on the boat said he [,] you will all have my property to fight and scratch about' alluding to our disturbances with Col Vason."[229] Ironically, Holt did die on this trip to Paris, and the family differences continued to go from bad to worse.

Even though William Vason and Jeff Thomas did not get along well, Gertrude seemed to make an effort to maintain her relationship with her sister. Family loyalty was important to her. "I intend that the enmity existing between Mr. Thomas and Col Vason shall not affect my feeling toward her [Sis Anne]." Ida Vason, a close relative of William Vason's, possibly his mother or sister, was visiting from Alabama when she and Gertrude had a misunderstanding. She was supposed to have repeated gossip about Gertrude, but Gertrude decided to drop the issue. "While I have never seen a person with whom I felt less congeniality she would have been the last person whom I would deliberately have traduced. Even if it had been my nature to have done so I have always been two clannish to have injured a person so intimately connected with Sis Anne's family."[230] The devotion to her family that Gertrude exhibited was not always reciprocated by her relatives.

Whatever old rivalries may have existed, they were not the primary cause of the present problems—the division of Turner Clanton's estate was the main issue. It was made even more urgent, especially for Gertrude and Jeff, because of the financial stress they were under, as they had hoped that whatever she received from the estate would improve their situation. For some reason, presumably because of money they had already received from the estate, they did not know if they would get anything else. In May 1869, Gertrude wrote, "I do not feel quite so desperate as I did last year when I did not expect anything from Pa's estate." It was decided that the children of Turner Clanton would hold a drawing to decide which plantation they would receive.

Gertrude got the Road Place and breathed a sigh of relief, writing, "I will at least have a home." She had been born there and had once jested she intended to send an artist up to sketch it. "I might become distinguished some day and it would be fortunate to have had it taken."[231] In the inventory of his property made when he died in 1864, the Road Place had been listed as one of Turner Clanton's plantations in Columbia County, consisting of 1,954 acres valued at $15 an acre.[232] Even though it was one of his larger plantations, the value per acre was lower, suggesting that perhaps the land was less desirable. In reality, this gift gave them more land, but there was not enough cash to pay taxes, hire workers, and buy supplies. However, Gertrude seemed grateful and did not complain. In fact, she was already trying to think of a way she could use her inheritance to repay Buddy. "If I knew that Mr. Thomas would be permitted to retain his other places and we could obtain a support from them I would be willing for Buddy to take the Road Place and keep it until we could pay what we owe him."

Gertrude also received four city lots, along with a sum of money, as a portion of her share of her father's estate. At one point she mentioned $1500 she had inherited at that time. All of this property she was willing to use if it would help get them out of debt. "I will be satisfied after a support for my family for all I have or can expect to have to assist Mr. Thomas in paying his debts. I wish I had more to aid him."[233] Unfortunately, all she had would not be enough to rescue them.

By 1869 Jeff's financial problems had been mounting steadily over the last few years. As Gertrude described them, "For two years Mr. Thomas has had this complication of affairs to worry him."[234] At one point Gertrude mentioned casually that he was being sued. An examination of the minutes of the Superior Court of Richmond County shows a number of cases where individuals or institutions were bringing him to court to get their money. A review of one of these cases illustrates the difficulties facing Jeff. In June 1868, in a case brought by E. Walton against J. Jefferson Thomas, the jury ruled in favor of the plaintiff for the sum of $5,625, with interest and the cost of the suit. From these simple facts and a few comments Gertrude made in the diary, one can begin to see a pattern that would be repeated a number of times. When Jeff had to come up with a large sum of money, he would appeal to a relative who still had money to lend. In this case it was Cousin Polly Walton. "Mr. Thomas made an arrangement with the man from New York by giving him a mortgage upon our lot in Augusta. It has been settled upon the children and I but there is a mortgage upon it for Cousin Polly for $5000." In order to repay Polly Walton in 1869, Jeff was forced to sell their home in Augusta to Mr. Campbell who bought it for $7,500.[235]

Gertrude could not tolerate this sense of obligation; it was a humiliation to her. "So deeply did I feel the obligation I was under to Mrs. Walton (Cousin Polly) that I was relieved when our house was sold and she was paid." She went on to say,

> I breathed freer, and afterwards when she sent me a small bag of butter beans which I had previously asked her for, I told Ma "to keep them. I did not want them." Ma said I was "foolish." Perhaps so, I only knew that never while I live do I wish

myself or one of my children to be under obligations to any person, (who has sued or advertised us) for as much as a pin point[,] treat them politely, courteously, but do not renew the intolerable sense of obligation.[236]

It was worse for Gertrude because she had a great sense of pride and had once been free of financial concerns. She was moved to say, "What I, the child of wealth and pride. I suffer such degradation."[237]

By the end of 1869 they had lost their home and their business in Augusta. When Gertrude began a new volume of her diary in November 1870, she attached two newspaper clippings on the first page advertising the sheriff's sale of both their plantations in Burke County. The notices were in the Waynesboro paper, and in an effort to avoid publicity they contained only the initials of the people involved. One plantation was 800 acres. "Said tract of land levied upon...to satisfy a mortgage fi fa...in favor of Julia E. Scales Administratrix of Nath'l Scales vs. J.J. Thomas" Julia Scales was Jeff's only sister and Gertrude's dear friend from her days at Wesleyan Female College. The other sale was for one tract of 800 acres and another of 250 acres to satisfy mortgages made by J. Pinckney Thomas, Jeff's brother, who had married Gertrude's sister, Mary. Gertrude was depressed. "At times I rebel. I say, [T]his is too hard. I suffered during the war. I lost a great deal after its close, but it was so general a loss that we could sympathise with each other, but this trial I am under going now is worse."[238]

There was to be no relief for Gertrude. In December of 1870, another disappointment was thrust upon her, and it was made even worse because it originated with her brothers and sisters. A suit was brought against Jeff for money owed Turner Clanton's estate. "In settling with Pa's estate Mr. Thomas was owing them I think four thousand dollars. Why this was so I do not know. He was owing some of it to Pa before his death and he was *expecting a large legacy* when the estate was divided and used some of the money of the estate." Gertrude knew she would spare her sisters' husbands such humiliation if she were in their position. "I know it is legal. I do not forget that. But this is against all nature. I get bewildered."

More than ever she felt isolated. "Why this is infinitely worse than Sherman. Then I was one of a crowd, now I am alone." She could not help thinking of *The Scarlet Letter*. "I remind myself of the woman in that powerful book of Hawthorne's who wore upon her breast the Scarlet Letter and yet she was no more of a heroine in her concealment than many a Negro woman who has concealed for the same cause the name of their child's father." She finally concluded, "But it was the publicity the being set apart, the being conspicuous the branding which was torture to a proud spirit."[239]

However, the most difficult news for Gertrude to hear at the end of 1870 was that they might lose Belmont. When she read of the sheriff's sale of their ninety-acre home in Richmond County, she could not believe what she was seeing. "[M]y home was levied upon, Belmont, the home upon which we have bestowed so much labor and love, the flower garden with its beautiful arch and often the subject of praise from Pa." It was originally set to be sold on the first Tuesday in January of 1871.There were numerous delays, and they would eventually be able to hold on to the property. But Gertrude did not know that in 1870. She wept, "Sobs such as hurt but do not relieve the over-burdened heart." She tried to pray but could not. "[S]omehow I wanted Pa worse than I did God and I stretched out my arms and called him."[240]

No one had ever been able to replace Pa in Gertrude's mind. Now in these times of trouble she felt that if he were alive things would be better. He would help her with his good judgment and cheer her with some kind word. In the present difficulties, Mary Clanton was buying clothes for Gertrude's children and allowing Turner and Mary Belle to live with her and go to school. Gertrude appreciated her mother's efforts. "I don't remember that I have ever devoted much time in the journals which I have kept to praising Ma." Gertrude said she admired her mother's "honest, truthful, self abrogating nature" but did not express it in words often.[241] At times her mother's words disappointed her, and, no matter what she felt now for her mother, it did not begin to equal the devotion she had had for her father.

Gertrude's feeling of alienation from her brothers and sisters was increasing. Early in 1870 she had written, "I expect I am morbid but my pride has suffered greatly of late…I have met with no expression of sympathy from one member of my family. None of them have been to see me." She did not believe that any "event except a death in my family would be apt to induce them to hire a conveyance to ride out six miles in the country to see me."[242] In December of the same year she remarked how her pride suffered when she thought of her children as the "poor relations of the family." Near Christmas at her mother's house Gertrude commented "at the dinner table Saturday (Ma was out of the room) that I should like to be off in a new place, far off from any one I knew, that I had become accustomed to never seeing my relatives, for unless I sought them I never saw them."[243] Gertrude admitted she was in an irritable state, but she did not believe her sisters had the ability to understand what she was experiencing.

Her husband was of no help to her either. Wrapped up as he was in his problems, he made no efforts to sympathize with his wife. He did not praise her attempts to save money by sewing or doing without needed articles. "I do not think he appreciates my puny efforts at trying to stop the floodgates of debt with which I feel that we are contending." She would try to make suggestions to help but they were never taken. At times she felt she could see what was wrong and would try to tell Jeff "not in a fault finding manner." She knew she was not supposed to intrude into his business. "I never attempt the slightest interference. I only advise him and this I seem to be unfortunate in my manner of doing." Trying hard not to be critical of her husband, she wrote, "[N]o living being has heard me utter one word of censure or complaint against Mr. Thomas for the manner in which our affairs are involved." But she finally could not resist confessing to her diary, "Yet in my own conscience I think a great deal of what we call bad luck is bad management."[244]

Jeff Thomas's low self-esteem and awareness of his own failures were becoming more and more apparent. A number of the remarks he made during this difficult period reveal how he felt about himself. When he received the papers that notified him he was bankrupt, his response had been, "I am the worst broken man in the world...I have none of my cotton out and nothing in the world to go on." He continually looked on the negative side of every turn of events. Gertrude wished he would be more optimistic. "If Mr. Thomas was more hopeful it would infuse new life and vigor into our little family circle."[245]

Finally in December of 1870, after she and Jeff had a heated conversation—as she called their arguments—about the ever-present financial problems, she described maybe his lowest moment. She wrote, "Mr. Thomas does not know what to do, talks about being a fit subject for the Lunatic Asylum and said tonight 'if I could get anyone to take care of me, he thought the best thing he could do would be to go to one.'" She felt he really did not mean a word of it, but it made a negative impact on her. When he went so far as to "use some irreverent expression" as she referred to profanity; she said, "Mr. Thomas

I have suffered a great deal for the last two or three days. Don't add to it by such remarks." He ended the conversation, "I have suffered two, said he, you can stay at home. I have to go out and face the world." Jeff and Gertrude were both having a very hard time, and, obviously, they were not able to help each other, nor were they getting help from anyone else.[246]

By March of 1871, Gertrude's feeling of isolation from her family was perhaps the greatest it had ever been. Jeff's affairs were again made public. His factor in Savannah, William H. Stark, had sued and there was a notice in the newspaper on March 9 about a sale of cows, mules, horses, and "a lot...of old hoes, ploughs etc" in order that he might be paid. Gertrude blamed her family. "I am sorry for him (Mr. Thomas)—I may be a strange woman but I do not dislike the loss of property as much as I do the fact that it is my own family who are having my husband sold out."

In her anger she sat down and wrote her mother a letter that she copied in her diary. Remembering the suit brought in November by Mr. Montgomery on behalf of her sisters, she wrote, "Dear Ma, ...I have read that advertisement and I have been trying to remember if in reality or fiction I have ever known of such an unnecessary humiliation being forced upon a woman, who staggering beneath her c[ro]ss, has this bitter cup pressed to her lip by—her sisters." She had read it over and over and wept bitterly. She remembered her mother saying that Mr. Montgomery was acting legally and the proceeds of the sale would not benefit the family. She wrote, "*As there* was *nothing to gain* my humiliation was unnecessary. One word from Sis Anne or Cora and the others, and it would have been prevented." Mr. Thomas had asked Col. Snead, Cora's husband, to stop the proceedings, and he had refused. "Sued by my mother, my sisters and brothers, Mr. Thomas' sisters and brothers, with Starks lien for which I am responsible added to it, I rebel and turning to my children for comfort, I think they two may sue me some day." She said she had been advised that she could "recover from Pa's estate by suing," but she had refused. She said there was a "higher tribunal" at which they would be judged. She remembered "Pa's dying charge to us 'to live in harmony' and Col Vason's promise of 'I will…to the best of my ability.'" Looking back on the letter the next day, Gertrude decided her sisters "knew not what they did." They did not understand how she was suffering. "Their husbands are their agents."[247]

It is impossible to unravel the myriad complexities of Jefferson Thomas's financial problems. Some of the lawsuits continued over many years, but Gertrude and her husband were able to hang on to Belmont longer than they had at first expected. It seems that Gertrude's brother, Buddy, rescued them more than once. Also, the trust fund that Turner Clanton had set up for her after her marriage enabled them to keep some possessions longer. After the bankruptcy, any remaining property was often put in her name. Repeatedly, Gertrude was being asked to sign papers with which she was uncomfortable. "I have been willing to sign when advised by Mr. Kerr, [an attorney or family advisor] (and not before) the claim or the interest of the money but I have tried so hard not to implicate myself. I have striven to preserve the little given to me in the division of the estate *for my children*." When a number of liens were placed on the property they had remaining, she said, "The arrangement could not be made without its being run in my name." In her anxiety, she wrote, "Ah my journal in my effort not to reduce my children to beggary…and my wish to oblige Mr. Thomas I have a hard time."[248]

There were no indications in the early 1870s that their financial problems would be solved, but Gertrude's mental outlook began gradually to improve. Perhaps she had just learned how to live and cope better with adversities. She stopped talking about her family difficulties long enough to record a lengthy description of an exciting incident in her life— an incident that revealed something about her growth and self-assurance. "The long deferred wish has been accomplished. Today I have seen and talked with President Davis! *At last!*"

Hearing that Jefferson Davis would be greeting Augustans at the Planters Hotel between noon and 1 p.m. on 26 May 1871, she took her ten-year-old son, Jefferson Davis Thomas, to meet the hero for whom he had been named. Beginning her entry, "I am writing history for you my children and your mother tells you now of her interview with the man whom she 'most' delights to honor." Gertrude wrote that Davis was much better looking in person than he was in his pictures, "so quietly elegant, so perfectly self possessed, not handsome but bearing about him that unmistaken air of a gentleman, without which the handsomest face would have no attraction to me." When she introduced her son to the former president of the Confederacy, he put his arm around the young boy, and remarked, "I cannot tell you Mrs. Thomas how highly I appreciate this compliment." He was even more gratified when Gertrude told him she had added Davis to her son's name when he was taken through Augusta a prisoner.

Gertrude went on to record a brief but revealing conversation she had with Davis. Placing his hand on Jeff's head, Davis remarked that he "had great faith in the southern women, that they would train the boys right…. It will come out right. I may not live to see it, but it is not in the nature of God to allow the best people he ever made to remain permanently under the rule of the meanest people he ever made." Despite the fact that Gertrude disliked the North for what they had inflicted on the South during the war, she did not agree with him. "President Davis was the courtly, elegant gentleman but not perfect. He has strong prejudices as that remark indicated, but he is mistaken. We are not the best, nor are the Yankees the worst nation God ever made." More than ever Gertrude was beginning to think for herself. The night before she had said Jefferson Davis was the "only man living whom [she] should be willing to kiss the hand of and feel honored in so doing," but that "remark gave me the key to understand why it was that it had not for one moment occurred to me to render the homage of kissing his hand as I had the night before said I would be willing to do."[249] She was becoming her own person and not automatically accepting what others said—not even the former president of the Confederate states.

Two days after her visit with President Davis, Gertrude arrived at the last page of her journal. It was a portion of her life that she would not want to live over again. When the question had recently been put to her, "You would be willing to begin again at seventeen, would you not Mrs. Thomas?" she had answered, with all honesty, "No said I for then my troubles began."[250] She was in a pensive mood, but, true to her nature, she refused to end that volume on a pessimistic note. In spite of the fact that her family's problems continued to grow, with more important lawsuits to be decided in the upcoming weeks, she would not dwell on them—at least for the time being.

Her children were a great comfort to her. She was now the mother of five children. A son, Julian, had been born on 23 January 1868, a date not covered in either this volume or the last. Fortunately he was healthy and had been a joy to her during hard times. He was now three years and six months old, Cora Lou was eight, Jeff ten, Mary Belle thirteen, and Turner was seventeen. Occasionally, she would mention the three children they had buried, but not too often. She was disagreeing with Jeff more than she had earlier in their marriage, but she did not entertain divorce—at least, not in the diary that has survived. Her sense of duty still compelled her to try to help him in any way she could.

Gertrude also had her faith to sustain her. "I believe in all ruling Providence and am willing to trust him for the future."[251] As she expressed it, she had a "dim consciousness" that the recent events in her life had enlarged and strengthened her character. Indeed, whether she was fully aware of it or not, she was growing stronger and more self-assured all the time. Already having considered the possibility of teaching, Gertrude was beginning to wonder if she could make money by writing. She had even mustered the courage to send off a couple of manuscripts. They had been rejected but, nevertheless, were tentative steps toward the publication of some of what she had written. Isolated from family and friends, she was learning to depend on herself. Years before she had said she wished she could meet an intelligent woman who had suffered and grown strong. She was becoming that woman.

Portrait of Ella Gertrude Clanton Thomas
in her second day dress after her marriage in 1852

Courtesy of F. Michael Despeaux, Great-Great Grandson of Ella Gertrude Clanton Thomas, Easley, S.C.

Gertrude's mother, Mary Luke Clanton (1812–1884)

Courtesy of the author, Carolyn Newton Curry, Atlanta, GA

Portrait of Gertrude's father Turner Clanton ca. 1837

Courtesy of William T. McGraw, Bogart, GA

WESLEYAN·COLLEGE·MACON·GEORGIA·
THE·PIONEER·COLLEGE·FOR·WOMEN·A·D·1836·

Painting by Athos Menaboni of original Wesleyan
depicting dresses students would have worn

Courtesy of Wesleyan College

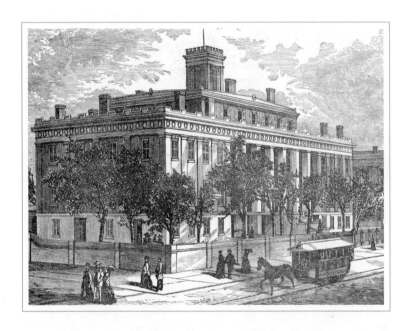

Original building of Wesleyan Female College as shown in the
college's catalogue for 1849, the year that Gertrude entered

Courtesy of Wesleyan College, Archives and Special Collections, Macon, GA

Portrait of J. Jefferson Thomas
thought to be painted in the late 1850s

Courtesy of F. Michael Despeaux, Great-Great Grandson of Ella Gertrude Clanton Thomas, Easley, SC

The three story, twenty-four room Clanton Mansion
on Greene St. in Augusta, Georgia had solid silver
hardware and doorknobs and was said to cost $50,000
when it was built in the 1840s.

Courtesy of Reese Library, Special Collections, Georgia Regents University, Augusta, GA

Children at play in front of the Clanton Mansion.

Courtesy of Reese Library, Special Collections, Georgia Regents University, Augusta, GA

Front view of Clanton Mansion
showing huge columns and ornate iron fencing
Library of Congress, Prints & Photographs Division, HABS GA, 123-AUG, 1-3

Old Colonial Home, Green Street, Augusta, Ga.

The Clanton Mansion was so beautiful it was used
on post cards celebrating the beauty of Augusta's homes.

Courtesy of Old Colonial Home, Green Street, Augusta and Environs Picture Post Cards in Color,
East Central Georgia Regional Library as presented in the Digital Library of Georgia

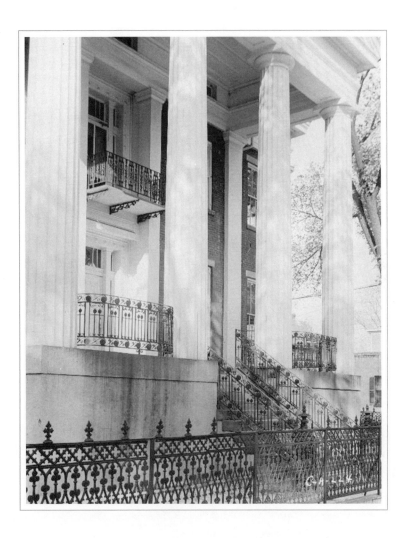

Detail of beautiful iron work ornamenting
the front of the Clanton Mansion

Library of Congress, Prints & Photographs Division, HABS GA, 123-AUG, 1-5

Foreign visitors such as William Makepeace Thackeray admired
the huge trees and wide streets of Augusta

The historic Augusta City Hall, originally built in 1820, and the
Signers' Monument, erected in 1848 to commemorate the three
Georgians who signed the Declaration of Independence

Cotton bales stacked on Broad Street as they would have
been in 1865 as Sherman was coming toward Augusta,
and everyone feared they "were packed to burn
at a moment's notice."

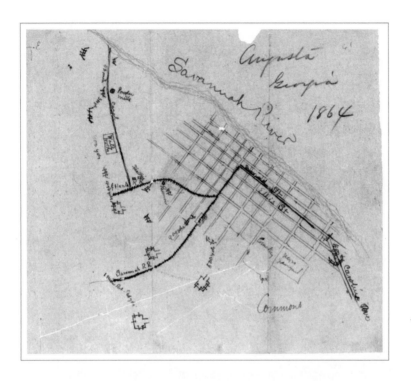

Hand written map of plans for fortification
of Augusta dated 1864 with Sherman written
in lower right hand corner

Library of Congress, Map Collection, Plans of Fortifications at Augusta, GA (1864), g3924a cws00047

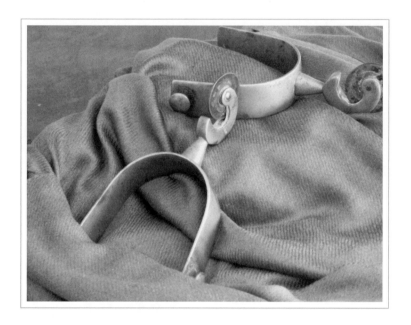

Spurs made from silver half dollars and pieces of brass
casing for the shells fired from Fort Sumter in the exchange
that started the Civil War

Courtesy of F. Michael Despeaux, Great-Great Grandson of Ella Gertrude Clanton Thomas, Easley, SC

J. Jefferson Thomas on his pony "Dixie Will Go"
that he often rode in parades to celebrate the Civil War
or the "Lost Cause" as it became known

J. Jefferson Thomas in his Confederate uniform
with knee-high leather boots and spurs

From the Princeton University Archives, Department of Rare Books and Special Collections,
Princeton University Library, Princeton, NJ

Collection of Gertrude's scrapbooks
with suffrage scrapbook dated 1894-1895 on stand

Courtesy of F. Michael Despeaux, Great-Great Grandson of Ella Gertrude Clanton Thomas, Easley, SC

Gertrude's voluminous suffrage scrapbook included
a picture of Susan B. Anthony, a picture of Anna Howard
Shaw, and an article about the second inauguration
of Grover Cleveland in 1893, along with many other
materials of interest to her.

Courtesy of F. Michael Despeaux, Great-Great Grandson of Ella Gertrude Clanton Thomas, Easley, SC

Mary Latimer McLendon worked with Gertrude first in the
Women's Christian Temperance Union and then in Georgia Woman
Suffrage Association, where she served as President from 1906 until
1921. She was the sister of Rebecca Latimer Felton.

Rebecca Latimer Felton and Ella Gertrude shared
enthusiasm for women's causes and often traveled
to conventions together. Felton is shown here in 1922,
when she became the first woman to serve
in the United States Senate.

Portrait of Ella Gertrude Clanton Thomas painted by
E.S. Jeter in 1899, the year Gertrude was elected President
of the Georgia Woman Suffrage Association

Obelisk marking Gertrude's grave in Magnolia Cemetery,
Augusta, Georgia, memorializing her death on May 11, 1907

Courtesy of Tim Owings, Augusta, GA

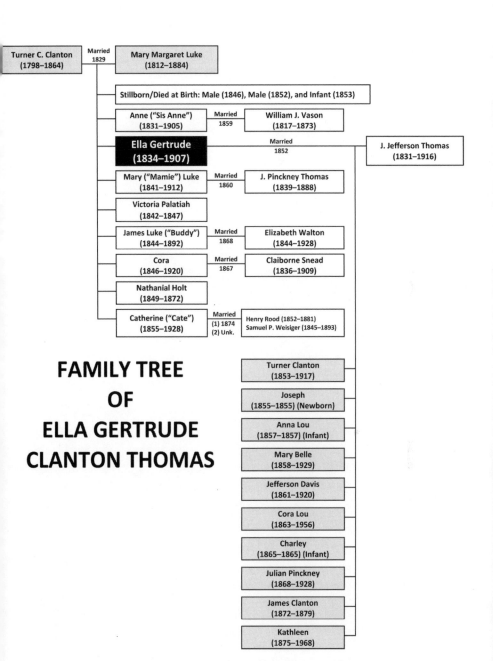

Turner C. Clanton (1798–1864) — Married 1829 — Mary Margaret Luke (1812–1884)

Stillborn/Died at Birth: Male (1846), Male (1852), and Infant (1853)

Anne ("Sis Anne") (1831–1905) — Married 1859 — William J. Vason (1817–1873)

Ella Gertrude (1834–1907) — Married 1852 — J. Jefferson Thomas (1831–1916)

Mary ("Mamie") Luke (1841–1912) — Married 1860 — J. Pinckney Thomas (1839–1888)

Victoria Palatiah (1842–1847)

James Luke ("Buddy") (1844–1892) — Married 1868 — Elizabeth Walton (1844–1928)

Cora (1846–1920) — Married 1867 — Claiborne Snead (1836–1909)

Nathanial Holt (1849–1872)

Catherine ("Cate") (1855–1928) — Married (1) 1874 (2) Unk. — Henry Rood (1852–1881) / Samuel P. Weisiger (1845–1893)

FAMILY TREE
OF
ELLA GERTRUDE
CLANTON THOMAS

Turner Clanton (1853–1917)

Joseph (1855–1855) (Newborn)

Anna Lou (1857–1857) (Infant)

Mary Belle (1858–1929)

Jefferson Davis (1861–1920)

Cora Lou (1863–1956)

Charley (1865–1865) (Infant)

Julian Pinckney (1868–1928)

James Clanton (1872–1879)

Kathleen (1875–1968)

8

Teacher and Writer

"I am a public woman now."

On 29 May 1871, when Gertrude made her final entry in
volume eleven, she was still living at Belmont, their beloved
plantation that they were unrealistically hoping to keep. When
she started volume twelve, she was living on what she referred
to simply as "The Farm." The date was 31 December 1878. She
testified to the fact that she had kept a journal in the
intervening years with the statement, "I have been reading
over my last journal, reading the record for the past three
years. I was eight years writing that book and this one has been
bought for months."[252] Unfortunately, nothing of what she
recorded during that eight-year period has survived.

Family tradition holds that portions of the diary were
destroyed and not lost.[253] It had been a very unhappy time for
Gertrude, and she had begun to say critical things more openly
in her previous volume. Could she have become so candid that
in later years family members thought it was best not to
preserve what she had to say? It is impossible to know, but
there are some clues as to what happened during the eight-year
interval.

One can be sure that the Thomases's financial condition did
not improve. A review of the records of the Superior Court of
Richmond County shows that the lawsuits continued. The
difficulties in the case involving Gertrude's sisters appeared on
the docket several times, particularly in 1872.[254] There were

ongoing debts and suits related to her husband's company, Mosher, Thomas, and Schuab. A jury ruled against J. J. Thomas and in favor of I. M. Dye and Co. for the sum of $3000 in June 1871, and in favor of Isaac Simon and Sons for $621.68.[255] But the most damaging court ruling came on 21 October 1872. In the case of *The National Bank of Augusta v. J. Jefferson Thomas*, judgment was rendered for the plaintiff, for the sum of $35,185.86 principal and $11,268.22 interest.[256] This sum, a staggering amount for that period of time, particularly on top of all the other rulings, must have brought the family to one of its lowest moments. No matter what course of action Jeff took, his affairs continued to deteriorate. At times he seemed to be able to figure out how to hold on to property, such as when he salvaged Belmont, for example. Unfortunately, even though they were able to maintain possession of this favorite home place, luck was not on their side. To their great disappointment—and under unexplained circumstances—Belmont burned sometime in the 1870s, and very little was saved.

The farm, which was very near the old site of Belmont, was a much more modest house than they were accustomed to having. The carpet had become so soiled that Gertrude had rolled it up and preferred the bare floors, despite the fact they were cold in the winter. The plaster was falling off the walls, and Gertrude was anxious to get it repaired. She was never particularly fond of living there, but, after a time, she grew sentimental. She began looking for a name for their home. At first she decided on Dixie Land for obvious connotations, but then changed it to Dixie Farm, "for it is literally a farm—on both sides are cotton fields and in front a piece of ground which during the winter is always green with oats or some green crop."[257]

During the intervening years Jeff and Gertrude's family had also grown. A boy, Clanton, had been born 16 September 1872, and a girl, Kathleen, had been born 4 January 1875. Gertrude was now the affectionate mother of seven children. With less money to feed and dress her children, Gertrude was busier than ever before in her life. But despite all she had to do, she kept looking for a way to add to the family income. She often wondered if she could make money with her writing, which was by far her first choice, but she finally decided that, with her children to care for and educate, she would operate a school out of her home.

Her neighbor and friend, Mrs. Carmichael, who had been in charge of the county school, had recently died. By January 1879, Gertrude made up her mind—somewhat reluctantly—to take over the county teaching job. "I am grateful and contented that I have an opportunity of adding to the comfort of my family.... I know that I will not be mistress of my own time but with that thought comes the reflection I shall be profitably engaged."[258]

Since they had been living on the farm, Jeff had moved an old barn, improved it, and made it into a wing room, joining it to the back porch. They had been using it as a kitchen. Now they added windows and a door facing the public road and made it her schoolroom. The county had provided a stove and desks, and Gertrude was to be paid $30 a month. This was in stark contrast to her earlier life. Before the Civil War she would never have thought about working for money—nor would she have considered how much anything cost. In her carefree youth, if she wanted a new dress, a book, or even a trip, all she had to do was ask her father. In fact, during her college days, she always exceeded her father's generous allowances because of her love for fine clothes. Once she had remarked she would like to appear in a new outfit every day. She still wanted beautiful clothes, especially for her daughters, but they were almost impossible to have. The days of not thinking about what things cost were gone forever.

Gertrude now began a habit in her diary of itemizing where every penny went. "Fifteen dollars of the first month's salary was paid out for the improvement of this room.... Ten more of that months salary [was] given for a black Tarleton for Mary Belle."[259] But she would list much smaller amounts individually. "I gave $1.50 for it [material for a dress for Cora Lou] and engaged the making of it with Mrs. Marsh for $3.00, bought two white table cloths for 3.25—trimmings for Cora Lou's dress for 85 cents, bought pins four papers for 10 cents, hair pins five papers for five cents. 10 cents candy. 10 cents dried figs." Obviously, she was trying very hard to dress her girls as she thought they should be dressed and give her children some small treats. But money was also spent on trying to maintain what they already had to make it last longer. "Paid for the cleaning of three pair of kid gloves 25 cents [and] 15 for the cleaning of a lace tie." She listed a teapot she purchased for thirty five cents. She even included the 10 cents she could manage to contribute when she went to St. James Church on that Sunday morning. Conscious of every penny, she was thankful prices were lower now, but "Oh the scarcity of money—The war times was nothing to it."[260]

Gertrude hated the idea of owing money to anyone. To her it was the most humiliating aspect of their financial situation. Her income enabled her to repay some of the smaller loans, and she took great pride and satisfaction in so doing. Before the war a Miss Sego had done some sewing, and Gertrude had owed her $5.00 since that time. Now, it had been more than ten years, but Gertrude could not forget. "I have always felt that she should be paid but how could I pay it? I called to see her, gave her the five dollars, found her sick and promised that Mr.

T would send her a load of wood, which has not been sent yet."[261]

To avoid publicity in the newspapers, Gertrude even undertook much bigger and more important debts. When they were in danger of "being levied upon" for back taxes on the plantation in Columbia County, she borrowed the money from her mother. She was very proud when she arranged to pay her mother back from her earnings. "I was bright and cheerful notwithstanding the fact that I had pledged myself to pay the amount I had, about fifty dollars." Her husband's response was not what she hoped. "I told Mr. Thomas and if I expected praise, commendation or anything of the kind, then or since, I was disappointed. Not one word of any thing of the kind, and this when I know he dislikes an advertisement of that kind in the papers as much as I do."[262] She had been hurt before when he was insensitive to her efforts to economize. Now, he did not seem to appreciate her efforts to repay their debts.

Disagreement about the management of their ongoing financial difficulties was getting worse. It appears from the diary that Gertrude was offering her opinions more often and being more adamant about them. Her comments indicate she was giving a considerable amount of thought as to how she and her husband could solve their problems. "I have been trying to persuade Mr. Thomas to consent to rent the land we own on the river.... We own the plantation in Columbia. The four houses in Augusta, this place and Belmont." She had a definite plan in mind. "I have proposed to Mr. Thomas that I teach and pay the drygoods bill of the family and some of the current expenses and to try to make a support out of the other places and if we can rent the river swamp let the money go toward paying the mortgage on this place or some other debt." Gertrude said Jeff's response to her ideas was, "Oh it seems to worry him so." Whether he could not agree with her or just did not like her making suggestions is not clear, and her response was to get "fretted" and have a sick headache.[263]

By now Gertrude was as overworked and frustrated as ever. Even though she was not particularly elated with teaching, she had decided it was her duty. As for their ongoing dilemma, she finally decided how she felt. "So far as I am concerned I have made up my mind that school teaching is to be my employment and if I were the only one to consult I would call my creditors together—make the best terms I could with them, try to secure some kind of support, give up everything and work the rest of my life. I would not have my existence so harassed."[264] By late 1879 she talked often of being tired, having bad headaches, and being quite nervous. She worried about her children not being able to travel to Catoosa Springs and such places the way she had as a young girl, and she felt envious at times of her family members who could afford to travel. Mr. Thomas had withdrawn from the church, but the thing that bothered her the most was his profanity in front of the children. She was not able to talk about these things with anyone, so she poured these thoughts into the privacy of the journal. But then, toward the end of the year, something far worse happened.

Just shy of his seventh birthday, Gertrude's son Clanton died, and she was faced, yet again, with the awful anguish of a child dying. This time was the worst of all because little Clanton was older and was so loved by all the family. He had ridden to their plantation in Columbia County with his father and brother Julian. When they returned, he was complaining of a headache, suddenly took a fever, and died within days. As was often the case with young children at this time, no one was sure what was wrong with him, and they were unable to help him. Gertrude was frustrated because she had to teach her classes and could not be with him constantly. Leaving Clanton in a nearby room, Gertrude came in during the morning to check on him. Then later, "I came in, changed his clothes at recess and I know now he was very sick then. He went to sleep and I returned to the school room leaving him with Cora Lou with instructions to call Mr. Thomas if she left him. When I came in again he *did not know me*. Oh my God that is so hard." Gertrude was guilt-stricken. "I was teaching other peoples children when I ought to have been with my own child."[265]

Gertrude grieved more over his death than she had over the deaths of her other children. "I have other children in the spirit world but my little earth child, my little seven year old darling is dearer than the other three who were so young." He was a gentle, sweet child, and Gertrude had thought he might become a minister someday. She could not be reconciled to his death. "Clanton my bright, beautiful boy. Where, oh where is he? I saw him die. I saw him after he was dead, but oh darling I want to see you *now, now*…. Oh how hard it is when we are so proud of our children to have them taken from us, and then I wept, oh so bitterly and have been weeping ever since."[266] This was written 16 November 1879, five weeks after Clanton had died.

In December of that same year, Gertrude reached one of her deepest depressions. She was still in mourning for Clanton. Tired from a week of teaching, she was sitting by the fire reading with the other children when, suddenly, Jeff came into the room and—with an oath—threw the newspaper onto the table. Just when she thought she could take no more, there was a column and a half on the front page of the *Augusta Chronicle* about her family. In a report on the decisions of the Supreme Court in Atlanta on December 9 was the case "J.J. Thomas, Trustee, and Gertrude Thomas, vs Jones and Norris, Complaint from Richmond." The company had brought suit to recover $992.36 due them from June 20 to 2 December 1874.[267]

The article stated that Jeff and Gertrude had failed to pay for provisions and wages for twelve laborers on a construction job. When Gertrude read the complex legal language, she did not understand everything she read, but her eyes filled with tears. To see her name and the names of her children listed in a lawsuit in the newspapers was embarrassing, and she could not utter a word for a long time. She sat before the fire and thought and thought until her brain was dazed. "I only felt that Mr. Thomas could not help me, the children could not. I had not one friend upon whom I could rely and before me seemed a dense high wall. Hope there was none for me and realizing this I sank on my knees by the sofa and said not one word. My heart and brain were alike [,] dumb utterance I had none." [268]

Finally after reading over the decision several times, she had one consoling thought, "Pa's will will hold good and that the property was secured for the children." As always in her life, even long after his death, her father was the only one who could bring comfort. "My life time interest may be sold but something from the wreck will be saved for them, and oh my father! Do you, can you know how grateful, how very grateful I am to you for this provision of your will." [269] Gertrude was partly correct. Records of the Richmond County Court show that in February 1880, Jeff, as trustee, was given permission to sell a portion of her estate to cover the debt. In this case, it was the city lots on the southwest corner of Taylor and Washington Streets as "is necessary to settle, compromise and discharge the said Execution of Jones and Norris." [270] This was an example of how her life estate began to slip away. But she was correct that it was only a portion and that much of it still remained for her children—at least for the time being.

Gertrude had reached the bottom, but the financial problems did not end with this recent suit. In fact, they would never end, and cases involving her name would remain in litigation through the last decades of her life. But it appeared that at this point, Gertrude's life began to move in a new direction. She started to let go of the past and look more to the future.

She had always had a need to achieve something—to be useful and not just spend her days doing mundane things. On 1 January 1880, she wrote, "Today I realize how old I am and how little I have accomplished…. I will be 46 and enter on my 47th year in April but the only way I can see of being useful to my family is by continuing to teach school."[271] Her school was going well, and she managed to keep approximately twenty children. But teaching young children elementary skills was not satisfying for her; she did it out of a sense of duty and not devotion. Her great love was writing—she wished she could earn money by publishing. At this point, she decided she would try to find a way to get her writing published whether or not she got paid for it.

Gertrude had already begun to make tentative steps in that direction. She and Jeff had joined the Richmond Vale Grange together back in the 1870s, and by 1875 Jeff was the secretary of the council. Even though there would only be a few women in attendance, Gertrude enjoyed going. Four essays she had written had appeared in *The Planter and Grange*. She was pleased and carefully posted two of them in a scrapbook. Dated 1876, one was entitled "Housekeeping" and one "Household Economy" and was signed E.G. Thomas. The tone was lofty. "Housekeeping began in the Garden of Eden. In Paradise our Mother Eve kept house without a care, no…consideration of 'what shall we eat, or where withal shall we be cloth[ed]'." Feeling some necessity to allude to her class, or rather former class, she added, "My idea of housekeeping does not consist in performing the work altogether, but in planning and 'looking well to the ways of her household' in seeing that it is well done by those whom we employ."[272] It was certainly not one of her favorite topics, but she was obviously proud that something she had written was in print.

During that summer Gertrude wrote about a subject much closer to her heart. She responded to an article in the *Chronicle* about President Jefferson Davis. The *New York Sun* had made the assertion that Mr. Davis had a great many namesakes in the South, and the editor of the Augusta paper had contradicted him. Referring to her journal, she described how she had named her son for the Confederate president and how she and her son had met and talked with him. In her letter to the editors, she conveyed her indignation and clearly made her point that she felt the *Chronicle* was wrong. On 10 August 1879 a Mr. Robinson complimented her on her "very fine piece" of last Monday.[273]

Gertrude was gaining confidence from the responses she was getting. She began to make more effort to get her opinions and descriptions in the newspaper. On 12 March 1880 she recorded, "Two weeks ago I wrote an article with regard to the improvements of our [Rosney] Chapel, signed my name Mrs. Gertrude Thomas, and it was published in the *Chronicle* and the *Constitutionalist*. I am a public woman now [and] would like for the patrons of my school to have an idea that I am capable of writing an interesting article."[274] It was significant that she signed her name Mrs. Gertrude Thomas and not Mrs. J. Jefferson Thomas. She was signing her name as herself and not as the wife of Jefferson Thomas. She called herself a "public woman," who was capable of having individual ideas worth publishing. Indeed, her public career would begin to blossom in the next decade. She would write less in her personal diary and spend more time writing articles for the groups in which she was involved.

The year 1880 was the last year that there were long and frequent entries in her diary. Some of the material may have been lost, but she admitted to not having the inclination to keep a record of her life. Since she had begun writing for publication, perhaps she no longer had the need to write in private. In the journal that she began in January 1881, she got into the habit of making entries around the time of her birthday and on holidays. The only exceptions would be incidents of great significance to her.

One such incident was her mother's death on 11 May 1884. Mary Clanton died, apparently of heart disease, in her home in Augusta at the age of seventy-two. Gertrude was stunned and could not write about her mother's death for several months. Then she confessed, "I who used to take so much comfort in writing have not written one word concerning my mother." She missed her mother, whom she had always taken for granted. "I was so happy in my mothers love, so blessed in her presence...." Her mother "had lived a life consecrated to the duties she was called upon to perform, that of a faithful wife and a devoted, conscientious mother."[275] Faithful to the nineteenth-century ideal of the quiet woman doing her prescribed duty, Mary Clanton had given birth to at least eleven children and had watched four of them die. She had lived through the difficulties of the Civil War, tried to mediate family feuds, and outlived her husband by twenty years. Now, perhaps, Gertrude felt somewhat guilty for not appreciating her mother more. For the first time in her life—or at least the first time she ever said it—Gertrude resolved to try to emulate her mother.

After Mary Clanton's death, there was again evidence of controversy in the family. Gertrude decided she would act in a way she thought her mother would like. "With that thought controlling every action, the division of my mother's furniture met my approval. My one idea was to preserve peace and family harmony—with the idea ever present with me, 'Ma would have approved it'."[276] With her mother's death there also passed the final source for family unity and sole link with a bygone era.

Mary Clanton's death in 1884 also brought another change of residence for Gertrude. She resigned from her position as schoolteacher, much to her relief, and, for the next three years, she and her family lived in the Clanton mansion on Greene Street in the city of Augusta. Perhaps it was because the family did not want the house empty and Gertrude's farm was not adequate. Gertrude loved the house and wished she could buy it, but, of course, that was impossible. The fact her father had built if for her mother and that her mother had loved it so much made Gertrude want it even more. But she was only able to rent it for $500 a year, which was to be deducted from her share when it was sold.

The Clanton mansion was a grand, twenty-four-room structure with stately columns that had been an elegant home before the Civil War. But the contrast to the years Gertrude had lived there as a young girl was stark; to maintain the house, she now had to take in boarders. "The second year I rented the parlours to Dr. and Mrs. Patrick for sixteen dollars per month.… Mrs. Allen rented the parlors for the year at eighteen dollars per month and in the spring for several months Mr. Wyam with his wife and two children and sister-in-law Mattie Nutting rented two rooms up stairs with the use of the parlor for 20 dollars p[e]r month." She went on to add, "I had forgotten to write that year before last Mr. Robert Brown and his wife and two children rented two rooms for two or three months for eighteen dollars per month." Obviously, the income these arrangements produced helped clothe her children and pay expenses, but she regretted "the privacy of my home was entirely destroyed."[277]

In addition to the loss of privacy, she was not well at this time. However, exactly what was wrong is difficult to know. She always referred to her "nerves," but she had a lot to unnerve her. Very unusual for that part of the country, on 31 August 1886, Augusta experienced an earthquake with serious aftershocks. The whole southeastern coast of the United States was affected, with Charleston, South Carolina, experiencing the most damage. There were thirteen shocks in Augusta over the next week or ten days, and aftershocks continued for several months.[278]

Gertrude took up her pen on 10 September 1886 to describe "last week's horror, the earthquake." Gertrude, Jeff, and their son Turner had driven out to Dixie Farm for a few days. She reported, "I was so far from well, tired heart, soul and body. The night before I had prayed in importunate, reckless manner 'Lift me higher, higher Lord to Thee.' I was so tired of life's cares, so impatient so dragged down by sordid care." But the next day she felt better cheered as she always was by "dear Mother Nature whom I so dearly love." However, as they were preparing for bed, she heard an awful noise. "Together we stood while the house shook and reeled like a drunken man, and still that awful, rushing, roaring sound is heard. I look, I see the piazzi sway to and fro (I seem to feel it now) and then as a man flees for his life I grasp Turner, and hand and hand we rush down the step and out into the front yard." She felt the earth moving. "Oh God! The horror of that moment! Just then I expect the earth to heave and swallow us up. Has the day of judgment come?" They stood in the yard holding each other expecting the house to collapse.

It seems that some people were made physically ill by the movements. Jeff and Turner were not victims, but Gertrude was. "I was conscious of an intolerable pain in my back, and an awful nausea, and from that time through the successive shocks I was sick like unto death." They stayed outside during that night, wrapped in blankets. Gertrude wrote, "Every shock made me sick like the throes of a woman in childbirth.... I could scarcely breathe." She said she was completely ignorant about earthquakes and thought the "earth would engulph us." She found out the next day that others had been sick like her as well. The following night, she confessed, "I said my prayers, undressed, tied my clothes securely together to grasp at a moment's warning, drank one teaspoonful of brandy and went to sleep.... I am a temperance woman but in a crisis like this is was better to drink the medicine than unnerve myself and others."[279]

The few entries that Gertrude was making during these years usually included something about her not being well. She referred to a "long illness...owing to the strain on my nervous system." Her "long illness" seemed to have been far more serious than the casual reference she made to it. Looking back on the summer of 1887, she recounted how she became a grandmother for the second time. Even though Gertrude made very few references in her diary to her first grandchild, whom Mary Belle had named Gertrude, she was very proud and looked forward to the birth of her daughter's second child. But when the baby boy Duncan was born, Gertrude was so weak from a long "malarial sickness" that the doctor would not even let her know about the birth. Female illnesses were frequently and, often incorrectly, attributed to nerves. That the illness was somehow related to her nervous condition, at least in her own mind, was confirmed by the way she recovered: She took an extended trip away from home. "My visit to Haywood White Sulphur [Springs] and Waynesville in N.C. prolonged my life."[280] She was physically and mentally revived.

With her renewed enthusiasm she could again take up her pen to describe what she experienced—but it was not in her diary: "I wrote home three letters, two for *Evening News* and one for the *Chronicle*." If she were weak and sick, her writing did not show it. She wrote something like a travel log for the newspapers, describing the scenery. She was enjoying herself, remembering an earlier visit, "I know of no place more delightful than Haywood White Sulphur Springs to spend the summer.... Since I have been here I have driven in every direction, and the mountains are with us everywhere. The trees are beginning to assume the autumn tints of yellow crimson and brown." Remembering a more carefree time in her own life, she wrote, "Large trees of chestnuts are heavily laden, and the chinquepin burs are bursting open and the pretty little reminders of my childhood are peeping out to give joy to these little blue-eyed North Carolina boys and girls." With an affirmative, joyful conclusion, she closed with "the heavens declare the glory of God." In this instance, she signed her name, "Mrs. J. Jefferson Thomas."[281]

Gertrude made brief references in her diary to the fact that she wrote similar travel logs and sent them back to the newspaper, but she made no mention at all of some other articles that she wrote around the same time. One of them was evidence of a far more assertive move on her part and of her interest in, and knowledge of, the political scene. Because of her concern for teaching, she wrote a strong, well informed editorial in support of the Blair Bill for public education. "Education should be compulsory. Nor would I permit a man to vote who could not read and write. I know little of politics, but I do not under-value the great privilege of the ballot box. Just after the war when my carriage driver and butler voted for men to fill positions of honor and trust, voted when I knew they could not read the name on the ballot, ...white men are seen affectionately associating with the colored man, whose votes they endeavor to secure." Giving them whiskey and flattering them, "[O]ften the ignorant negro man is the dupe of the designing white man." She said education would prevent that abuse. She finished by saying, "[L]et us remember we owe the colored race a debt of gratitude, I would rather be taxed to educate the colored families whose fathers labored faithfully for us, than to pay a pension to support the Union soldiers who fought again us...."[282]

Here, Gertrude was getting into issues that were being widely discussed at the time. She even alluded to being "tempted to claim the privilege [of the vote]" for herself. Written in 1887, this article showed how Gertrude was beginning to be outspoken in her views. She was also foreshadowing her wider interests in suffrage and temperance, as well as education. What she was saying was extraordinary for 1887 in the South, namely that "colored families" should be educated because the former slave owners owed it to them in gratitude for their fathers' service. No longer tentative or hesitant, Gertrude had begun to make bolder statements. In fact, the pieces she composed for the reading public were much stronger than her private writing. By this point, she felt her opinion was significant enough that it should be published for all to read.

The short diary excerpts of 1887, of which there were only four, have a different tone. "Yesterday was April the 4th, my birthday.... I am fifty three years old." Mentioning a friend who had recently died at age seventy four, Gertrude wondered, "Do I realy wish to live that long?" Trying to make an effort at being more optimistic, she was reminded of Victor Hugo's words that "fifty was the old age of youth and the youth of old age." But she had to admit that the last few years had "not been years of unalloyed happiness." Tired and frustrated, Gertrude yearned for faith and submission to God's will. She closed that entry in the diary with the prayer she had recently read, "Save us oh God! Thine ocean is so large and our boat so small."[283]

Growing older, Gertrude frequently mentioned feeling that she had not achieved anything significant. She was now seeking access to a public forum, something that would serve her personal as well as charitable interests. In this state of mind, Gertrude came into contact with an organization for women that was relatively young and geared perfectly toward her growing interests—the Women's Christian Temperance Union. It would be an avenue of change and growth for many women, as well as for Gertrude.

Gertrude never wrote about the WCTU in her diary but, fortunately, she described how she became associated with the group in an article she wrote for the *Augusta Chronicle* dated 7 November 1887. She said that "a number of years ago" Mrs. Sallie F. Chapin from South Carolina came and spoke in Augusta at the Christian Church. In her appeal to win support for the temperance movement, Mrs. Chapin wanted "to save the boys of our dead soldiers from pitfalls more destructive than bullet or ball." She aroused two of the strongest emotions in Gertrude's nature, "love of country and a mother's love." The next morning Gertrude called at the home of her friend and relative, Mrs. William Sibley, and "enrolled [her own] name for Temperance."[284] She became an enthusiastic and vocal worker for the cause.

Her friendship with Mrs. William Sibley was a fortunate coincidence that would result in years of a productive partnership. Before her marriage, Mrs. Sibley was Jane Elizabeth Thomas, daughter of Judge Grigsby E. Thomas of Columbus, Georgia, and a cousin of Jeff Thomas. She visited with Gertrude and Jeff occasionally and is mentioned in the diary. Her friendship with Gertrude went back to early in Gertrude's marriage. In 1858 when Gertrude was pregnant with her daughter Mary Belle, Jane came to visit, and Gertrude wrote, "I notice…last spring while cousin Jane Thomas was with us. She spent the month of April and a few days in May with us. I found her extremely pleasant and had it not been for the excessive nausea I was suffering from at that time I would have enjoyed her visit very much indeed."[285] In 1860 Jane married William C. Sibley, a member of a prominent Augusta family and owner of Sibley Mill. The couple remained good friends with Gertrude and Jeff and are mentioned on one occasion after the war when they came to visit. They were present for an evening with family and friends, "Major Sibley, Cousin Jane [and others] danced and appeared to enjoy themselves very much."[286] Their long friendship enabled Gertrude to trust her judgment and follow Jane's lead into this newfound organization.

Gertrude was soon caught up in the center of activity. In 1887 Jane Sibley was state president of the WCTU. Gertrude and Jane had worked together on church projects, and Gertrude had grown to admire her even more. "To name Mrs. Sibley is to praise her; to know her intimately is a revelation of noble womanhood. She is charming alike as the gay, witty leader of social entertainments, or as the earnest Christian woman ready alike to lift a church indebtedness or preside as state president in the Temperance Union, an organization which claims on this side of the Atlantic nearly 300,000 members."[287] Gertrude was finally involved and working with women who provided her with positive role models. She had often expressed her wish in the diary to know intelligent, strong women with whom she could talk, and now she was finally satisfying that wish.

Gertrude was honored to go with Jane Sibley to represent Georgia at the fifth annual convention of the WCTU in Columbia, South Carolina, in November of 1887. It was at this meeting that Gertrude met and reported on another very important figure of the movement, Frances Willard, the national president of the organization. Willard had first established the Union in Cleveland, Ohio, in 1874, but it soon found fertile ground in the states of the Old South. Miss Willard was quick to recognize this fact and traveled widely in the South recruiting new followers. Gertrude was most impressed with Frances Willard and found her to be a "representative woman, one of whom her sex may be proud." Gertrude was enthralled, "She has a wonderfully earnest, magnetic nature. A trained elocutionist, she brings hereditary talent to assist in making arguments masculine in strength, while her gentle, womanly nature asserts itself in every graceful gesture."

Willard was obviously a gifted speaker with charm and charisma, "One moment her voice thrills you with pathos indescribable, and the next you smile with pleasure as some arch look, or graceful compliment wins its way to the sterner sex and you instinctively recognize the fact that Miss Willard has scored another victory for the WCTU." Gertrude's description of this powerful leader is evidence of why the leader of the temperance movement was so successful and how she won over so many followers.

Earlier in her life, Gertrude had been offended when a woman was bold enough to speak in church, thus violating St. Paul's instructions that women were to remain silent. But she had obviously changed her mind. Gertrude was won over by this woman and came away from the convention with the zeal of a religious convert. "Since I have attended that convention I have a consciousness of enlarged views, of greater love for humanity." It was women who suffered silently at the hands of drunken fathers and husbands, but it was also the women who were going to have to bring about the change in society. Gertrude was a forceful crusader. "Oh! Mothers, wives, sisters, daughters, women to whom the commission was first given, 'Go tell my disciples,' do women's work, worthy of women, not by the ballot box, but by the influence of example." Gertrude used the religious image of the women at the tomb of Christ who had found that he had risen. The women were the messengers to the disciples and the rest of mankind. She continued her plea, "You surely do not care to drink. Abstain and teach men so to do. By your example, strengthen erring, fallen men and women, and by exerting individual responsibility unite in the great moral work of reformation and temperance."[288]

Finally, Gertrude had found her passion. For the time being, women did not have the ballot and would have to strive for change through example and influence. But Gertrude had found something "worthy of women"—something that helped her forget her personal problems.

It seems very unusual that there was no mention in the diary of the Women's Christian Temperance Union, since in her public statements she was so enthusiastic about her newly found cause. But there were only four entries in the diary for 1887, one in January, two in April, and one in August. Other than mentioning her granddaughter and the fact that Julian was going to graduate from the Medical College in Augusta, the mood was grim.

With business cares pressing upon her, Gertrude felt she had grown much older in the last couple of years. She said she often thought of death. "How strange a thing is death and how strange a thing is life. I look out and the trees look as they did the spring Pa died. That was twenty years ago and ever since I have hoped to meet my father again. My mother two I trust to see and I am trying to realize the idea and accustom myself to the inevitable destiny which awaits me."[289]

She made only one entry in the diary in 1888. As had become her custom, she wrote it on April 3, the eve of her birthday. "Tomorrow I will be fifty four years old and I could not obtain credit for fifty dollars. I own land, much of it, and it does not support my family. For three years we have had complete failures on our river lands from high waters. There is nothing to be obtained from my mother's estate. Spring has come and I cannot buy a dress for Cora Lou or Kathleen." Over the years, nothing much had changed. Being land rich and cash poor had been their problem since immediately following the war. Gertrude still could not buy new clothes for her children, and the much hoped for proceeds from her mother's and father's estates had not materialized. She concluded, "A pitiful confession to make to you my journal. I have written so little because I did not like to give expression to such trials *for they are trials*."[290] She went on to say that she had had only one servant in the last month because she could not bear to owe money that she could not pay. She was now sending the clothes out to be laundered while she and Cora Lou were doing the housework.

As they had always been, her children were the bright spots in her life. By this date Julian had graduated from medical school and had gone north to work at Christ Hospital in Jersey City Heights, New Jersey. His title was house surgeon. Turner was in the insurance business in Augusta, while Jeff worked in an express company and lived in Savannah. Mary Belle was happily married to Fred Ingraham, and they had two children, Gertrude and Duncan. Cora Lou and Kathleen were still living at home. She was proud of them and expressed her thanks.

"Oh God I thank Thee for my children and my grandchildren."[291] There was no mention of her husband.

Gertrude made only two brief entries in 1889, both of which were written in August. By this time, the Thomases had moved back to Dixie Farm. She was concerned about what might be the fate of her diary. "What is to become of my journals? If you ever wish any one to read them you will have to have them printed said one of my sisters. I notice that my children are interested in reference to their childhood."[292] Gertrude had always stated that she was keeping an account of her life for her children to read. This is the only mention in the diary that she ever made on the subject of having it printed, but it seems that she never seriously considered doing so. Her diary had been her consolation more than anything else. In addition, she had become more honest regarding the family's financial hardships, and she would not have wanted other people to know about such personal matters.

Gertrude was now far more interested in outside activities than she was in keeping a record of what had become mostly trials and tribulations in her private life. Writing about her personal life depressed her, unless she was recalling the achievements of her children, but, when she wrote about one of her new causes or groups, Gertrude was invigorated. She did not need her diary as she once had. So often she had referred to it as "dear friend," but now she had new friends in women whom she admired.

In the last entry of her diary, dated August 1889, she was recounting a day with her children. Her son Jeff had come home from Savannah, and the young people played croquet on the lawn. Gertrude gave them watermelon and apples, and they enjoyed listening to Jeff sing. It was a relaxed and happy time for Gertrude, but her final comments in the diary refer to her writing and one of her new interests. A literary society had been formed called the Hayne Circle, in honor of local poet Paul Hamilton Hayne. The group would gather and present papers they had written on works of literature. Gertrude had embraced the group enthusiastically, often reading her essays and having them published. "I also received the subscription for *The Old Homestead* a magazine published in Savannah. In the August number was a paper I wrote on *Henry IV*. In September will be a paper on Ophelia from the play of *Hamlet*. I read both of them before the Hayne Circle." She closed her diary with one of her present references to writing. "I have received many complimentary notices but little substantial encouragement to write."[293]

Thus, Gertrude ended her diary of forty-one years. Perhaps there was more that was either lost or destroyed, but one feels that she stopped keeping the diary because her new activities were taking up much of her time. She herself had talked often of going for long periods without writing. In order to know what Gertrude did for the next eighteen years of her life, one must go to her scrapbooks, the court records, and other available sources.

Gertrude was a fifty-five year old grandmother who thought her life was almost over. She did not know that within the next ten years she would leave Augusta and begin a new life for herself. She would be intimately involved in embryonic activity of organizations that would have wide ramifications in women's lives and would finally realize her lifelong goal of achieving something worthwhile outside her domestic sphere. She was in the "youth of old age" and she had only just begun to become a public woman.

9

Awareness and Commitment

"In touch with everything that concerns her sex"

"A scrapbook is a curiosity shop—a repository for odd and interesting things which appear in print. They savor of the past, and preserve the curios of literature until they become valuable." This anonymous newspaper quotation was carefully glued on the inside cover of one of Gertrude's many scrapbooks, and a more appropriate description of these fascinating books could not be found. Indeed, they are made up of an assortment of "odd and interesting" things, which for one reason or another, she wanted to keep. A careful study of these books and their contents tells the story of Gertrude's later years.

Because the contents are not always in chronological order, one has the impression that Gertrude saved items over a span of time, perhaps even years, and then sat down and glued them meticulously into place. Almost all of the scrapbooks are filled with newspaper clippings. Many are articles she had written herself and are the ones that reveal what she was thinking and for which causes she was working. Other than pieces about family and friends, the majority of the other articles have one unifying characteristic—they are about women and their welfare. Through her own life experiences she had become genuinely concerned about the wellbeing and accomplishments of her own sex.

One can also see a pattern that developed in the scrapbooks. The earlier ones, containing material from the 1870s, reflect her love of literature; poems and essays about writers—perhaps those she wanted to emulate—fill the pages. Also included are her first published pieces that had to do with home and family and, on occasion, with one of her trips. During the late 1880s and early 1890s, however, as she was becoming more active in various organizations, the articles reflect a shift in emphasis. Earlier, Gertrude had tried to conform to what historians of the nineteenth century have called the "Cult of Domesticity" or "Cult of True Womanhood."[294] In this widely accepted and understood system, women stayed strictly in the home in order to provide a haven for men, who were the ones who took care of any activity in the outside world. Women were expected to be pure, subservient, silent, and obedient to their husbands. Also included in the female sphere was the moral guardianship of the family.

But in the 1890s Gertrude's outside activities increased, as did her willingness to express her own opinions. As she became more concerned about women, she grew willing to be associated with organizations that advanced their interests. She would finally throw herself into the Georgia Woman Suffrage Association that challenged the circumscribed roles of women in the South, and was, therefore, considered radical for the time.

The path that Gertrude took toward this end was also typical of the one followed by other women of her era in the South: It began in the church. Since her conversion at Wesleyan College, Gertrude had always been active in the Methodist Church. After the Civil War, when she came to question the validity of the Bible, and when she was embarrassed by her family's problems and publicity in the newspapers, she did not attend church regularly. Despite these times of doubt, however, she never abandoned the church and for many years belonged to St. John Methodist in Augusta.

As was expected of women, Gertrude took the responsibility for her family's salvation very seriously. Her husband Jeff had always been a concern to her. In her diary she had complained about his many depressions and his use of profanity, especially around the children. That he was not always interested in attending church upset her. On several occasions she had recorded those times when he had shown any evidence of wanting to be converted. She had also been anxious for each of her children to show interest and join the church, and if one of them made the decision, she happily recorded it in her diary. It was in her church that Gertrude found one of her first opportunities for expression.

She had attended Sunday school and taught there, but the women's organizations became the church activities that were to have the most lasting meaning to her. During the nineteenth century women had gradually begun to have prayer groups where they were allowed to meet on their own, and they soon learned they could raise money for missions and other work of the church. Mission societies became popular avenues for women, and they would be the ones that Gertrude would follow. She became a member of the Ladies Missionary Society and was a delegate to the meeting of the Woman's Board of Missions of the Southern Methodist Church when it convened at St. John Methodist in 1886.[295] It was there that she began to meet women with organizational skills and to develop friendships with women who had interests similar to hers. Even though her commitments would broaden and she would never be conventional in her thinking, she always remained loyal to the Methodist Church and to its women's organizations.

Where religion was concerned, however, Gertrude was not content to work quietly. By 1891 she could not resist expressing her views on a controversial issue: the female evangelist. Mattie Gordon was a woman Gertrude had mentioned only briefly in the diary, saying simply she had heard her speak in Augusta. But Gertrude had been impressed by Miss Gordon and so would naturally notice news of her from Atlanta. Some young people at the First Baptist Church in Atlanta had invited Miss Gordon to speak, and she had been able to do so, but only after much effort on the part of the young advocates. When Gertrude heard that "the older and more influential members" of the church objected to a female speaking, she felt she had to take a stand. She argued that the Women's Missionary Union of the church had, the previous year, raised $15,000 and the church had accepted this amount. She asked, "[D]id the rules of the church enforce the acceptance of money, but command a woman to be silent in meetings?"[296]

Gertrude used this opportunity to take her argument one step farther and in a controversial move, criticized the Southern Baptist Convention for not allowing female delegates at its annual meetings. She said that a few years earlier when the SBC had assembled in Augusta, "I will never forget the interest created by the effort to have two ladies admitted as delegates to the convention. The husband of one of them pleaded and argued for their admission, but in vain. The ladies, of course, said not one word." Gertrude had been a visitor only but felt moved by the proceedings. "I, a member of another church, sat and listened and do you know I felt humiliated? It was an object lesson. It taught the women of that church that they were yet in a state of bondage—it taught the children that mother was not the equal of father."[297] Written on 29 May 1891, this statement was one of the strongest she had made on the subject of equality for women and was evidence of her growing dissatisfaction with the position of women in Southern society.

Much of Gertrude's boldness seemed to have come from her association with the Women's Christian Temperance Union, evidence of which can be found in her article defending Mattie Gordon that indicated Gertrude was growing accustomed to hearing strong women express their viewpoints in public. She compared Mattie Gordon with Mrs. Mary F. Lathrop, who during the National WCTU convention had addressed a group of men and women at a Baptist church in Atlanta. "Mrs. Lathrop is a wonderfully gifted woman. She, like Miss Gordon, has a mission to speak words which 'Shall waken a new nature in the weak and sinful souls of men'."

Gertrude had been a member of the WCTU for several years and had attended the annual convention in Columbia, South Carolina, in 1887. Augusta had a particularly strong organization because it was the home of the state president and Gertrude's good friend and relative, Mrs. William Sibley. So active was Gertrude that in 1889 that she was elected vice president and, later that year, district president for the tenth district, which was Augusta.

In Gertrude, the union gained a willing and capable spokeswoman for temperance. Utilizing the argument so often put forth by the WCTU, she spoke against alcohol consumption because of what subsequently happened to women and children. She confirmed her belief that men had personal freedom to do as they pleased but, "The only restraint I would place upon him would be, take care, don't let your indulgence of personal liberty interfere with the rights of your wife, your child, or your neighbor." She argued that men could take care of themselves, "It is for the wife and child I plead. God pity the woman exposed…to the mercy of an infuriated drunken husband. I would lose faith in the belief in the goodness and justice of God, did I not firmly believe that hereafter such women will be compensated for misery and wretchedness endured in this life."[298] Signed Mrs. J. Jefferson Thomas, the article was dated August 1889.

Gertrude's pleas were so heartfelt that one cannot help but think she was speaking from her own experience. Even though there were no specific references to Jeff drinking in the diary, it is believed that this is one of the secrets Gertrude was keeping from her journals. It has been conjectured by historians and supported by family tradition that Jeff had a drinking problem. "There is little doubt that Gertrude Thomas's dedication to the temperance movement was influenced by personal experience—speculation confirmed by family members."[299] Alcohol was a huge part of the Southern culture, and men who had suffered during the war felt entitled to drink. There are no figures to support the assumption, but it is probable that many of the women dedicated to the WCTU were facing the same problem at home.

Although women were the moral custodians of the family, they were limited by how much they could say and do. The WCTU, however, was an organization that had "Christian" in its name. It was considered proper for women to get dressed up in their hats and gloves and have their say against "demon rum." Even though it had its origin in the North and was beginning to question male supremacy, it is not at all surprising that it was so popular in the South.

Not only did Gertrude believe in the cause, she seemed to enjoy traveling, meeting interesting women, and, especially, being the spokeswoman. By May 1890 she was again traveling on behalf of the WCTU. This occasion was the eighth annual convention of the Georgia WCTU held in Rome, Georgia. She wrote a report detailing the activities of the Augusta delegation and also described the beautiful city and its gracious people.

Returning to Augusta via Atlanta, the group attended the national convention, which was meeting there.

It was in Atlanta that Gertrude met another influential woman in the organization, one who would go on to become well-known in Georgia history: Rebecca Latimer Felton. Gertrude's words show her admiration, "Poetry and legend will tell in future ages of that memorable scene when Mrs. Dr. Felton, 'the member from Bartow,' arose and with trained parliamentary eloquence pleaded from a mother's heart to the voters of our country to save our sons from a drunkard's fate."[300] Rebecca Latimer had been born in 1835 on a plantation in DeKalb County, Georgia. During the war they lost their plantation to invading troops, and their slaves had also been emancipated. The life she and her husband shared soon went in a new direction. In 1874 she had had her first taste of politics by helping her husband—who had served as a surgeon during the war—when he ran for Congress to represent Bartow County. She had worked behind the scenes, writing speeches and managing her husband's campaign, but even this kind of political equity between husband and wife was criticized. Politics was an area strictly denied to women in the 1870s and 1880s. But when Rebecca Latimer Felton discovered the WCTU, she found a place where she could speak as a woman and be heard—and speak she did, with fearless, bold speeches and editorials about the WCTU and later the suffrage movement. She was not deterred by criticism. "I was called a 'petticoat reformer' and subject to plenty of ridicule, in public and private."[301] She would go on to become one of the foremost spokespersons for women's suffrage in the state and would spend her life speaking and writing for her various causes. In 1922 at the age of 87, when Senator Tom Watson died, Georgia's governor Thomas Hardwick appointed her to serve out his unexpired term, making Felton the first woman to sit in the United States senate. Her tenure would be the shortest in history—one day—but, nonetheless, she will always be remembered as the first woman to be seated in this all-male bastion.

There is no doubt that all of these women were having a profound impact on Gertrude and her thinking about politics. After hearing Rebecca Latimer Felton speak, and dining in the Markham Hotel, the WCTU delegation visited the capitol in Atlanta. Gertrude reported, "When I enquired what was the basis of representation in senate and legislature, there was discovered a great amount of ignorance among the WCTU ladies, who know little of politics and only care for it when it involves the happiness of home."[302] Gertrude was irritated with these women for not being informed about such important things and was moving away from the idea that politics was off limits to women.

Dating back to 1848, to the first women's rights convention in Seneca Falls, New York, women in the North had always been ahead of women in the South as far as suffrage and women's equality were concerned. Northern women like Frances Willard were running the national WCTU meetings and were more progressive than their Southern counterparts, but it was obvious to both that their petitions and speeches were falling on the deaf ears of legislators. When Willard spoke at the national convention in Atlanta, which Gertrude attended, she spoke forcefully about women entering politics. Directing her remarks to the men present, she said, "My brothers, do not misunderstand us, we are not overstepping our sphere, we are only laboring to get to one end of the line while you stand at the other, to help you lift the burdens of the world." Later in the convention, other speakers endorsed the vote for women specifically and were greeted by a standing ovation and waving of handkerchiefs.[303]

Jane Sibley, the Georgia WCTU president, was also at the meeting with Gertrude and left convinced "for the first time I publicly declare myself in favor of woman's ballot, and I will do my best to get the Georgia WCTU to adopt a franchise department." The WCTU had not publically endorsed suffrage, but the idea was gaining ground.[304]

Talk of suffrage divided men and women in Georgia in their attitudes toward the WCTU. This was especially true of the clergy and conservative Christians, who still felt that the Bible taught that women were to be silent. In 1892 an interesting correspondence occurred between Jane Sibley and Warren A. Candler, who was president of Emory College at the time and who would become a bishop of the Methodist Church in 1898. On 29 April 1892, while cautiously deciding how to handle the issue of suffrage, Sibley wrote to Candler inviting him and his wife to attend the WCTU convention in Milledgeville, Georgia. Sibley told him, "There has been a marvelous religious awakening in all the churches and one of the outcomes of it is a *desire for reform.*" Sibley went on to say, "I trust your good wife who it seems has become alarmed on the 'suffrage & political party question' will attend our convention. She need not be afraid. Let her come and see and speak for herself." She also asked for his counsel, "We would be glad to have an address from you. Will you not come? Come and advise on these very questions," and then went on to assure him, "They never have been mentioned in our convention sessions and we have never adopted either of them of course, though there are many converts in their favor." She said she had been "holding off" these many years despite pressure from the national organization.

On May 2, Candler responded in a three page, hand-written letter to Sibley, and he was very emphatic about his views. He reassured her that he was a total abstainer and uncompromising prohibitionist but that he and his wife would not be associated with the WCTU until "the suffrage business is stopped." He went into some detail and listed three reasons: First, the Northern organization was hurting the cause in the South and furnishing "enemies of prohibition with a stick to beat us." Second, the women suffragists had already made a "fissure in the northern Methodist Church and they will make a similar fissure in the southern Methodist Church." He went on to say that the Methodist Church had given "cordial cooperation" to the WCTU, unlike the Presbyterians and the Baptists, and the Methodists would "catch the burden of this load when it comes." Third, if suffrage were adopted and supported by the WCTU, it would set back the prohibition movement fifty years in the South. Leaving no doubt as to the church's position, he wrote, "We will fire back in earnest. We are not willing to furnish churches for meeting places, give pulpit advertising and moral support.... Besides we believe the whole suffrage movement unscriptural and sinful." He ended his letter with precise instruction, "Our Georgia women should cut loose from the National WCTU and let them go on their way."[305]

Candler's words created a huge dilemma for the WCTU. These women truly believed they were doing God's will and had dedicated years of work to the cause. In her letter to Candler, Sibley wrote, "All these years of prayer and effort and waiting and hoping, God has opened the way for us in a way in which there can be no mistaking. There never has been a time more propitious." Many people had given their support, including some ministers. "We have been out assessing the people with our petitions and find great enthusiasm and encouragement.... I do not know what will be the outcome. God only knows that but the prospects are very bright for success."[306] If they could no longer meet in the churches, and the ministers would not announce their events from the pulpit, the prospects of the WCTU would definitely not be as good.

Candler was not the only prominent minister who came out against the WCTU. Dr. J. B. Hawthorne of the First Baptist Church in Atlanta publicly criticized Frances Willard and the national organization for speaking in favor of ordaining women into the clergy. He charged that her statements ran "contrary to the teachings of the preachers and leaders, contrary to the Scriptures," and he even went so far as to say that they would create "a subversion of the relations between women and marriage."[307]

Of course, these prominent church leaders were influential and began to make many women have second thoughts about their involvement with the WCTU. Attendance started to decline, and long discussions were held at the conventions about what the position of the Southern organization should be toward the Northern counterpart. In 1893 the Southern WCTU reached a compromise by deciding to reaffirm its loyalty to the Northern organization, but stated, "[W]e hereby believe that woman's suffrage is not conducive to the best interests of temperance work in Georgia."[308] The result was that the WCTU lost some members, but it did not die. There was no doubt that many still thought that while it was appropriate for women to speak up and organize about the issue of temperance, talking about politics and the vote for women was strictly off limits. The WCTU would never publicly endorse the vote for women. If women were going to get the vote, they would have to go in another direction with leaders who were strong enough to withstand criticism. Gertrude would join Rebecca Latimer Felton, her sister Mary Latimer McLendon, and others who were willing to take the lead in this controversial move.

In the meantime, Gertrude kept up her many activities. She had always been more interested in politics than most other women around her and had made references to her interest in suffrage on more than one occasion in her diary. This was especially true during the Civil War when, for her, patriotism and country meant the South. As was thought proper, she had remained loyal to the "lost cause" and its heroes, particularly Jefferson Davis. During this period, Gertrude was working to commemorate the war and its heroes. She had embraced the Ladies Memorial Association enthusiastically, a society that worked to get a Confederate monument built in Augusta. As often happened in any organization she was a part of, Gertrude became its spokeswoman, and, by 1891, she was serving as treasurer of the LMA and published its financial report in the newspaper.

She was also corresponding with another well-known woman of the period: Mary Gay. Gay was just a few years older than Gertrude and had been born in Jones County, Georgia, but moved to Decatur, Georgia, where she had lived during the hardships of the war. Her only brother Thomas was killed toward the end of the war in Franklin, Tennessee, so Mary became the breadwinner for her widowed mother, her sister, her sister-in-law, and her young nephew. Unconventional but necessary, Mary Gay spent much of her life traveling around the state commemorating the memories of the Confederacy and selling her books. In 1892 she achieved something Gertrude had always wanted to do: She published one of three books, called *Life in Dixie during the Civil War*, which is supposed to have influenced Margaret Mitchell in her creation of that most famous woman in Southern fiction—Scarlett O'Hara. Certain scenes in the 1939 movie *Gone with the Wind* are said to have been drawn directly from Gay's memoir.[309]

Gertrude probably came to know Mary through her sister Missouria, who was a leader in the Atlanta and state WCTU.

Mary did not see the advantage in joining reform groups—perhaps because she was too busy being the family breadwinner—but she did join in efforts to commemorate the memory of Civil War heroes. She worked hard to establish the Alexander H. Stephens Monument in Crawfordville, Georgia. Gertrude joined Mary's effort, and on Memorial Day collected money at the gates of the cemetery on behalf of the Stephens Monument. Gertrude was pleased to be able to send Mary $20 on behalf of the women of Augusta.

Gertrude was in the middle of planning and promoting these activities but would take the time to voice other sentiments, if she felt it necessary. For instance, she was outraged when, upon the death of Jefferson Davis, the secretary of war refused to order the American flag flown at half-staff. She was also mystified that "the people of the South are indifferent to the fancied slight of the secretary of war." The *New York Herald* had written that Davis had "scorned to seek forgiveness for what history had already pronounced a crime...." Gertrude's response in the *Augusta Chronicle* was strong. "I voice the opinion of Southern women and a united South when I assert that Mr. Davis did not wish the North to forgive him or posterity to excuse him. He had no apology to render."[310] Gertrude may have had mixed emotions about Davis during his lifetime, but once he was deceased, she felt he should receive proper respect—yet another example of Gertrude's willingness to express her opinion and, more importantly, feel that she was speaking on behalf of others, in this case "Southern women" and even the "united South."

In fact, Gertrude became so busy in the early 1890s that one has to wonder how she had time to do all she had undertaken. In addition to being a wife and mother, she was involved in the Missionary Society at St. John's, the WCTU, and LMS, but she also continued to write essays to be read at Hayne Society meetings. She presented one on Sidney Lanier and another on Ophelia in *Othello*; her essay on *Henry IV* brought special praise. As reported in the newspaper,

> It was prepared with careful thought and arranged with admirable precision and strength. Mrs. Thomas has a way of grouping her ideas in an orderly and striking manner. She is also a clear, forcible reader. The picture of the play was so well given that the subject was admirably developed for general discussion. Mrs. Thomas is a writer who is well known to the press and people of Augusta. Her pen is always active in good causes and for deserving enterprises.[311]

It was certainly true that Gertrude's pen was "always active" during this period. One area of concern for the WCTU was prison reform, especially concerning the treatment of women inmates. As district president of the WCTU from Augusta, Gertrude reported at the 1890 annual convention in Rome, Georgia, that they had visited the jail but gave no details.[312] However, on 27 March 1891, she wrote a strong editorial in support of prison reform. She said she was disgusted to find that male and female prisoners incarcerated in Columbus, Georgia, were not separated. She argued for separation of sexes, as well as races, and urged that women not be made to do manual work. "It is time for some woman to protest when the men of the land, the law makers, fail to protect women from shame, from ignominy, it is time to assert the right to say, 'Thus far shalt thou go and not farther'."[313] If the elected officials were not going to speak up, it was going to be up to the women, and Gertrude would speak for them.

As busy as she was, Gertrude never forgot her beloved Wesleyan. When she was able, she attended the alumnae meetings held every three years. Despite her many activities, she was in attendance at Macon in 1891. Becoming more comfortable in front of an audience, she had been one of the speakers at the opening meeting. She was again elected an officer of the association. The following note appeared in the *Augusta Chronicle*, "Mrs. Thomas was elected second vice president of the association for the next three years. Her address was an excellent compilation of reminiscence and history of that venerable institution, which has the honor of being the oldest seminary in the world for the education of women."[314]

Gertrude was perhaps more fulfilled than she had ever been in her life. She was constantly writing, something she had always wanted to do. She also belonged to a number of organizations doing important things and from them she gained a feeling of accomplishment. Why then would she and her family suddenly decide in 1893 to leave their hometown of Augusta? She loved the city and had lived in the vicinity all her life. She was also fifty-nine years old, not an easy age to adjust to change. To answer that question—or attempt to answer it— one must look back into her personal life.

Since Gertrude had stopped keeping her diary in 1889, one has to examine other sources and make assumptions based on her past experiences. The Thomases's previous financial problems immediately come to mind, and an examination of the records of the Superior Court in Richmond County indicates that Jeff and Gertrude had never been able to work their way out of legal entanglements. They had experienced a number of foreclosures, and, despite the fact they still owned land, they could not make a profit from it. The court records indicate that a pattern had begun that was triggered by a seemingly insignificant decision. Back in 1873, when Gertrude and her husband had been in dire need of money, Gertrude had been persuaded or advised to "convey to him J. Jefferson Thomas" part of her life estate. The key phrase here was "convey to him."[315] As a result, the separate estate "not liable for her husband's debts" that Turner Clanton had set up for his daughter and her heirs was no longer invulnerable from claims by creditors. This decision enabled Jeff to borrow money more easily, but it also allowed creditors far more access to the property, if he could not pay his obligations. With this transaction, Turner Clanton's wise provision for his daughter was undone. She would have been able always to maintain possession of her inheritance had this not happened.

In the years following 1873, more and more creditors were successfully suing and collecting money from the estate. For example, in 1878, when the Superior Court had ruled in favor of Jones and Morris against J.J. Thomas, it had found "for the plantiff against the trust estate…as the trust estate is liable for the debt and its payment."[316] It was as if the floodgate had been opened. By 1889 Gertrude and her heirs had petitioned the court to sell land from the trust in order to pay taxes. She still owned the Road Place, city lots in Augusta, and one-sixth of the Clanton Warehouse on Reynolds Street, which had eventually come to her after her mother's death. But to prevent a forced sale by the sheriff, they had to pay taxes and interest in the amount of $1400, and the money was not available. In February 1890, when the court authorized them to negotiate a loan and to secure it, they had to deliver to the lender a deed for the Road Place.[317]

What must have been far more devastating to Gertrude than the family's precarious financial situation was the deterioration of family relationships. There had been what Gertrude had called "enmity" between William Vason and Jeff Thomas. Gertrude had worked to preserve her relationship with her older sister Anne, but there had been difficulties through the years. Judge Vason had died 10 August 1873, but Anne still lived in Augusta, and, as family tradition has it, was better off financially than the other Clanton children.[318]

Even though Gertrude hated owing anyone, she had borrowed money from relatives in the past. The Thomases's circumstances were so desperate, however, that she had borrowed $1,000 from Anne in April 1886, putting up as collateral her one-sixth interest in the Clanton Warehouse and sixty-eight acres she had inherited from her brother N. Holt Clanton. By January 1893, Gertrude had been able to repay only $250 of the $1000. The note was renewed for $750, but there must have been hard feelings at that time. The renewal was a sixty-day note at eight percent interest; Gertrude could not repay it.

This was 1893, the year Gertrude and Jeff left Augusta. The eventual outcome must have been particularly difficult for Gertrude, who was so sensitive to publicity about her private problems. In the April 1895 session of the Richmond County Superior Court, Anne Vason sued her sister, Gertrude Thomas, for $750. The court ruled in favor of Anne and ordered Gertrude to pay the principal $750, interest $193.28 and attorneys' fees of $94.28. Execution was stayed for one year from 25 November 1896.[319] It is possible that Gertrude and Jeff had given up any hope of straightening out their financial problems, and embarrassment over the publicity in the newspapers would have made a move appealing. Gertrude had been born into one of the most prestigious families in Augusta, but she had seen position and wealth slip away. Occasionally she had mentioned in her diary that her family was now treated differently. Several times she had appealed to her childhood neighbor, John Phinizy, for a job for young Jeff. She felt slighted when he did not do her the courtesy of responding. Despite the fact that he had the reputation as the best horseman and rifleman in the county, her son Turner had been passed over for command of the Richmond Hussars. Whether or not these snubs were directly related to their loss of status in the community, Gertrude certainly believed they were, and said so in her diary.

Back in 1870 when the lawsuits by family members were beginning, Gertrude said at the Christmas dinner table, "I should like to be off in a new place, far off from any one I knew, that I had become accustomed to never seeing my relatives, for unless I sought them I never saw them."[320] She was still being sued by family members in the 1890s, and she finally got her wish to move "far off." Certainly Atlanta was not that far from Augusta, but it was far enough. She would not know everyone, and everyone would not know her family and their personal business.

It is difficult to be exact about the date on which Gertrude, Jeff, and the two younger girls, Kathleen and Cora, left Augusta and went to live with their son Julian in Atlanta. The move from a small farm outside Augusta into the rapidly growing, young metropolis of Atlanta would have been exciting in the 1890s. Promoted as the commercial and industrial leader of the New South by the editor of the *Atlanta Constitution*, Henry W. Grady, Atlanta was now the capital and the largest city in the state. Electric streetcars had been installed in 1888, and the suburbs of West End and Inman Park were growing. Peachtree Street was already seeing the construction of stately mansions, but to make it even more attractive to the Thomas family, their son was becoming an established doctor in the community.

Julian Pinckney Thomas had graduated from the Medical College of Georgia in 1887, and, after a short sojourn in New Jersey, had gone to Atlanta to begin his practice. In an article dated 1892, Julian was called a "specialist in Skin Diseases and Cancers" and was described as having "a large practice in Atlanta and rapidly becoming known all over the South." The Atlanta city directories for 1896 and 1897 show Julian Thomas living at 102 North Pryor Street. He did not stay solely in that line of medicine, however, because he soon formed the Atlanta Hygienic Institute with one Dr. Alexander. Its creation must have necessitated a move because in 1899 his residence and office were listed at 82 North Forsyth Street. Considered very progressive for that period, the doctors specialized in a kind of preventive medicine and advocated physical exercise and the taking of Turkish baths. They performed minor surgery and treated facial blemishes. "The institute very strongly appeals to common sense, and is enjoying a constantly increasing cliente[le]. Its treatment has been singularly effective, and among other things the gymnasium department has done wonders in reducing over-fleshy patients."[321] As a mother, Gertrude would have been very proud of him and all he had accomplished.

Gertrude must have settled relatively quickly into her new city home because the flow of her articles hardly slowed at all. It seems she immediately threw herself into a whirlwind of activity, connecting with her WCTU friends and getting busy with her many areas of concern. She had written earlier about prison reform, and, on 12 February 1893, she sent an editorial to the *Chronicle* making a plea for police matrons. Still thinking of herself as an Augustan, she asked, "Messrs Editors, is there a police matron in Augusta? If not, the good women of our city should never be content until there is one." A new police station in Atlanta was to open March 1, and Gertrude listed the number of cells for white women and black women, as well as those for white men and black men, an arrangement for which she had argued previously. She concluded, "In Atlanta the police matron's room will adjoin the room occupied by the female prisoners. Let every Georgia city follow Atlanta's example in this respect. Wherever there is a police station, insist upon the necessity for a female matron."[322]

Only five days later, Gertrude wrote a searing comment on a crime that she believed was not punished with nearly enough harshness—domestic violence. Many men felt that they had the right to beat their wives. Under the influence of alcohol, these men could badly wound or even kill their wives, and the temperance women were serious about getting something done. Gertrude said that a legal system that treated such abuse with "less severity than the theft of bread or the shooting of game" could not pretend to be a friend of the female sex. She also argued that domestic violence was not confined to the lower classes. In her view, the legislation of the sale of whiskey caused the problem and left women helpless victims of drunken men. Gertrude appealed to the legislators, "Think of the sacred obligation violated—the example and subsequent degradation of the children, but above all think of the utter humiliation of the wife. Reflect on this subject, men of Georgia, and in the name of mother, wife and sister, make such laws as will protect a class of people who cannot make laws for themselves." The title of the article left no doubt whatsoever as to the seriousness of the crime: "A Coward and Brute who Beats His Wife Deserves to be Shot."[323] In this passionate article one can see how women in the WCTU were moving more and more toward the necessity of the vote for women. Gertrude was reminding her readers that women were at the mercy of male lawmakers who were not doing their job to protect women.

As wrapped up as she was in her own family situation and the wrongs of the justice system, however, Gertrude still did not abandon her interest in those things that lifted the human spirit, such as literature and religion. Another advantage of moving to Atlanta was exposure to cultural events that may not have been available in Augusta. The Chautauqua Movement that had started in 1874 at Lake Chautauqua in New

York State, where writers, teachers, musicians, and lecturers shared their art in outdoor, summer programs, had grown very popular in America. Gertrude was able to attend the Atlanta Chautauqua on 15 July 1893 and wrote, "Who can estimate the influence for good that has been accomplished? To many 'it has been a feast of reason and a flow of soul,' a continued intellectual banquet." She delighted in the concerts and lectures that inspired her. She described the object of the series as being to raise humanity to a higher plane and to teach men and women to think and to reflect. In her opinion, it was a privilege to listen to the words of wisdom from eloquent orators. "I think that the minds of ordinary persons receive truth, or instruction, more readily from the lips of others." Whether Gertrude realized it or not, she was testifying to the origin of some of the changes that had occurred in her life. She had learned to lift herself to a higher plane of concern and empathy.[324]

No matter how busy she was—and because of her years at Wesleyan—education for young women would always be on her mind. When she got to Atlanta, she renewed her work with Mary Latimer McLendon, her co-worker in the WCTU and Rebecca Latimer Felton's younger sister. They were both very interested in encouraging support for the Industrial School for Girls in Milledgeville, Georgia. Since females were not allowed at the state university in Athens, the school in Milledgeville was an attempt to provide teacher education for women. It would later become the Georgia State College for Women and is today Georgia College & State University. In the beginning this school was supported by the Fulton County Education Loan Association that met the first Wednesday of every month at the Governor's Mansion. Mrs. William J. Northen, the governor's wife, was president, Mary McLendon was secretary, and Gertrude was producing press releases.

On 3 August 1894 Gertrude wrote, "If there is one cause dearer to the writer than another, it is that of the girls of our state. What is to be done for them? How can they support themselves? It is one of the problems of the hour." She appealed for financial help, "It requires a loan of $200 a year to educate a young man at the State University; $100 will support a young girl at the Milledgeville school for the same length of time. Will some liberal man or woman remember the Fulton County Loan Association and 'give the girls a chance'?" Since dormitory space was inadequate for the large number of girls applying, the women decided to present a petition to the legislature for an appropriation. Gertrude's appeal was published. "The legislature will have many subjects presented to it during this session, but there will be none more worthy of attention than the Girls' Normal and Industrial College at Milledgeville."[325]

Not only did Gertrude spend her time strengthening women's education, but she also was active in the Methodist Church. In 1894 she joined the First Methodist Episcopal Church South in Atlanta, now the First Methodist Church. Records show that Gertrude, her two daughters, Cora and Kathleen, and her son Dr. Julian Thomas were members and that Gertrude and her daughters were living at 191 Courtland Street.[326] There is no record of her husband Jeff joining, however, something that Gertrude would have regretted. Whether or not he joined, to Gertrude the church had always been important and would remain so all her life.

When the quarterly mass meeting of the Woman's Parsonage and Home Mission Society was held on 24 July 1894, Gertrude was vice president of the North Atlanta district. As had become customary with any organization with which she was associated, she was at the heart of the group. She presented a report of the society's resolutions at the annual meeting and wrote about them for the newspaper. The members were asking that parsonages be exempt from tax so that ministers' wives might "possess what all women prize—a home." Gertrude's work did not go unnoticed. When the Woman's Parsonage and Home Mission Society met in Milledgeville, the following notice was published in the *Milledgeville Chronicle*: "One of the best known and most dearly beloved women of the convention is Mrs. J. Jefferson Thomas, of Atlanta. She is broad-minded and generous and in touch with everything that concerns her sex."[327] One cannot help but be reminded that Gertrude knew only too well what it meant to have a home of her own and to have had it taken from her.

By 1894 there was evidence that Gertrude had gained a reputation for public service and for writing that went beyond Augusta and Atlanta. A weekly paper in Jackson, Mississippi, edited by Kate Markham Power, included a piece on female writers in Georgia. Miss Power noted, "the high character the women of Georgia enjoy in the world of letters" and made specific reference to several women "well known in the South." She included Rebecca Latimer Felton, "invincible in a controversy," Mrs. William Sibley, "a writer of great force," and Mrs. J. Jefferson Thomas, "a lady of exalted character and wide influence."[328]

For a number of years Gertrude had been willing to speak her mind and think for herself, but now, in the 1890s, her awareness, especially as far as women were concerned, had reached a new high. All of the organizations for which she had worked in the past had been considered proper for women because they were associated with morality and religion in some way—things in which women were supposed to be interested and activities that did not intrude into the male domains of business and politics. She would not be protected or be "on a pedestal" like women in the Old South were; she would be a New Woman of the New South, willing to make a commitment of her time and energy, even if her decision to do so was controversial. The South had been slow to accept new ideas about the proper place for women, but Gertrude had the ability and courage to change that—and she would ask other women to join her. Despite the fact she was sixty-one years old, she would throw herself into a radical cause: the fight for women's suffrage.

10

Suffragist and New Woman

"His equal in the work of the world"

By the late nineteenth century there were many suffrage groups throughout the United States with large memberships and solid financing, but the Georgia Woman Suffrage Association had a late and very humble beginning. It had been formed in 1890 in Columbus, Georgia, by Miss H. Augusta Howard, and its first members were Howard, her mother, and her four sisters. Augusta Howard had never heard or seen a woman speak about suffrage for women, but she had seen the difficulty her widowed mother had experienced after her husband's death. Her sister, Miriam Howard Dubose, said years later that her motivation was, "Her mother's yearly inescapable taxes [her father had died during her childhood] without representation compelled her realization of gross injustices done hundreds of thousands of women assisting in supporting a government, politically classing them with minors, lunatics, idiots, traitors, and felons."[329] Thus, with little know-how but strong commitment, the Georgia Woman Suffrage Association got its beginning. Membership was open to like-minded persons of either sex who agreed about the injustices done to women and who wanted to correct them. They met monthly in the Howard residence in Columbus. Because of the hostility of most Georgians toward the idea of the vote for women, however, the organization had very limited success and attracted few members in the early years.

The Howard women were victims of ridicule and sarcasm from men, who made fun of the principle of equal rights for women, and from women who said they had all the rights they needed or wanted. Some years later, a citizen of Columbus said that the Howard women were "almost run out of town."[330] In spite of these attitudes, they did gradually enroll a few new members, both male and female. One of the men who came out for women's vote was William C. Sibley of Augusta, the husband of Gertrude's friend Jane Sibley. In addition there was Walter B. Hill of Macon, who later became chancellor of the University of Georgia. In 1892 Mary Latimer McLendon and Kate Mallette Harwick of Atlanta joined the group. But the number of organized suffrage members remained very small, and by January 1894 it was estimated that there were only about twenty in the whole state.[331]

To offset some of the criticism and to get attention from the press, Augusta Howard and two of her sisters, Miriam Howard Dubose and Claudia Howard Maxwell, decided to make a bold move. They would go to Washington DC to the 1894 national meeting of the National American Woman Suffrage Association and invite the group to come to Atlanta for their 1895 annual meeting. It was a Herculean task, and they were up against delegates who wanted the meeting in Cincinnati, Detroit, or back in Washington.

Augusta Howard addressed the convention and was very persuasive. She said they could hold a thousand conventions above the Mason and Dixon line and the people of the South would never hear a word of it. She said, "The Georgia papers and the far Southern papers still insist that women do not want the ballot. Until you hold a convention in the South and prove to them that this is not so, they will keep on saying it is."[332] She assured them that if they came to Atlanta, she would secure the Grand Opera House, which was one of the largest auditoriums in the United States and that it would be packed. A convention of women would be a great curiosity in the South and newspapers would publish stories for and against it. Even though some would come to laugh, she believed many would leave the convention as members.

Fortunately for the Georgia delegation, one of the most prominent members of the convention, Anna Howard Shaw, came out in support of Atlanta. In 1880 Shaw had become the first woman in America ordained as a Methodist minister, and, in 1886, she had received an MD degree from Boston University. A close friend of Susan B. Anthony and an outspoken advocate for women's rights, Shaw had just spoken in Atlanta at a WCTU meeting and been well received. She was also concerned that there were so few suffrage groups in the South. When the vote was taken, Atlanta got a majority, and it was decided that the 1895 National American Woman Suffrage Association would meet there. The Howard sisters were overjoyed.

Augusta Howard immediately started courting publicity, and she was not shy about expressing her views. When the twenty-eight-year-old woman was interviewed by the *New York Sun*, she said, "Why, down in Georgia women are simply afraid to say they are suffragists. If they are married their husbands threaten to get a divorce from them, and if they are unmarried, they know that they can't get any husbands at all. You don't know how far behind the times Georgia is! That's why I wanted the National Convention to meet in Atlanta next year. It will open the eyes of the few blind down there."[333]

The young Georgia Woman Suffrage Association had accomplished something few thought was possible. They were soon very encouraged when, on 21 March 1894, Margaret Chandler and Mary Latimer McLendon, organized the Atlanta Equal Suffrage Association. Its membership of forty men and women more than doubled the number of organized suffragists in the state.[334] It is not known if Gertrude was an original member, but, because of her friendship with McLendon and subsequent positions of leadership, her association probably began very early after its formation. Mary Latimer McLendon was elected president, and, over the next few years, she and Gertrude would be in the forefront of efforts to win support for the vote for women in Georgia.

On 31 January 1895 the annual convention of the National American Woman Suffrage Association convened in Atlanta, with headquarters at the Aragon Hotel. Just as the women hoped, they began to draw attention in the press. As the convention was about to begin, the *Atlanta Constitution* took a poll of citizens' opinions on woman suffrage. "Some of them smiled, some laughed, some blushed, some looked grave, others sour, and some of them looked unutterable things. A great many said they were emphatically against it. Some said that they did not especially care, and quite a few refused to say anything at all."[335]

Captain J. W. English said that he did not believe in suffrage for our American women. He said it might be proper for women in other countries where women were less respected, but not here. He went on to say, "When women assume the voting responsibility, they must take up all other duties of citizenship. They must be soldiers, be eligible for places in Congress, for governorships, and for the presidency.... I, for one, do not want any petticoat government. I do not want women to be soldiers, and I certainly don't want them at such places as our average polling places."[336]

Some people objected to women's suffrage, saying women's minds were not suited for politics. Women were too emotional and voting was not a part of women's domestic sphere. In addition there was opposition from the clergy, who still argued that women should keep silent. As has been noted, Warren Candler of the Methodist Church had said that suffrage was not scriptural and was actually sinful.[337] As the convention was getting under way, J. B. Hawthorne of First Baptist Church of Atlanta preached a sermon that was widely quoted. He said that the suffrage women were attempting to defy the Bible and the laws of God and they outraged social sentiment "which despises every woman who confesses to such unwomanly aspirations." He went so far as to say that any "advocate of equal suffrage must have a feeble-minded husband."[338] The suffrage women came to believe that his remarks were so outrageous that he unintentionally helped the group. Many Atlantans, even those who were opposed to women's suffrage, were embarrassed and issued apologies to the delegates for the discourtesy shown to the guests in their city.[339]

The most vehement opponents would organize the Georgia Association Opposed to Woman Suffrage and issue extreme claims in their publications. In a speech given at the Hotel Dempsey in Macon, Georgia, by Eugene Anderson, president of the Georgia-Alabama Business College, he stated that women's suffrage would ruin home-life, destroy the moral code, undo the federal government and even "unchain the demons of the lower world."[340]

There is no doubt that all of this negative publicity discouraged some women from joining. But if some women were afraid to say they believed in suffrage for women, Gertrude Thomas was not one of them. She attended this historic meeting in Atlanta, not as an official delegate, but as a "fraternal delegate from the Atlanta WCTU."[341] She kept two scrapbooks that she labeled "Suffrage" and wrote "1894–1895" on the covers. They are filled with articles on that subject and particularly on the convention of 1895.

Despite all the excitement, the convention went quietly about its business. When the first session convened there were ninety-three delegates, representing twenty-eight states, along with a number of visitors from all over the United States. The morning and afternoon sessions were devoted to state reports and other business issues while the special evening speeches were held in DeGive's Opera House. The DeGive's Grand Opera House was opened in 1893 at Peachtree and Forsyth streets and could accommodate more than two thousand people in its palatial, ornate setting. In later years it became the Loews Grand Theatre, famous for the 1939 premiere of the movie *Gone with the Wind.* Proud of its Southern hospitality, Atlanta must have impressed these women as it threw open the doors to this grand hall.

The opening remarks were given by the president, Susan B. Anthony. She said, "I hope the good men of Atlanta will understand that we [women] do not claim to be the better half of creation but we do claim to be half."[342] She reported on the progress that had been made in Colorado, where women had received the vote in 1893 and where there were now three women in that state's legislature. Mary Latimer McLendon, representing the young Atlanta Equal Suffrage Association, also spoke that night and outlined some of the difficulties women were having in Georgia. There were even a couple of men who welcomed the delegates to the city and spoke on behalf of suffrage for women.

Later in the convention, a memorable address was given by Mrs. Josephine K. Henry of Kentucky, who outlined some of the wrongs being done to women. She said that throughout history women had had no say whatsoever on the laws that governed them. Women should have co-guardianship of their own children, equal pay for equal work, and a single standard of morals that would do away with the double standard.

Women did not have possession and control of their own inheritance and earnings. As she closed her remarks, she insisted that women needed and wanted the ballot, the only protection against these wrongs.[343]

Other speakers at the convention included Alice Stone Blackwell of Massachusetts and Carrie Chapman Catt of New York, both prominent leaders in the movement. On Sunday, the indomitable Anna Howard Shaw spoke to the convention in the Opera House with two thousand people present. As the first female minister of the Methodist Church, she told of the discrimination against women in the church and of the prejudice against female preachers, no matter how worthy and accomplished they were. She challenged the notion that equal suffrage went against nature and God's law. The following day, Susan B. Anthony presided over a mass meeting of the Atlanta Equal Suffrage League.

Augusta Howard had obviously achieved her goal; the convention had brought the most outstanding women in the suffrage movement to Atlanta. Anna Howard Shaw and Carrie Chapman Catt would go on to lead the national organization, and Susan B. Anthony was already a nationally prominent spokesperson for the movement. These women were challenging wrongs that had been accepted by society for generations. Gertrude Thomas and like-minded women were there to meet these women, hear their speeches, and take up the fight in Georgia.

As was expected, the convention did receive publicity all over the state but none of the big newspapers endorsed female suffrage. The *Atlanta Constitution* stated in an editorial that Atlanta was happy to have welcomed the suffragists to the city and to have had an opportunity to show "southern hospitality and southern enterprise," but concluded by saying, "Georgia women had influence in politics through their masculine connections, could enter the business world, and had all the rights they needed."[344] But, as these suffrage women knew, women in Georgia did not have the rights they needed. They did not have co-guardianship rights to their own children, could not own their own wages, and the age of consent or, as it was called in 1895, the age of protection, for girls was only ten years of age. Women in Georgia would not get the vote until 1920 with the Nineteenth Amendment to the United States Constitution, and the age of consent would go up to only fourteen years of age in 1918. Georgia still had a long way to go, and it would not be an easy path for Georgia suffrage women to follow. Even though the suffrage movement had received a lot of publicity, they had only picked up thirty-four members from the convention.[345]

Even so, Gertrude had been inspired, and the women she had heard speak had strengthened her resolve. She was soon speaking up about the issue and being quoted around the state. On 30 May 1895 an article appeared in the *Atlanta Constitution* titled, "They Want to Vote." A meeting was held at the Unitarian Church and was called the "most interesting and entertaining of all the meetings yet held by the Atlanta Woman's Suffrage Association." The debate was whether women should have full voting rights exactly like men and whether there should be education or property requirements. It was reported, "Mrs. Thomas believed that women should be allowed to vote on all occasions just as men vote but she was sure admission of uneducated women to the ballot box would be a public calamity." She stated that there had been enough experience with ignorant male voters in the South to know they did not want to make that mistake when women got the vote.[346]

For years Gertrude had been an advocate for compulsory public education for whites and had even alluded to compulsory black education. The article stated that the attendance at this meeting was large, and many names were added to the membership list. Between 1895 and 1899, Gertrude was completely caught up in all the issues surrounding suffrage and kept herself very busy with her various activities in Atlanta. Perhaps all of these activities were a distraction from her personal life.

It was during this period that her myriad financial problems in Augusta, which had stretched over almost her entire adult life, were finally resolved. The outcome was not good. It appears that after Gertrude left Augusta, the remainder of her estate had been transferred to her oldest son Turner, who was acting as representative for the heirs (all of Gertrude's children). Turner actually sued his mother. In the case *Turner C. Thomas v. Gertrude Thomas*, 6 July 1897, the court records stated, "[S]aid life tenants [Gertrude and Jeff] had committed acts tending to the permanent injury of the Estate of the remaindermen [the heirs—Gertrude's children] such as allowing the property to get out of repair and allowing a part of it to be sold for taxes, and that thereafter, on the same day, to wit, February 12, 1895, all of said parties sold and conveyed as aforesaid, all of said property to Turner C. Thomas."[347]

It was true that Gertrude and Jeff had not been able to take care of the property, and the children's inheritance had certainly been damaged. It is impossible, though, to know how much hostility there was between the parents and some of the children. Jeff and Gertrude had left Augusta to live with their son Julian in Atlanta; they had not stayed with Turner in Augusta. The fact remains that Turner, her oldest son, was suing his mother to get what he could from the estate for himself and his siblings. It is interesting to note that back in 1871, when Gertrude was sued by her family members, she had written in a letter to her mother, "Sued by my mother, my sisters and brothers, Mr. Thomas' sisters and brothers,.... I rebel and turning to my children for comfort, I think they two may sue me some day."[348] Perhaps suing family members had become so commonplace in the family, that it was not thought all that unusual. Nonetheless, it must have been very sad for Gertrude.

A careful examination of the records of the case *Turner C. Thomas v. Gertrude Thomas* that came before the Equity Court in April 1898 in Richmond Count tells the story.[349] Turner was petitioning the court to sell the life estate, which then consisted of "Belmont and Dixie Farm, and ... the other property set out in the petition, to wit: the Road Place in Columbia County and four lots in the city of Augusta on the southwest corner of Taylor and Washington Streets." Turner was trying to work out the legal entanglements and salvage something from the estate. However, there were problems with taxes and liens. Henry Cumming had a lien on the Road Place and William K. Miller had one on the town lots. The court gave Turner ten months to dispose of the property and instructed him to sell the Road Place, which consisted of 1,000 acres at that time, for not less than $3.50 an acre; Belmont and Dixie Farm for not less than $50 an acre; and the town lots at not less than $2,500. He was then to pay the taxes and liens and keep the remainder for himself and the other heirs.

The sale of the 320 acres of Belmont and Dixie Farm, combined with the 1,000 acres left in the Road Place plantation, along with the four city lots should have brought a total of $22,000, based on the prices suggested by the court. It would have allowed Turner to pay all the debts and still have a sizable amount left. But by the 1898 April term of the court, Turner stated "after diligent effort," he had succeeded in an "offer of $4,900 for all of the property." The court was satisfied that Turner had done his best and ordered him to sell all the property to one Albert W. Anderson. The $4,900 was less than one-fourth of what the court felt he should get for the land.

The $4,900 was divided in the following manner: $2,719.49 to Henry Cumming, $1,864.77 to William K. Miller, $50.43 for state and county taxes, $144.69 for city taxes, and $50 for court costs. The total debt payment came to $4,829.38. The balance of $70.62 was to be paid to Turner Thomas. Thus, after all the years of court battles, fighting to pay taxes, and numerous foreclosures all that remained was $70.62.[350]

It is sad to see the total loss of Gertrude's inheritance. She had lost her home in Augusta and now she had lost Dixie Farm, Belmont, the Road Place, the city lots, and any cash parcels she had inherited. What happened was exactly what her father Turner Clanton had tried to avoid. Of course, he could not have foreseen the difficulties created by the Civil War, but he did know how men used their wives' property to satisfy their own debts. The separate estate had not helped, and there was now nothing left for her children, something Gertrude had always hoped to avoid. Had her father lived, perhaps some of it could have been saved with better management. But that was all conjecture now.

Even though the resolution left nothing for the heirs, Gertrude's financial problems were, thankfully, finally over. She was free for the first time in years, and she seemed to let go and throw herself into even more activity. She was writing, making meaningful contributions to society, and she soon began travelling more than she ever had. She also began to be recognized for her efforts, something that must have given her joy and satisfaction.

Some of that recognition came from an organization that Gertrude had joined after she came to Atlanta—the United Daughters of the Confederacy. Having been formed in 1894, it was still a very young group but had quickly grown popular in the South. With her background in the Ladies Memorial Association in Augusta, it followed that Gertrude would be interested in an organization devoted to perpetuating the memory of the South and the Civil War. But, equally important, she liked the idea that the group was devoted to helping widows of the war and educating their children.

She enjoyed travelling to attend UDC meetings in different parts of the country, and one of Gertrude's scrapbooks is devoted to itemized lists of addresses of its members and money she spent on trips. As was always the case with Gertrude, she quickly assumed positions of leadership. She went to Baltimore in 1897 to the fourth annual convention and kept a news clipping report of the delightful trip she took on the Southern Railroad with her friend and mentor, Rebecca Latimer Felton. "A pleasant party were on the train, among them Mrs. Wm Felton, who the next day read before the convention an admirable paper upon the necessity of higher education for the southern white girl." The article ended, "Upon motion of Mrs. J. J. Thomas of Georgia, the paper was received by a standing vote of thanks."[351]

The following year, Gertrude was again travelling with the UDC delegation to its national convention in Hot Springs, Arkansas. Another newspaper article reported, "Mrs. J. Jefferson Thomas of Atlanta, Ga., is the national treasurer, having been re-elected last year at the Baltimore convention. Mrs. Thomas the previous year was general recording secretary and has for many years been intimately connected with memorial work." The article finished with, "She is one of the oldest Daughters of the Confederacy, and is a most distinguished personage."[352] She was also given a medallion at the Hot Springs meeting with a resolution praising her "kindness, courtesy and efficiency."[353] She must have enjoyed the salute given to her at the reunion of the UDC. "Col. Bennett

H. Young of Louisville, Kentucky, moved that the Kentucky Confederate Glee Club give three cheers for Mrs. Thomas, and they were given with a will."[354]

Gertrude enthusiastically served the UDC and seemed to be truly devoted to its work. It was a popular organization and acceptable for women in the South to pursue. It was a group looking back in time, remembering the war years and celebrating those who had sacrificed for the "Lost Cause," as the war became known. At the same time, Gertrude was embracing suffrage for women, which was far more progressive and not nearly as acceptable for women to support. But for women like Gertrude, such as Mary Latimer McLendon and Rebecca Latimer Felton, however, they saw no conflict and embraced both groups with the same drive and determination.

There is evidence that Gertrude was active in a number of other organizations in Atlanta. She wrote articles back to Augusta about the American Library Association expressing gratitude for Andrew Carnegie's gift of $100,000 to build a library in Atlanta. She also wrote articles and attended meetings of the Woman's Club and the Women's Press Club, both of which had started in Atlanta.[355] However, it was in the Georgia Woman Suffrage Association that Gertrude reached the pinnacle of her public career. By 1896 she was serving as recording secretary and stayed in that position until 1899 as the organization prepared to have its first state convention. By then there were two hundred members on the roster of the Atlanta Equal Suffrage Association, and local clubs were beginning to be organized around the state. The communities of Waynesboro, Fitzgerald, and Demorest had formed organizations. If there were no local club in their area, women could join the state organization. Such at-large members came from Columbus, Conyers, Douglasville, Rome, and Fitzgerald, Georgia. Although the organization was still considered radical by many and did not have nearly as many members as the WCTU, it was slowly beginning to increase its membership and recognition in the state.

The women planning for the first state convention in Georgia followed the example of the 1895 national meeting that had been held in Atlanta. If they wanted to get publicity for the vote for women and educate people in the state about the need for suffrage, they were successful. On 29 November 1899 there was an almost full-page story in the *Atlanta Journal* about the meetings of the convention, its speakers, and the election of new officers. Instead of the Opera House, the opening session was held in the hall of the House of Representatives. "A large and cultured audience of ladies and gentlemen assembled with the chosen champions of the Georgia Woman Suffrage Association now assembled in the city holding their first annual convention although organized in 1890." The paper also reported on a "fair sprinkling of legislators and club women in the large and well-filled hall."

President Mary Latimer McLendon opened the session by introducing Gertrude to give the welcoming address to the convention. Despite the fact that the paper incorrectly gave Gertrude's age as seventy-five instead of sixty-five, it gave a lengthy summary. "Mrs. J. Jefferson Thomas who, crowned with the dignity of 75 years of useful and honored life, spoke impressively. Mrs. Thomas took occasion to speak forcefully of her work in behalf of equal rights, as she welcomed the members of the convention." She made a lasting impression on those attending, "She reminded the audience that woman was not taken from the head of man—she is not his superior; she was not taken from his foot—she is not his inferior; but she was taken from his side, and there she should stand, his equal in the work of the world."[356] In her speech Gertrude went beyond suffrage and even dared to claim equality for men and women—a bold statement for 1899.

Unfortunately, a complete copy of her remarks has not survived, but she must have made a powerful and persuasive speech that was well received. Martin V. Calvin, the representative from Richmond County, wrote an informative comment on it that was published in the *Augusta Chronicle* on December 5. "Mrs. J. Jefferson, of whom old Richmond should ever be proud, delivered an address of welcome. Mrs. Thomas was greatly at ease and gave a talk brimful of good sense and rare good humor."[357]

There were several other notable speeches that evening; one was given by Mrs. F. C. Swift, president of the Atlanta Equal Rights Association. Mrs. I. W. Parks, speaking of the "New Woman," said progress had been made in the past fifty years but much more was needed. She said the "trouble was that for a long time the world had been going on with one-half of its people one hundred years in advance of the other half.... The state needs the whole intelligence of its people. Woman needs the development of her full powers for the training of her children and for the betterment of the world."

These women were serious about what they were saying, but they often said it with humor and good spirit. Miss Frances E. Griffin of Alabama gave a speech that the paper labeled "The Hit of the Evening." Saying Miss Griffin had a "bright and spicy manner," she said, "When men ask me why I want to vote, I tell them it is none of their business! It is, moreover, none of their business to say whether or not I shall vote. I am a human being just as a man is a human being, and in common justice it is not the place of one-half the human beings in the world to say what the other half should do, much less to ask them why they want to do it!"[358] After Miss Griffin was cheered and applauded throughout the hall, the meeting was adjourned.

The next morning they had their business meeting and resolutions were drawn up. They quoted the authority of the Bible, "God...created man and woman in His own image and gave them dominion over the earth and all things." They also declared that because the Constitution of the United States said, "All persons born or naturalized in the United States...are citizens...and that government derives its powers from the consent of the governed" that women were being taxed without representation, which had to end. They then listed the resolutions that would be presented to the legislature. The first and foremost, of course, was the enfranchisement of women. They also asked that the University of Georgia be opened to women, that women become members of the boards of education, and that women physicians be placed on the staff of physicians of the State Lunatic Asylum. Motions were unanimously adopted asking the governor and legislature to appoint a woman as president of the Georgia Normal and Industrial College and to give women positions on the board of trustees. They also asked for women to be exempt from paying property taxes until they were allowed to vote.[359]

The other big item of business was the election of officers. The next day, 30 November 1899, the *Atlanta Journal* reported on the previous afternoon's session devoted to that task. Mary Latimer McLendon announced that she would not serve another term as president at that time. She said that in her opinion "rotation in office was the best method in all associations." She was then unanimously elected honorary president, "a deserved compliment to one who has proven herself thoroughly devoted to the cause." The convention then elected its new officers: Mrs. Claudia Howard Maxwell, sister of the founder Augusta Howard, was elected Secretary, and the new president was Mrs. J. Jefferson Thomas.[360]

Being elected president of the Georgia Woman Suffrage Association the first time it met in convention was certainly the high point of Gertrude's public career—the culmination of all she had worked for through the years. At the evening closing session of the convention, Gertrude was seated on the platform with the other newly elected officers. Mary McLendon introduced them to the convention "in a most happy manner." The resolutions that had been adopted were read and "received with applause by the delighted audience which seemed to be in thorough sympathy with the Suffragists." The program concluded with a moving rendition of "Praise God from Whom All Blessings Flow," which everyone joined in singing. As one observer described, the women felt "His benediction was upon this movement for the uplift of woman, and through her the uplifting of humanity,"[361] Gertrude would have certainly shared this sentiment. It was probably one of the happiest and most fulfilling evenings of her life.

As president of the Georgia Woman Suffrage Association Gertrude was chosen to attend the thirty-second annual convention of the National American Suffrage Association that was meeting in Washington DC. On 14 February 1900 she wrote an article back to the *Augusta Chronicle* describing her trip and the wonderful experience it was for her:

> I came from Atlanta on the Seaboard...Line and had an enjoyable ride on an elegant car.... Yesterday was an ideal Sabbath. The air was invigorating and the sun was shining brightly, the little birds are singing in the trees and the parks and all nature seems in unison with the animate crowds of pedestrians who crowd the streets of this beautiful city. I attended the Methodist Church a few blocks from the White House and heard an eloquent sermon.

She went on to say that the delegates visited the National Library that afternoon. "It was a pleasure to look upon the beautiful pictures, frescoed walls, historical collections and innumerable objects of interest." In the evening she heard her friend Anna Howard Shaw and wrote, "She is a wonderful woman."[362] She attended the sessions of the association, visited in the president's home, and attended a reception at the Willard Hotel. As was her custom, Gertrude found fulfillment in her work and was encouraged by the women she met.

It became customary for the association to hold its annual meeting in November and to get national leaders to be keynote speakers. They were fortunate in 1901 to get Carrie Chapman Catt, who had succeeded Susan B. Anthony as president of the National American Woman's Suffrage Association, to be the principal speaker. Again they met in the House of Representatives and, now as honorary president, Gertrude gave the address of welcome. On November 26, the *Constitution* reported, "Mrs. J. Jefferson Thomas...spoke with warmth and cordiality that made the delegates from the different parts of the state feel at home; and in the course of her remarks gave some very good reasons why she was a suffragist."[363] Clearly, Gertrude had become a polished speaker and she was reaching the women who might not have otherwise been drawn to suffrage.

It is not known exactly how long Gertrude was able to stay active in the GWSA. A brief note in the *Constitution* on 18 April 1902 said, "Mrs. J. Jefferson Thomas...is recovering from a severe attack of illness,"[364] the nature of which was not disclosed. However, when the GWSA met again in November 1903, Anna Howard Shaw was the guest speaker and Gertrude was there as honorary president, but this time she only gave the prayer.[365] She may have begun to curtail her activities due to poor health. By this time in her life, Gertrude had become well known for her suffrage work not only in Georgia but also nationally. She was made a life member of the National American Woman Suffrage Association. In appreciation, they sent her a copy of volume four of the *History of Woman Suffrage* with a personal note to Gertrude from Susan B. Anthony.

> Mrs. Gertrude C. Thomas
> Atlanta—Georgia
> I present you this huge volume *IV*—because you are a *Life Member* of the *National Association*—and because I hope you will be able to place this book—together with its three huge companions—in the *public libraries* of your cities and towns—your colleges, your high schools—your normal schools etc—Where every student may find them and learn the facts about women during the 19th century—facts that they can find *nowhere else*—
> Yours truly,
Susan B. Anthony
Rochester, N. Y.
Feb. 15, 1903[366]

Gertrude must have cherished this gift. Susan B. Anthony had been president of the National American Woman Suffrage Association and was one of the women in the country who most personified the movement in the United States. It was also a compliment to Gertrude that Anthony saw her as an ambassador for the movement. Indeed, she was a worthy ambassador and knew the facts about women during the nineteenth century better than most.

As Gertrude was beginning to slow down her activities, she could be proud of her achievements in her many organizations, but she also had another area of satisfaction in her life—her children. Whatever disagreements there may have been with some of them about the inheritance would hopefully be resolved and forgiven. She had always taken great pride in her children, and it would have given her joy to see them all mature and either married or settled into their careers. Mary Belle was married to Fred L. Ingraham, Cora Lou to Patrick J. Farrell, and Kathleen to George McMillan. The three girls would all settle in Atlanta and raise families. Mary Belle, more than the other children, seemed to have shared her mother's interests and love of writing, occasionally publishing articles and commentaries. Gertrude's oldest son, Turner, would remain single and work in the insurance business in Augusta. Jefferson Davis, who had started out in an express business between Macon and Savannah, would end up dividing his time between Macon and Augusta. Julian would eventually marry and move his medical practice to New York. One of the privileges of Gertrude's later years was to be a grandmother and watch another generation of her descendants begin to mature. Gertrude had always been very caring and loving toward her children. Her grandchildren would have been an equal pleasure to her.

Jeff and Gertrude stayed together until their deaths. Even though Gertrude was frustrated with him because of his drinking and cursing, she did not believe in divorce. He had never shown any interest in her diary and may not have shown much interest in her other activities. In particular, her suffrage activity may have caused dissension. When, in 1894, Augusta Howard wrote about married women that, "their husbands threaten to get a divorce from them," her statement was not all in jest.[367] It is known that in 1892 Nicholas McLendon, the husband of Gertrude's close friend, Mary Latimer McLendon, moved out of the family home in Atlanta as Mary gave more and more of her time to her public career.[368] It seems that they did not get a divorce but did live separately the rest of their lives. In the case of Jeff and Gertrude, they seemed to go their separate ways, with him living in the past and Gertrude looking to the future.

Gertrude was said to have suffered a stroke at some point that seriously incapacitated her. According to family tradition, she lost the ability to talk and made a great effort trying to regain her speech. Her daughter Cora devoted much of her time to helping her.[369] Gertrude spent the last few years of her life in a wheelchair, and it was not unusual to see her being pushed up and down Peachtree Street in Atlanta. She was living at 54 East Alexander Street when she died on 11 May 1907 at the age of seventy-three. Her death certificate recorded immediate cause of death to be "apoplexy 3rd attack," with contributing cause being "apoplexy & paralysis."[370] Thus, Gertrude had suffered previous strokes, and it was a massive one that finally ended her life.

Jeff outlived Gertrude by nine years, dying on 17 December 1916, while living at 81 Waddell Street in the Atlanta suburb of Inman Park with Cora and her husband. At eighty-six, he was the oldest Princeton graduate in Georgia and regularly attended alumni meetings. He was well known for riding around Atlanta in his Confederate uniform on his horse, "Dixie Will Go." He would ride in parades, sporting prized knee-high leather boots and spurs that were made out of brass shell casing that had held the balls fired from Fort Sumter. As late as 1 March 1916, an article appeared in the *Princeton Alumni Weekly* calling him one of the "most picturesque graduates" and "Notwithstanding his advanced age, he is still in vigorous health…. [A]t his country place outside of Atlanta he still sleeps in a tent and three times a week in the summer he is wont to take a swim in the lake at Piedmont Park."[371] Until the end of his life, Jeff was active in the affairs of the United Confederate Veterans and was commander of Camp 159. It was as if he were literally reliving the war years. Jeff had only served on active duty for nine months in a war that went on for three more years after he had purchased a substitute, but this fact seemed to have been forgotten. So loyal was he to the memory of the "Lost Cause" that he asked to be buried in the old grey uniform he had worn in the war.

Both Jeff and Gertrude's bodies were returned to Augusta and buried in the Magnolia Cemetery. The *Augusta Chronicle,* the newspaper to which Gertrude had directed so many of her articles and that had covered the demise of her wealthy family, at this time gave extensive, complimentary coverage to her obituary and burial. Articles appeared on May 12, 13 and 14, saying that Gertrude "was one of the most prominent women of Georgia and one of the most highly regarded.... She was almost an indisputable authority on Southern affairs.... and regarded as one of the most brilliant...women of her time."[372] A simple list of all the offices she had held in local and national organizations of the WCTU, UDC, the Wesleyan Alumnae Association, along with the presidency of the Georgia Woman Suffrage Association, testify to her years of service.

Gertrude had been born to wealth and privilege in the traditional Old South, but when all of that was taken away from her during and after the Civil War, she never quit striving to accomplish things that gave her life meaning. Most of her achievements as a "public woman" came late in life, when most people would have given up active roles and grown unable to accept new ideas. She did not live to see many of the changes that she worked so hard to achieve. In fact, in 1920 when the Nineteenth Amendment passed Congress and was sent to the states for ratification, Georgia was one of the states that never ratified it. Gertrude had been one of those leaders among that small group of women who had kept the fight going, even if it meant being ridiculed at times. It took tremendous courage and determination, but Gertrude had become the woman she had sought to be early in her life, one that had "suffered and grown strong."

Her work in the nineteenth century helped point the way for the women who followed in the twentieth century—women who would be called New Women of the New South. As she had said in her address to the 1899 GWSA convention, women did not want to be better than men, they did not want to be less than men, they wanted to be "equal in the work of the world."

Conclusion

Gertrude Thomas lived seventy-three years, which was a long life for the turn of the century, when life expectancy was only about forty-nine years, but it was short compared to some of the other women activists of her era. Her good friend, Mary Latimer McLendon, lived to be eighty-one, Mary Gay lived to be eighty-nine, and Rebecca Latimer Felton lived to the ripe old age of ninety-five. When she was appointed the first woman in the United States Senate, Felton was active and healthy at the age of eighty-seven. One cannot help but wonder what Gertrude might have achieved had she lived longer. Early in life, Gertrude began to measure her life by what she had accomplished. Although she did not live as long as the other women, Gertrude had a life of comparable service, and she should be remembered alongside the others.

Gertrude also accomplished something that makes her unique: She managed to keep a revealing account of her life and times in her diary for the amazing length of forty-one years. Other Civil War diaries, such as *Mary Chesnut's Civil War*, or *The Civil War Diary of a Southern Woman* by Sarah Morgan, along with others, only cover the period of the war years.[373] By including the fifteen scrapbooks and the legal records, one can put together a record of the intellectual and spiritual struggle of one woman's life for almost sixty years, starting with the antebellum and continuing through the protected nineteenth century and into the more progressive twentieth-century New South.

In the early years, Gertrude recorded what she wore, where she went, and the books she read, but as life became more difficult, she wrote about the war, loss of property, and deaths of loved ones. After a traumatic event she intuitively knew the benefit of getting her thoughts out, by talking, by crying, or—in Gertrude's case—by writing.[374] In the most difficult times, when other people let her down and she felt alone, she actually personified the diary, referring to it as "old friend." The changes she experienced, the adjustments she made, and the way in which she worked through them, are laid out for examination. Even though some of the diary was lost or destroyed, a wealth of material survives that gives one of the most vivid portraits we have of the real life of a nineteenth-century Southern woman.

Gertrude would probably have been surprised at how well known her diary would become. Unlike diarists such as Mary Chestnut, who knew hers was to be published, and who carefully revised it, Gertrude was writing for her children, especially for her girls. She often complained that no one, particularly her husband, was interested in her diary. Despite the lack of interest shown by others, the diary was enormously important to Gertrude, and she continued to pour her thoughts into it. Fortunately for us today, the result is the genuine, candid way in which she expressed herself.

There were times when she was cautious about what she wrote about her husband, because she hoped her children would read her words someday, and there are historians who have thought that she was not being completely honest about miscegenation and Jeff's drinking problem. Historian Nell Painter wrote an interesting introductory essay to the edited diary when it was published in 1990. She believed that Gertrude was withholding some things that can be detected in what psychologists call "deception clues" and "leakage," which could be seen in her "highly charged material." Painter suggested that when Gertrude talked about the many mulatto children on her father's plantation and her own, she suspected her husband and father of what was, in her eyes, a grave sin—miscegenation and even adultery. That may or may not have been the truth, and, as Painter said, the "self-deception is not entirely clear in the journal."[375] What we can be certain of, however, is that Gertrude did not want to see it, and she lived in denial like the other women of the antebellum South. She might have talked about it happening in other families, but her own family was strictly off limits. One must note that she never lost respect for her father, but she was critical of her husband. This might be the most telling of whom she suspected. Despite this one area of secrecy, one can sense an overall candor and basic truth in Gertrude's words.

Many historians have quoted from Gertrude's diary, but they are so numerous I will only mention a few. Anne Firor Scott, with her groundbreaking book, *The Southern Lady: From Pedestal to Politics 1830–1930*, was the first I saw that quoted from it.[376] She was also the well-known historian who recommended that I put my dissertation "on the back burner" until I could come back to it. She thought the story of Gertrude's relatives was interesting, and she wanted me to talk about "the family." I will always be grateful for her advising me years ago. I must also mention Elizabeth Fox-Genovese who read my dissertation and spent hours talking to me about it here in Atlanta. She used Gertrude's diary in her book, *Within the Plantation Household: Black and White Women of the Old South.*[377] She thought the entries in the diary from 1848 to the outbreak of the war, where Gertrude talked about what she read and thought were important, too. Those innocent, carefree days of reading and thinking started her on her path of always examining her life.

The Civil War turned the issues of gender, class, and race in the Old South upside down, and they have been favorite topics of historians. Studies such as LeeAnn Whites's *The Civil War as a Crisis in Gender: Augusta, Georgia 1860–1890,* and Drew Gilpin Faust's *Mothers of Invention: Women of the Slaveholding South in the American Civil War,* are two excellent examples that make frequent use of Gertrude's diary as they look at these issues.[378]

The struggle Gertrude had with her husband Jeff has been examined numerous times. Jeff was destroyed by the war and thought himself "fit for the insane asylum." He spent the rest of his life living in the past and riding around Atlanta in his Confederate uniform while celebrating a Lost Cause that he had actually abandoned. In contrast, by throwing herself into her women's activities, Gertrude was able to move on and look to the future. In fact, she embraced the most progressive issues of her time such as the vote for women and gender equality.

The progression of Gertrude's thoughts on slavery is fascinating, too. She started out accepting it, as did her father and all members of the planter aristocracy. After all the Bible justified it. But then she began to question it, and the plight of the slave women performing manual labor while pregnant made her more sympathetic. Also, the shared suffering in childbirth and the help from the wet nurses made Gertrude more sensitive. By the end of the war, she could see that slavery had been wrong and was actually glad the slaves had been freed. This was another point on which Jeff and Gertrude always differed; he could never admit that the slaves should have been freed. In an article she wrote in 1887 endorsing public education, Gertrude even said that former slave owners owed a debt of gratitude to the slaves who had served them and should educate their children. Compared to other diarists of the war period, she was far more liberal in her thinking about race.

The greatest loss for Gertrude was that of wealth and class; she talked about it all the time. More than once she lamented that she was a child of wealth and pride and she had been brought to such degradation. Her identity as a young woman was tied to her privileged class, and when she lost it, she had to figure out what to do with her life. That struggle is central to the diary and to Gertrude's survival. The very fact that she kept writing about it and trying to make sense of it all was what saved her in the end. Of course, had she not lost her fortune, she probably would never have reached the heights of understanding and compassion she developed for the well-being of other women.

Another loss that was critical was the loss of family, and the unraveling of this all-important structure was vital to Gertrude's life story. Life in the Old South, especially on the plantation, centered on a mythical family comprising a master/patriarch who took care of a huge family that included his wife and children and even his slave family. Gertrude's father, Turner Clanton, was the epitome of the powerful master, and, from what we know of him, seemed to have been generous and caring, particularly to his wife and children. Gertrude was secure and wanted for nothing as long as he was alive. She was supposed to grow up and remain a Southern lady, protected and conforming to certain standards of behavior. But with her father's death in 1864 and the defeat in war, all of that changed. Gertrude's husband, Jeff, was not a good businessman nor was he encouraging to her the way her father had been. Jeff Thomas could never live up to the example set by Turner Clanton, and Gertrude found herself ever more unprotected by a strong male figure. Over the years she was repeatedly disappointed by her family.

Family and kinship ties have always been important in the South where, as the old saying goes, families "trace their ancestry back to Noah." Who is related to whom and who is descended from whom is very important and often discussed. But when it comes to money in the family, all of that falls by the wayside. Gertrude's story is an excellent and well-documented history of one family's demise. The acrimony and bitterness in the family following lawsuit after lawsuit broke down those kinship ties. As Gertrude describes in the diary, she found herself alienated from her family and more and more alone. Continually looking for some "strong, intelligent women" with whom she could share her innermost feelings and concern, she was forced to think for herself and become more self-sufficient. Indeed, she did "suffer and grow strong."

Finally, it was her early relationship with that strong father figure, whom she loved and adored more than any other person in her life, that helped to make her the woman she was to become late in life. She and her father had a special bond. Fortunately, he was able to recognize her intelligence and love of learning. At a time when most people thought education for women was unnecessary, he investigated the new college for women, Wesleyan Female College, and decided she should attend. It was she, and not her older sister, who was chosen to go. Her father visited her while she was there and even sent her back on a visit during the war to cheer her up. He seemed to be genuinely interested in her well-being, and it gave her confidence. He became her role model instead of her mother, who was the epitome of a Southern lady. There are other examples of strong women who emerged in the nineteenth century who had a close relationship with a strong father figure.[379] Gertrude said more than once that she wanted to be like her father—decisive, strong, and intelligent. It was these very traits that enabled her to survive and even thrive.

Gertrude's gradual transition from one side of the spectrum to the other unfolds in her diary and scrapbooks; yet, she was still a product of her times in some ways. Even though she was more liberal toward race than other Southerners, she still worked primarily for the vote and education for white women, not all women. She held anger against the "Yankees," who had scorched the earth of her home state, but she could see that Southerners were not necessarily "the best people God ever made." Her wide reading of different sides of issues helped her to be more rational than others of her time. Finally, late in her life, she was able to think for herself—a trait rare in any age.

Having been born in the Old South, which taught women to be silent and to not speak in public, Gertrude found her voice and the courage to speak out about the most controversial issues concerning women at the end of the nineteenth century. Early in her life she had been critical of a woman who stood up in church to address the congregation. Late in her life she would stand before hundreds in the House of Representatives and say that not only should women get the vote, but they also should be "equal [to men] in the work of the world." It was at this moment, in 1899, that Gertrude had come full circle. She was no longer a Southern lady; she was a New Woman of the New South.

Acknowledgments

Where do I begin thanking those who have been helpful to me along the way? It is not an easy task. First and foremost, I have been blessed with many wonderful teachers who encouraged me and recognized something in me that maybe I did not see in myself. From Miss Bolton, Mrs. Hughes, and Miss Miller in elementary school and from Mr. Stuart, Miss Taylor, and Dr. Felder in high school, I learned to experience the joy and satisfaction of learning. Dr. Miriam Felder encouraged me to attend her alma mater, Agnes Scott College, a woman's college in Decatur, Georgia, and that made all the difference. I became an English major because of two great professors: Dr. George P. Hayes and Dr. Margaret Pepperdene. I loved the literature, but it was the stories about the lives of the writers themselves that fascinated me the most. After a ten-year break during which time I got married and had two children, I went back to graduate school knowing that I wanted to major in history and study these stories.

Back in the 1970s there was not much written about women in the history books, so finding the women became my task. I had wonderful professors at Georgia State University who helped me along the way. Dr. Douglas Reynolds, Dr. C. L. Grant, and Dr. Diane Willen taught wonderful courses and awakened new interests for me. When I started looking for a dissertation topic I was grateful that my adviser, Dr. John Matthews, encouraged me to go to Duke University and look at the diary of Ella Gertrude Clanton Thomas. Reading that diary started me on a long, interesting journey that came to fruition in this book. The staff at the Perkins Library at Duke was most helpful and directed me to Gertrude Threlkeld Despeaux, Ella

Gertrude Clanton Thomas's great-granddaughter. Enthusiastic and trusting of my abilities to tell the elder Gertrude's story, Gertrude Despeaux was very generous with both her time and the valuable scrapbooks she had in her possession. Madge Rood, another family member, was also very helpful when I visited her in Augusta. Gertrude Despeaux's son Michael and his wife, Mary Sue, the current custodians of the portraits and scrapbooks, have also been very generous and allowed me to visit in their home and photograph these prized items. Gertrude Despeaux's daughter Patricia Seraphine also allowed me to photograph a wonderful portrait of Gertrude that was in her home. Mary Ann Longshore, a friend with a passion for photography, spent hours riding with me to make pictures that I would never would have been able to capture as well as she did. I would also like to thank an old friend, Tim Owings, who answered my appeal for help with a photography assignment in Augusta. Also, Charles Gardner and Carol Colly were helpful looking up records at First Methodist Church in Atlanta. Thanks also goes to librarians at Princeton University, Emory University, Georgia Regents University, the University of Georgia, and Georgia State University who helped find other pictures and rare information.

Although I did not try to publish my dissertation when I first completed it, I must thank those who encouraged me to keep thinking about that possibility. Richard Wentworth at University of Illinois Press was very supportive. I must thank those who read it then and gave me helpful comments that I kept on file all these years. Anne Firor Scott at Duke University made very thoughtful remarks, as did Jacqueline Dowd Hall at The University of North Carolina. Some years later, Elizabeth Fox Genovese was most generous with her time. I must add that she was also a mentor and adviser to my daughter Kristin Hunter, who got her PhD at Emory University. Other readers I must mention who have kept me going are Kent Leslie, Kathy Seeley-Fuller, Carolyn Clarke, Dot Addison, Ron Greer, and Karen Greer. Special recognition must go to my friend Betty Mori who read my dissertation then recommended to President Ruth Knox and other friends at Wesleyan College that I make a speech about Gertrude. It was the spark I needed to get going again on publication, and I will always be grateful to her, along with Sybil McNeal, Cathy Snow, and Mary Ann Howard at Wesleyan.

I want to thank women at my alma mater, Agnes Scott College, who have always expressed enthusiasm for this project: President Elizabeth Kiss, Alumnae Director Kim Vickers, members of the Atlanta Alumnae Steering Committee, classmates, and others too numerous to name. I want to mention some of the women from Women Alone Together® who have shown interest and given support: Sharon Pauli, Janet Browning, Helen Maddox, Gloria Payne, Jean Hyman, Lucy Molinaro, Terri Roland, and others.

I am indebted to Pete and Susan Wellborn who gave support to this project in numerous ways. They were interested from the beginning, listened to my stories, read my manuscript, and provided technical support. Pete led me through the mysteries of the computer universe. I know I could not have done all that I needed to do without him. I would also like to express gratitude to my friend Jeff Battcher who has given his expertise and advice to the project.

My friends and supporters at Georgia State University were enthusiastic and believed it was important that I tell this story. I can only mention some of them: Morna Gerrard, Michelle Brittain, Natalie Blake, Nan Seimans, Laura Voisinet, Amy Hunter, Denita Hampton, and Denita Clark.

Of course, I want to thank Marc Jolley, Director of Mercer University Press, publishing assistant Marsha Luttrell, who patiently answered all my questions and guided me through this process, and Mary Beth Kosowski, director of marketing. I could not have done it without them.

Finally, I want to thank my family, beginning with my ninety-two-year-old mother, Frances Newton, who was the first strong woman in my life. She and my father, Weyman Newton, who died last year at the age of ninety-three, planted the idea that education was important to life. Following in that tradition, our daughter Kristin is a marvelous teacher. She and her husband, Bob, are raising the next generation of intelligent, delightful, young women Evelyn and Claire. Never one to shy away from a task, our son Bill, Jr., and his wife, Kelly, are raising four equally smart, energetic young men: Alex, Elliot, Brett, and Jack. As a daughter, mother, and grandmother, I am truly blessed.

How can I say thank you to my husband Bill for all he has done? For more than fifty years we have shared life's great adventure. He has listened to my dreams, understood them better than anyone else, and loved me through them all. Love and thanks I give to him with all my heart.

Notes

[1] Anne Firor Scott, *The Southern Lady From Pedestal to Politics* 1830–1930 (Chicago: University of Chicago Press, 1970).

[2] Mary Elizabeth Massey, "The Making of a Feminist," *The Journal of Southern History* 39 (February 1973): 3–22. Note: even though Gertrude is her middle name, I know from articles she signed, listings in legal documents, and use of name by descendants that she went by Gertrude.

[3] Ella Gertrude Clanton Thomas, *The Secret Eye: The Journal of Ella Gertrude Clanton Thomas 1848–1889*, ed. Virginia Ingraham Burr (Chapel Hill: University of North Carolina Press, 1990).

[4] Edward J. Cashin, *The Story of Augusta* (Augusta GA: Richmond County Board of Education, 1980).

[5] J. William Harris, *Plain Folk and Gentry in a Slave Society: White Liberty and Black Slavery in Augusta's Hinterlands* (Middletown CT: Wesleyan University Press, 1985) 14.

[6] *Augusta Daily Constitutionalist* (Augusta GA) 4 April, 21 October, 23 November 1858.

[7] Harris, *Plain Folk,* 15–16.

[8] Florence Fleming Corley, *Confederate City: Augusta, Georgia, 1860–1864* (Columbia: University of South Carolina Press, 1960) 6.

[9] Fredrika Bremer, *The Homes of the New World: Impressions of America,* trans. Mary Howitt, 2 vols. (New York: Harper & Brothers, 1853); reprinted (New York: Johnson Reprint Corp., 1968) 372–73.

[10] Corley, *Confederate City,* 8.

[11] Corley, *Confederate City,* 7.

[12] Interview with Mrs. Robert Rood, daughter-in-law of Kate Clanton, Ella Gertrude's younger sister, on 16 February 1986 in Augusta, Georgia.

[13] Corley, *Confederate City,* 11.

[14] Ella Gertrude Clanton Thomas, *Journal of Ella Gertrude Clanton Thomas,* 13 vols., Manuscript Department, William R. Perkins Library, Duke University, Durham, North Carolina, vol. 6, p. 97, hereafter cited as *Journal.*

[15] Dr. H. R. Casey, "Reminiscenses," *Columbia Sentinel,* compiled by Janette S. Kelley in *Our Heritage: Personalities 1754–1983 Columbia County, Georgia* (Thomson, Georgia, n.d.), 22 March 1984, 39. Gift to Georgia Department of Archives and History, Morrow, Georgia, hereafter cited as GDAHMG.

[16] Ibid., 40.

[17] Will of William B. Luke, Columbia County, Georgia, Drawer 91, Box 11, p. 79, GDAHMG.

[18] *Christian Index 1848*, Drawer 204, Box 26, p. 395, GDAHMG.

[19] Will of Elizabeth Luke, Columbia County, Georgia, 1848, Drawer 192, Box 5, p. 186, GDAHMG.

[20] Will of Turner Clanton, Richmond County, Georgia, 1864, John H Ruffin, Jr., Court House, Augusta, Georgia, hereafter cited as JHRJCH.

[21] "Magnolia Cemetery Sexton's Records," *Ancestoring: A Journal of the Augusta Genealogical Society*, vol. 3 (Augusta GA: Augusta Genealogical Society, 1842, 1846): 53, 56; vol. 4, 48; vol. 5, 62.

[22] Casey, "Reminiscenses," 35.

[23] Deed, Columbia County, Georgia, Jephemiah Athey grantor to Holt Clanton grantee, 12 February 1803, Book N, p. 329, GDAHMG.

[24] Deed, Columbia County, Georgia, George Dent to Holt Clanton, 13 December 1805, Book N, 323; and Marmaduke Ricketson to Holt Clanton, 7 January 1804, Book N, 321, GDAHMG.

[25] Deeds, Columbia County, Georgia, 1809–27, Books O, P, R, X, Y, GDAHMG; and *Index to the Headright and Bounty Grants of Georgia 1756–1909* (Vidalia: Georgia Genealogical Reprints, 1970) 109.

[26] Nathaniel Holt Clanton was the father of James Clanton, who was a general in the Civil War and an adopted son of the state of Alabama. He was involved in politics in that state, and his career was rising when, during the days of Reconstruction, he met a violent death in a street row in Knoxville, Tennessee. See Casey, "Reminiscenses," 35.

[27] Casey, "Reminiscenses," 35.

[28] United States Bureau of the Census, Census of 1830, GDAHMG. Twenty-nine males were listed by age, with nine being between 24 and 36, and five between 36 and 50. The rest were in their early twenties, teens, and younger. Twenty-two females were listed, with nine being between 10 and 24 and two between 24 and 36. There were only four older female slaves, with the remainder being under ten years of age.

[29] Deed, Columbia County, Georgia, Executors of John Campbell to Turner Clanton, 14 January 1830, Book Z, p. 56, GDAHMG.

[30] Tax Digest, Columbia County, Georgia, 1846, GDAHMG. Land lots: 202 acres in Gwinnett County, 202 acres in Laurens County. According to the Richmond County Digest, "First quality land consisted of Sea Island, marsh and tide water acreage; Second quality land was river swamp; third quality was oak and hickory land; and fourth quality was pine-covered."

[31] United States Census Bureau of the Productions of Agriculture, Columbia County, 1850, 1860, Drawer 13, Box 76; and Drawer 14, Box 1, GDAHMG.

[32] Deed, Richmond County, Georgia, Milton Antony to Turner Clanton, 2 August 1841, Book Z, JHRJCH.

[33] Interview, Mrs. Robert Rood, 16 February 1986, Augusta, Georgia.

[34] United States Census 1850, Richmond County, Georgia, GDAHMG.

[35] Lease agreement, Turner Clanton to Clarke Cook, 5 March 1847, Book CC, p. 319, JHRJCH.

[36] Hitchcock and Ingalls to Turner Clanton, 3 January 1857, Book LL, p. 575; Hitchcock and Ingalls to Turner Clanton, 5 January 1858, Book MM, p. 358. JHRJCH.

[37] Mortgage deed, Eliza Robinson to Turner Clanton, 9 February 1857, Book LL, p. 637. JHRJCH.

[38] *Augusta City Directory 1859*, Archives, Regents College, Augusta, Georgia.

[39] Will of Turner Clanton, Richmond County, Georgia, 1864, JHRJCH.

[40] James Oakes, *The Ruling Race: A History of American Slaveholders* (New York: Norton, 1998) xvi, 229.

[41] Will of Turner Clanton.

[42] Trust deed, Turner Clanton to Trustees Joseph Thomas, James L. Clanton, Jefferson Thomas, and Thomas McMillan, 6 January 1854, Book JJ, pp. 212–14, JHRJCH.

[43] Trust deed, Turner Clanton to Trustees Jonathan Pinckney Thomas, James Jefferson Thomas, James L. Clanton, and Nathaniel Hold Clanton, 18 December 1860, Book PP, pp. 179, 181, JHRJCH.

[44] Trust deed, Turner Clanton to Trustees William Vason, James L. Clanton, et al., 7 November 1859, Book NN, pp. 451–53, JHRJCH.

[45] Eleanor M. Boatwright, "The Political and Civil Status of Women in Georgia, 1783-1860," *The Georgia Historical Quarterly* 25 (December 1941): 310.

[46] Suzanne Lebsock, *The Free Women of Petersburg: Status and Culture in a Southern Town, 1784–1860* (New York: Norton, 1984) 55.

[47] *Augusta Chronicle* (Augusta, Georgia) 14 April 1864.

[48] Undated newspaper clipping, family Bible belonging to Mrs. Robert Rood, 1206 Anthony Road, Augusta, Georgia.

[49] *Journal*, vol. 2, 20.

[50] *Journal*, vol. 10, 143.

[51] Ibid.

[52] *Journal*, vol. 1, p. 1. Quotes from the diary will be made using Gertrude's spelling and punctuation. She uses *two* for *too* consistently and misspells some words more than once. Original diary was difficult to read at times, and one cannot be sure of spacing and punctuation.

[53] Ibid., 2.

[54] Ibid.

[55] Ibid.,16.

[56] Identified as *History of the United States—on a New Plan Adapted to the Capacity of Youth (1836)*, by Jesse Olney in Thomas, *The Secret Eye*, 77, hereafter cited as *The Secret Eye*.

[57] *Journal*, vol. 1, pp. 25, 51.

[58] Ibid., 4, 12, 13, 25.

[59] Ibid., 3, 5, 6, 7.

[60] Ibid., 8, 26.

[61] Ibid., 6, 45.

[62] Carroll Smith-Rosenberg, "The Female World of Love and Ritual: Relations between Women in Nineteenth-Century America," *Signs*, vol. 1 (1975): 1–29. Rosenberg comments on the significance of such relationships.

[63] *Journal*, vol. 1, pp. 39, 42.

[64] Ibid., 36.

[65] Burr, *The Secret Eye*, 78.

[66] *Journal*, vol. 1, pp. 36, 37.

[67] *The New Testament* (Philadelphia: National Bible Press, 1941) 349.

[68] Richard W. Griffin, "Wesleyan College: Its Genesis 1835–1840," *Georgia Historical Quarterly* (March 1966): 54–73. Also Florence Fleming Corley, "Higher Education for Southern Women: Four Church-Related Women's Colleges in Georgia, Agnes Scott, Shorter, Spelman and Wesleyan, 1900–1920," (PhD diss., Georgia State University, 1985).

[69] Ibid., 71.

[70] Samuel Luttrell Akers, *The First Hundred Years of Wesleyan College 1836–1936* (Macon GA: Beehive, 1976) 67.

[71] Griffin, 67.

[72] Akers, 61.

[73] *Journal*, vol. 1, p. 46.

[74] Ibid., 47.

[75] Ibid., 46.

[76] Elizabeth Barber Young, *A Study of the Curricula of Seven Selected Women's Colleges of the Southern States* (New York, 1932) 48; reprinted New York, 1972.

[77] *Journal*, vol. 2, p. 13.

[78] Ibid, 1.

[79] Virginia Lee Nelson, ed., *Loyally, A History of Alpha Delta Pi from the founding of the Adelphean Society in 1851 at Wesleyan Female College, Macon, Georgia through 1964* (Atlanta: Alpha Delta Pi Sorority, 1965) 16.

[80] *Journal*, vol. 2, pp. 22, 39.

[81] Young, *A Study of the Curricula*, 52.

[82] Ibid., 54–55.

[83] *Journal*, vol. 8, p. 97.

[84] Ibid., 108–13.

[85] *Journal*, vol. 2, p. 37.

[86] *Journal*, vol. 8, p. 99.

[87] *Journal*, vol. 2, p. 47.

[88] *Journal*, vol. 8, pp. 97–98.

[89] *Journal*, vol. 2, p. 1.

[90] Nelson, *A History of Alpha Delta Pi,* 16; and *Journal*, vol. 2, pp. 26–27.

[91] *Journal*, vol. 2, p. 35.

[92] Ibid., 5–6.

[93] Ibid., 27.

[94] Wesleyan College, Special Collections, Wesleyan College Library.

[95] Ibid., 28.

[96] Ibid., 52.

[97] Young, *A Study of the Curricula*, 58–59.

[98] Ibid., 52.

[99] *Journal*, vol. 8, p. 51.

[100] *Journal*, vol. 9, p. 22.

[101] Ibid., 111–12.

[102] *Journal*, vol. 2, p. 1.

[103] *Journal*, vol. 6, p. 7. As mentioned earlier, Gertrude will almost always refer to her husband as Mr. Thomas.

[104] Will of Joseph Thomas. Richmond County, Georgia, 1858, Drawer 48, Box 74, pp. 181–82, Georgia Department of Archives and History, Morrow, Georgia, hereafter cited as GDAHMG. Subsequent references to Will of Joseph Thomas.

[105] *Journal*, vol. 3, p. 5.

[106] Ibid., 11.

[107] *Journal*, vol. 5, p. 21.

[108] Ibid., 20.

[109] *Journal*, vol. 3, p. 41.

[110] Mary Elizabeth Massey, "The Making of a Feminist," *The Journal of Southern History* 39 (February 1973): 6.

[111] *Journal*, vol. 5, p. 6.

[112] Will of Joseph Thomas.

[113] Will of Joseph Thomas, Richmond County, Georgia. 1859. Division of Estate Drawer 48, Box 74, pp. 280–88. GDAHMG.

[114] *Journal*, vol. 5, pp. 22, 25.

[115] *Journal*, vol. 6, p. 8.

[116] Ibid., 9.

[117] Ibid., 23, 83.

[118] Ibid., 23, 83–84, 119.

[119] *Journal*, vol. 7, p. 10.

[120] Ibid., 18.

[121] *Journal*, vol. 6, pp. 8, 55.

[122] Ibid., 55, 126–27, 98.

[123] *Journal*, vol. 7, pp. 4, 10.

[124] Ibid.,18, 36.

[125] Ibid., 51.

[126] Ibid., 52.

[127] *Journal*, vol. 6, pp. 13, 53–54, 61.

[128] *Journal*, vol. 7, pp. 9–10.

[129] Mary Boykin Chesnut, *Mary Chesnut's Civil War,* ed. C. Vann Woodward (New Haven and London: Yale University Press, 1981) 29.

[130] *Journal*, vol. 7, p. 71.

[131] Ibid., 71–72.

[132] Ibid., 72.

[133] Ibid.

[134] *Journal*, vol. 6, p. 122.

[135] *Journal*, vol. 7, p. 44.

[136] Ibid., 14.

[137] *Journal*, vol. 6, p. 130.

[138] Ibid., 50.

[139] Ibid., 36.

[140] *Journal*, vol. 7, pp. 32, 33.

[141] *Journal*, vol. 6, p. 15–16.

[142] *Journal*, vol. 7, p. 69.

[143] Ibid.

[144] *Journal*, vol. 8, p. 14.

[145] Ibid., 5–6.

[146] Ibid.

[147] Ibid., 17, 21.

[148] Sarah Case, "Mildred Lewis Rutherford (1851–1928): The Redefinition of New South White Womanhood," *Georgia Women: Their Lives and Times,* vol. 1, eds. Ann Chirhart and Betty Wood (Athens: University of Georgia Press, 2009) 273–74.

[149] *Journal,* vol. 8, p. 24.

[150] Ibid., 87–88.

[151] Ibid., 104.

[152] Harriet Bey Mesic, *Cobb's Legion Cavalry: A History and Roster of the Ninth Georgia Volunteers in the Civil War* (Jefferson NC: McFarland & Co., 2009) 305.

[153] *Journal,* vol. 8, pp. 127, 192.

[154] Ibid., 159.

[155] Ibid., 175, 177.

[156] Florence Fleming Corley, "Higher Education for Southern Women: Four Church-Related Women's Colleges in Georgia, Agnes Scott, Shorter, Spelman and Wesleyan, 1900–1920," (PhD diss., Georgia State University, 1985) 41.

[157] *Journal,* vol. 8, pp. 173–76.

[158] *Journal,* vol. 6, p. 70–71.

[159] *Journal,* vol. 8, p. 6.

[160] Ibid., 7.

[161] Ibid., 110.

[162] Ibid., 118–19.

[163] Ibid., 123.

[164] Ibid.,37.

[165] Sally McMillan, "Mothers' Sacred Duty: Breastfeeding Patterns Among Middle and Upper-Class Women in the Antebellum South," *The Journal of Southern History* (August 1983): 355.

[166] *Journal,* vol. 8, pp. 143, 153.

[167] Ibid., 144, 148.

[168] Ibid., 181.

[169] Ibid., 101.

[170] Ibid., 165.

[171] Ibid.

[172] Ibid., 122, 188.

[173] Ibid., 194, 195.

[174] Ibid., 195.

[175] Ibid., 201.

[176] *Journal*, vol. 9, p. 4.

[177] Ibid., 3, 8.

[178] Ibid., 10.

[179] Ibid., 3–4.

[180] Ibid., 18.

[181] See Bruce Catton, *The Civil War* (New York: Houghton Mifflin, 2004).

[182] *Journal*, vol. 9, pp. 7, 17.

[183] Kenneth Coleman, ed., *A History of Georgia* (Athens: University of Georgia Press, 1977) 201.

[184] *Journal*, vol. 9, pp. 21–23.

[185] Ibid.

[186] Ibid., 25.

[187] Coleman, *A History of Georgia,* 203.

[188] *Journal*, vol. 9, p. 39.

[189] Ibid., 37–38.

[190] Ibid., 130.

[191] Ibid., 43, 44.

[192] Ibid., 42, 53.

[193] Ibid., 90, 91.

[194] Ibid., 65, 70.

[195] Eugene Genovese, *Roll, Jordan, Roll: The World The Slave Made.* (New York: Random House, 1972) 111, 112.

[196] *Journal*, vol. 9, pp. 67, 70, 71.

[197] Ibid., 85.

[198] Ibid., 55.

[199] Ibid., 80.

[200] Ibid., 89.

[201] Ibid., 98, 132.

[202] Ibid., 89.

[203] Ibid., 123,124, 133.

[204] Ibid., 73, 75.

[205] Ibid., 58, 67.

[206] Ibid., 51.

[207] Ibid.,139.

[208] Martin V. Calvin, *Calvin's Augusta and Business Directory for 1865–66* (Augusta GA: Constitutionalist Job Office, 1865) 69. Special Collections, Reese Library, Georgia Regents University, Augusta, Georgia.

[209] E. H. Pughe, *Pughe's Directory for the City of Augusta and its Vicinity.* (Augusta GA: E. H. Pughe Printer, 1867) 55, Special Collections, Reese Library, Georgia Regents University, Augusta, Georgia.

[210] Georgia, Vol. 1B, p. 187, R. G. Dun & Company Collection, Baker Library, Harvard University Graduate School of Business Administration, Cambridge, Massachusetts.

[211] *Journal,* vol. 9, pp. 101, 102.

[212] Ibid., 107, 109.

[213] Ibid., 58.

[214] Among dozens of important studies, see Drew Gilpin Faust, *Mothers of Invention: Women of the Slaveholding South in the American Civil War* (Chapel Hill: University of North Carolina Press, 1996); Anne Firor Scott, *The Southern Lady From Pedestal to Politics 1830–1930* (Chicago: University of Illinois, 1970); and LeeAnn Whites, *The Civil War as a Crisis in Gender: Augusta, Georgia, 1860–1890* (Athens: University of Georgia Press, 1995).

[215] *Journal,* vol. 9, pp. 61, 67, 126.

[216] Ibid., 143.

[217] *Journal,* vol. 10, p. 6.

[218] Ibid.,6, 10.

[219] Ibid., 7.

[220] Ibid., 8.

[221] Ibid., 15.

[222] Ibid., 3–5.

[223] *Journal,* vol. 11, p. 28.

[224] Ibid., 51.

[225] *Journal,* vol. 10, p. 19.

[226] Georgia, Vol. 1B, p. 128, R. G. Dun and Company Collection, Baker Library, Harvard University Graduate School of Business Administration, Cambridge, Massachusetts.

[227] *Journal,* vol. 10, pp. 75, 76.

[228] *Journal,* vol. 7, p. 42.

[229] *Journal,* vol. 10, pp. 20, 126.

[230] Ibid., 24, 41.

[231] Ibid., 89.

[232] Will of Turner Clanton, Richmond County, Georgia, 1864, John H Ruffin, Jr., Court House, Augusta, Georgia, hereafter cited as JHRJCH.

[233] *Journal,* vol. 10, p. 80.

[234] Ibid., 29.

[235] Ibid., 33, 151.

[236] *Journal,* vol. 9, p. 6.

[237] *Journal,* vol. 10, p. 133.

[238] *Journal,* vol. 11, pp. 3, 5.

[239] Ibid., 17, 20, 21.

[240] Ibid., 23, 24.

[241] *Journal,* vol. 10, p. 32.

[242] Ibid., 142.

[243] *Journal,* vol. 9, p. 52.

[244] *Journal,* vol. 10, pp. 121, 136, 162.

[245] Ibid., 28, 151.

[246] *Journal,* vol. 9, p. 26.

[247] Ibid., 107–09.

[248] Ibid., 110–11.

[249] Ibid.,139–44.

[250] Ibid., 145.

[251] Ibid., 146.

[252] *Journal,* vol. 12, p. 4.

[253] Gertrude Threlkeld Despeaux, great-granddaughter of Gertrude, testified that she saw her Aunt Cora, one of the daughters of Jeff and Gertrude, destroy parts of the journal.

[254] Minutes of the Superior Court of Richmond County, 1872–74, Book 25, pp. 341–43, John H Ruffin, Jr., Court House, Augusta, Georgia, hereafter cited as JHRJCH. Subsequent references to Minutes SCRC.

[255] Minutes SCRC, 1870–71, Book 24, p. 629, JHRJCH.

[256] Minutes SCRC, 1872–74. Book 25, p. 229, JHRJCH.

[257] *Journal,* vol. 12, p. 104.

[258] Ibid., 4.

[259] Ibid., Note tarlatan was a thin, plain-weave cotton fabric, finished with stiffening agents and sometimes glazed. Also can be tarlatane, a kind of cloth originally imported from India. *The Random House Dictionary of the English Language Second Edition Unabridged.* (New York: Random House, 1987).

[260] Ibid., 14.

[261] Ibid.

[262] Ibid., 15.

[263] Ibid., 114–15.

[264] *Journal,* vol. 13, p. 47.

[265] *Journal,* vol. 12, p. 42.

[266] Ibid., 38–40.

[267] *Augusta Daily Chronicle and Constitutionalist* (Augusta GA), c. 12 December 1879, p 1.

[268] *Journal,* vol. 12, p. 46.

[269] Ibid., 48.

[270] Minutes SCRC, 1878–80, 24 February 1880, 534–39, JHRJCH.

[271] *Journal,* vol. 12, p. 53.

[272] Scrapbook 1, 7 October 1876, unnumbered page.

[273] *Journal,* vol. 12, p. 29.

[274] Ibid., 74.

[275] *Journal,* vol. 13, pp. 51, 53, 57.

[276] Ibid., 55.

[277] Ibid., 80.

[278] Thomas, *The Secret Eye,* 437.

[279] Ibid., 438–40.

[280] *Journal,* vol. 13, pp. 80, 81.

[281] Scrapbook 1, 63.

[282] Ibid., 65.

[283] *Journal,* vol. 13, pp. 75–77.

[284] Scrapbook 1, 70.

[285] Burr, *The Secret Eye,* 162.

[286] Ibid., 266.

[287] Scrapbook 1, 70.

[288] Ibid.

[289] *Journal,* vol. 13, p. 76.

[290] Ibid., 79.

[291] Ibid., 80.

[292] Ibid., 83.

[293] Ibid., 85.

[294] Nancy F. Cott, *The Bonds of Womanhood: "Women's Sphere" in New England 1780–1835* (New Haven, 1977); and Barbara Welter, "The Cult of True Womanhood, 1820–1860, *American Quarterly* 18 (1966): 151–74.

[295] Scrapbook 4, 53.

[296] Scrapbook 1, 59.

[297] Ibid.

[298] Scrapbook 2, unnumbered page.

[299] Thomas, *The Secret Eye,* 451.

[300] Scrapbook 1, 71.

[301] LeeAnn Whites, "Rebecca Latimer Felton (1835–1930): The Problem of Protection in the New South," *Georgia Women: Their Lives and Times,* vol. 1,

eds. Ann Short Chirhart and Betty Wood (Athens: University of Georgia Press, 2009) 231.

[302] Scrapbook 1, 71.

[303] Stacey Horstmann Gatti, "Mary Latimer McLendon (1840–1921): Mother of Suffrage Work in Georgia," *Georgia Women: Their Lives and Time*, vol. 1, eds. Ann Short Chirhart and Betty Wood (Athens: University of Georgia Press, 2009) 252.

[304] Ibid., 253.

[305] J. E.Sibley to Warren Candler, 29 April 1892; and Warren Candler to J.E. Sibley, 2 May 1892, Warren Candler Papers, Special Collections, Archives and Rare Book Library, Robert W. Woodruff Library, Emory University.

[306] Ibid.

[307] Gatti, 257.

[308] Ibid., 258.

[309] Michele Gillespie, "Mary Gay (1829–1918): Sin, Self, and Survival in the Post-Civil War South," *Georgia Women: Their Lives and Times*, vol. 1, eds. Ann Short Chirhart and Betty Wood (Athens: University of Georgia Press, 2009) 201.

[310] Scrapbook 1, 81.

[311] Ibid., 56.

[312] Minutes of the 8th Annual Convention of the Georgia WCTU, Special Collections, Archives and Rare Book Library, Robert W. Woodruff Library, Emory University, Atlanta, Georgia.

[313] Ibid., 62.

[314] Ibid., 58.

[315] Turner Clanton v. Gertrude Thomas, 6 July 1897, *Minutes SCRC, Georgia,* Book 37, pp. 203–07, John H Ruffin, Jr., Court House, Augusta, Georgia, hereafter cited as JHRJCH.

[316] Jones and Norris v. J. J. Thomas, Trustee et al, 6 November 1878, *Minutes SCRC, Georgia,* Book 27, pp. 661–2, JHRJCH.

[317] Gertrude Thomas v. J.J. Thomas, 2 October 1889, *Minutes SCRC, Georgia,* Book 33, pp. 533–39, JHRJCH.

[318] Mrs. Robert Rood, daughter-in-law of Kate Clanton, Gertrude's younger sister, interviewed by author, Augusta, Georgia, 16 February 1986.

[319] Anne Vason v. Gertrude Thomas, April 1896, *Minutes SCRC, Georgia,* Book 36, pp. 429–31, JHRJCH.

[320] *Journal,* vol. 9, p. 52.

[321] Scrapbook 1, 64, 69.

[322] Ibid., 67.

[323] Ibid.

[324] Ibid.,66.

[325] Scrapbook 1, 74.

[326] Interview, the Rev. Charles Gardner, First Methodist Church, Atlanta, Georgia, 21 May 2013.

[327] Ibid.

[328] Scrapbook 3, 21.

[329] A. Elizabeth Taylor, "The Origin of the Woman Suffrage Movement in Georgia," *The Georgia Historical Quarterly* 28 (June 1944): 64.

[330] Ibid., 66.

[331] Ibid.

[332] Ibid., 69.

[333] *New York Sun*, 1894, suffrage scrapbook, unnumbered page.

[334] Ibid.,72.

[335] Ibid., 72, 73.

[336] *Constitution* (Atlanta), 29 January 1895.

[337] Warren Candler to J. E. Sibley, 2 May 1892, Warren Candler Papers, Special Collections, Archives and Rare Book Library, Robert W. Woodruff Library, Emory University.

[338] *Constitution* (Atlanta), 28 January 1895.

[339] Taylor, 74.

[340] Eugene Anderson, "Unchaining the Demons of the Lower World or a Petition of Ninety-Nine Per Cent Against Suffrage," speech given at meeting Georgia Association Opposed to Women Suffrage, Macon, Georgia, n.d., Georgia Department of Archives and History, Morrow, Georgia, hereafter cited as GDAHMG.

[341] Suffrage scrapbook 1895, unnumbered page.

[342] Taylor, *The Origin of the Woman Suffrage Movement in Georgia,* 74.

[343] Ibid.,76.

[344] *Constitution* (Atlanta), 6 February 1895.

[345] Taylor, *The Origin of the Woman Suffrage Movement in Georgia,* 77.

[346] "They Want To Vote," *Constitution* (Atlanta), 30 May 1895.

[347] Minutes of the Superior Court of Richmond County, Book 37, pp. 203–07, John H Ruffin, Jr., Court House, Augusta, Georgia, hereafter cited as JHRJCH. Subsequent references to Minutes SCRC.

[348] *Journal* vol. 1, pp. 108–09.

[349] Minutes SCRC, 15 July 1898, Book 38, pp. 302–05, JHRJCH.

[350] Ibid., 304.

[351] Scrapbook 2, unnumbered page.

[352] Ibid.

[353] Mary Elizabeth Massey, "The Making of a Feminist," *The Journal of Southern History* 39 (February 1973): 21.

[354] United Daughters of the Confederacy Scrapbook, unnumbered page.

[355] *Augusta Chronicle,* 14 May 1899; and *Augusta Chronicle* (Augusta GA), 25 June 1899.

[356] "Women Suffragists Still in Session," *Atlanta Journal* (Atlanta), 29 November 1899.

[357] Minutes of the Georgia Woman Suffrage Association, 28, 29 November 1899, Atlanta, Georgia, 16. Judicial Library, Georgia State Library, GDAHMG. Subsequent references to Minutes GWSA

[358] *Atlanta Journal* (Atlanta), 29 November 1899.

[359] Ibid.

[360] *Atlanta Journal* (Atlanta), 30 November 1899.

[361] Minutes GWSA, 7.

[362] *Augusta Chronicle* (Augusta GA), 14 February 1900.

[363] "Women Suffragist of Georgia in Session," *Constitution* (Atlanta), 26 November 1901, 4.

[364] *Constitution* (Atlanta), 13 April 1902.

[365] "Anna Shaw Arrived Today," *Constitution* (Atlanta), 18 November 1903.

[366] Interview with Gertrude Threlkeld Despeaux, Gertrude's great-granddaughter, October 1986, Atlanta, Georgia. Book is now in possession of Gertrude's great-great-great-grandson David Laurens Despeaux in Mount Pleasant, South Carolina.

[367] *New York Sun,* 1894, suffrage scrapbook, unnumbered page.

[368] Stacey Horstmann Gatti, "Mary Latimer McLendon (1840–1921): Mother of Suffrage Work in Georgia," *Georgia Women: Their Lives and Times,* vol. 1, eds. Ann Short Chirhart and Betty Wood (Athens: University of Georgia Press, 2009) 253.

[369] Interview with Gertrude Threlkeld Despeaux, February 1986, Atlanta, Georgia.

[370] "Return of a Death, Mrs. Gertrude Thomas," Vital Records Service, Fulton County, Atlanta, Georgia, 13 May 1907.

[371] *Princeton Alumni Weekly,* 1 March 1916, Princeton University Archives, Department of Rare Books and Special Collections, Princeton University Library, Princeton, New Jersey.

[372] *Augusta Chronicle* (Augusta) 12, 13, 14 May 1907.

[373] See Mary Boykin Chesnut, *Mary Chesnut's Civil War,* ed. C. Vann Woodward (New Haven and London: Yale University Press, 1981); Sarah Morgan, *Sarah Morgan: The Civil War Diary of a Southern Woman,*ed. Charles East. (Athens: University of Georgia Press, 1991).

[374] James W. Pennebaker, *Opening Up: The Healing Power of Expressing Emotions* (New York: Guilford Press, 1990), revised 1997 by James W. Pennebaker.

[375] Nell Painter, "Introduction. The Journal of Ella Gertrude Clanton Thomas," in *The Secret Eye: The Journal of Ella Gertrude Clanton Thomas 1848– 1889.,* ed. Virginia Ingraham Burr (Chapel Hill: University of North Carolina Press, 1990) 56.

[376] Anne Firor Scott, *The Southern Lady from Pedestal to Politics 1830–1930* (Chicago: University of Chicago Press, 1984).

[377] Elizabeth Fox-Genovese, *Within the Plantation Household: Black and White Women of the Old South* (Chapel Hill: University of North Carolina Press, 1988).

[378] LeeAnn Whites, *The Civil War as a Crisis in Gender: Augusta, Georgia 1860–1890* (Athens: University of Georgia Press, 1995). Drew Gilpin Faust, *Mothers of Invention: Women of the Slaveholding South in the American Civil War* (Chapel Hill: University of North Carolina Press, 1996).

[379] See discussion of social learning theory and role models in Elisabeth Griffith, *In Her Own Right: The Life of Elizabeth Cady Stanton* (New York: Oxford University Press, 1984) 219–225.

Bibliography

Manuscript Sources

Ella Gertrude Clanton Thomas Journal. 13 volumes. Manuscript Department, Robert R. Perkins Library. Duke University. Durham, North Carolina.

Princeton Alumni Weekly. "President Hibben's Trip to the West and South," 1 March 1916. Princeton University Archives. Department of Rare Books and Special Collections. Princeton University Library. Princeton, New Jersey.

R. G. Dun & Company Collection. Baker Library. Harvard University Graduate School of Business Administration. Cambridge, Massachusetts.

Warren Chandler Papers. Manuscript, Archives, and Rare Books Library. Emory University. Atlanta, Georgia.

Commencement programs and catalogues. Archives and Special Collections. Lucy Lester Willet Memorial Library. Wesleyan College. Macon, Georgia.

Private Collections

Scrapbooks of Ella Gertrude Clanton Thomas. 15 volumes. Courtesy of Mrs. Gertrude Threlkeld Despeaux, Atlanta, Georgia. Now in possession of her son, Michael Despeaux, Easley, South Carolina.

Interviews

Gail Threlkeld Despeaux, great-granddaughter of Ella Gertrude Clanton Thomas. Series of interviews in fall of 1985 and spring of 1986.

Mrs. Robert Rood, daughter-in-law of Gertrude's younger sister, Kate. Interview on 16 February 1986.

Letters

Franklin M. Garrett, Atlanta Historical Society, to author dated 6 July 1987.

Virginia I. Burr, great-granddaughter of Ella Gertrude Clanton Thomas, and editor of Journal, to author dated 26 January 1988.

Newspapers

Atlanta Constitution
Atlanta Georgian
Atlanta Journal
Atlanta Journal & Constitution
Augusta Chronicle
Augusta Daily Constitutionalist

Columbia Sentinel

Birth and Death Certificates
Office of Vital Statistics. The Health Department. Fulton County, Georgia.

Tax and Census Records
Columbia County, Georgia. Tax Digest, 1846. Georgia Division of Archives and
   History. Morrow, Georgia
United States Bureau of the Census. Census of 1830. Columbia County, Georgia.
   Georgia Division of Archives and History. Morrow, Georgia.
———. *Census of 1840. Columbia County, Georiga.* Georgia Division of
   Archives and History. Morrow, Georgia.
———. *Census of 1850. Richmond County, Georgia.* Georgia Division of
   Archives and History. Morrow, Georgia.
United States Census Bureau of the Productions of Agriculture. Columbia County,
   Georgia 1850 and 1860. Drawer 13, Box 76 and Drawer 14, Box 1. Georgia
   Division of Archives and History. Morrow, Georgia.

Legal Records
Minutes of the Superior Court, Richmond County, Georgia. John H. Ruffin,
   Jr., Court House. Augusta, Georgia.
E. Walton v. J. Jefferson Thomas, Petition to foreclose mortgage, 20 February
   1868, 527.
E. Walton v. J. Jefferson Thomas, Rule to foreclose mortgage, 16 June 1868, 582.
Harmon Rowley v. Mosher, Thomas & Schaub, Makers, James L. Clanton, Endorser.
   Verdict, June 1868, Book 24, 9.
Savings Bank of Augusta v. J. Jefferson Thomas, Maker, James L. Clanton, Endorser.
   Verdict, 17 June 1869, Book 24, 156.
John H. Nesmith v. J. Jefferson Thomas, 7 March 1870, Book 24, 289.
Richards & Bros v. J. Jefferson Thomas. Verdict, 7 March 1870, Book 24, 291.
Abraham Sego v. J. Jefferson Thomas, 17 June 1870, Book 24, 376.
I.M. Dye & Co. v. Mosher, Thomas & Schaub, 14 June 1871, Book 24, 629.
Isaac Simon Sons v. J. Jefferson Thomas, 14 June 1871, Book 24, 629.
The National Bank of Augusta v. J. Jefferson Thomas, 21 October 1872, Book 25,
   229.
J. Sibley and Sons v. J. Jefferson Thomas, 21 October 1872, Book 25, 285.
Harmon Rowley v. J. Jefferson Thomas, 21 December 1872, Book 25, 228.
W.W. Montgomery v. J. Jefferson Thomas, 21 December 1872, Book 25, 341.
W.W. Montgomery v. J. Jefferson Thomas, 21 December 1872, Book 25, 343.
Harmon Rowley v. J. Jefferson Thomas, 21 April 1873, Book 25, 402.

J. Sibley & Sons v. J. Jefferson Thomas, 4 October 1873, Book 25, 569.

Jones & Norris v. J. Jefferson Thomas, 6 November 1878, Book 27, 661.

J.J. Thomas, Trustee, Gertrude Thomas et al, Petition to sell Trust Property, 27 February 1880, Book 28, 534–39.

Wm. J. Vason et al Exes of Turner Clanton v. Mary Clanton et al In Equity, 27 April 1880, Book 28, 588–89.

Gertrude Thomas et al v. J. Jefferson Thomas Proceedings to change Trustee, October Term 1889, Book 33, 533–39.

Sallie E. Griffrida v. Gertrude Thomas, Petition and Rule Nisi on Foreclosure of Mortgage on Realty, 27 May 1891, Book 34, 261–62.

Sallie E. Griffrida v. Gertrude Thomas, Mortgage Foreclosure, 4 November 1891, Book 34, 455–56.

Ann Vason v. Gertrude Thomas, Mortgage FC [foreclosure], April Term 1895, Book 36, 288–90.

Ann C. Vason v. Gertrude Thomas, Rule Absolute Mortgage FC [foreclosure], 5 November 1896, Book 36, 429–31.

Turner C. Thomas v. Gertrude Thomas et al, 6 July 1897, Book 37, 203–07.

Turner C. Thomas v. Gertrude Thomas et al, 15 July 1898, Book 38, 302–05.

Wills and Deeds, Columbia County and Richmond County, Georgia.

Will of Holt Clanton, Columbia County, Georgia, 1826. Georgia Division of Archives and History. Morrow, Georgia.

Will of Littlebury Clanton, Columbia County, Georgia 1828. Georgia Division of Archives and History. Morrow, Georgia.

Will of Mary Luke Clanton, Richmond County, Georgia 1884. John H. Ruffin, Jr., Court House. Augusta, Georgia.

Will of Turner Clanton, Richmond County, Georgia, 1864. John H. Ruffin, Jr., Court House. Augusta, Georgia.

Will of Elizabeth Luke, Columbia County, Georgia, 1848. Georgia Division of Archives and History. Morrow, Georgia.

Will of William B. Luke, Columbia County, Georgia, 1844. Georgia Division of Archives and History. Morrow, Georgia.

Will of Joseph D. Thomas, Richmond County, Georgia. 1856. Georgia Division of Archives and History. Morrow, Georgia.

Deeds, Columbia County, Georgia
Georgia Division of Archives and History, Morrow, Georgia.
Holt Clanton–Jephemiah Athey. 12 February 1803, Book N, 329.
———–Marmaduke Ricketson. 7 January 1804, Book N, 321.
———–George Dent. 13 December 1805, Book N, 323.

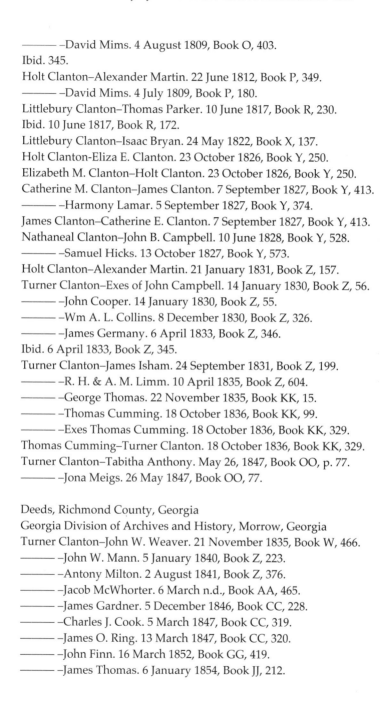

————— –David Mims. 4 August 1809, Book O, 403.

Ibid. 345.

Holt Clanton–Alexander Martin. 22 June 1812, Book P, 349.

————— –David Mims. 4 July 1809, Book P, 180.

Littlebury Clanton–Thomas Parker. 10 June 1817, Book R, 230.

Ibid. 10 June 1817, Book R, 172.

Littlebury Clanton–Isaac Bryan. 24 May 1822, Book X, 137.

Holt Clanton-Eliza E. Clanton. 23 October 1826, Book Y, 250.

Elizabeth M. Clanton–Holt Clanton. 23 October 1826, Book Y, 250.

Catherine M. Clanton–James Clanton. 7 September 1827, Book Y, 413.

————— –Harmony Lamar. 5 September 1827, Book Y, 374.

James Clanton–Catherine E. Clanton. 7 September 1827, Book Y, 413.

Nathaneal Clanton–John B. Campbell. 10 June 1828, Book Y, 528.

————— –Samuel Hicks. 13 October 1827, Book Y, 573.

Holt Clanton–Alexander Martin. 21 January 1831, Book Z, 157.

Turner Clanton–Exes of John Campbell. 14 January 1830, Book Z, 56.

————— –John Cooper. 14 January 1830, Book Z, 55.

————— –Wm A. L. Collins. 8 December 1830, Book Z, 326.

————— –James Germany. 6 April 1833, Book Z, 346.

Ibid. 6 April 1833, Book Z, 345.

Turner Clanton–James Isham. 24 September 1831, Book Z, 199.

————— –R. H. & A. M. Limm. 10 April 1835, Book Z, 604.

————— –George Thomas. 22 November 1835, Book KK, 15.

————— –Thomas Cumming. 18 October 1836, Book KK, 99.

————— –Exes Thomas Cumming. 18 October 1836, Book KK, 329.

Thomas Cumming–Turner Clanton. 18 October 1836, Book KK, 329.

Turner Clanton–Tabitha Anthony. May 26, 1847, Book OO, p. 77.

————— –Jona Meigs. 26 May 1847, Book OO, 77.

Deeds, Richmond County, Georgia

Georgia Division of Archives and History, Morrow, Georgia

Turner Clanton–John W. Weaver. 21 November 1835, Book W, 466.

————— –John W. Mann. 5 January 1840, Book Z, 223.

————— –Antony Milton. 2 August 1841, Book Z, 376.

————— –Jacob McWhorter. 6 March n.d., Book AA, 465.

————— –James Gardner. 5 December 1846, Book CC, 228.

————— –Charles J. Cook. 5 March 1847, Book CC, 319.

————— –James O. Ring. 13 March 1847, Book CC, 320.

————— –John Finn. 16 March 1852, Book GG, 419.

————— –James Thomas. 6 January 1854, Book JJ, 212.

———–John P. King. 23 March 1854, Book JJ, 654.
———–Nancy P. Farron. 10 March 1856, Book LL, 342.
———–H. H. Cumming. 25 July 1856, Book LL, 342.
———–Hitchcock & Ingalls. 3 January 1857, Book LL, 575.
———–Eliza Robinson. 9 February 1857, Book LL, 637.
———–Turner C. Thomas. 18 June 1857, Book LL, 716.
———–Hitchcock & Ingalls, 5 January 1858, Book MM, 358.
———–Thomas L. Metcalf. 1 June 1858, Book NN, 108.
———–Lewis Lovell. 14 June 1858, Book NN, 139.
———–J. Jefferson Thomas. 27 October 1859, Book NN, 451.
———–James L. Clanton. 3 December 1859, Book OO, 340.
———–J. P. Thomas. 6 December 1860, Book PP, 179.
———–Adolphus P. Bignon. 10 April 1861, Book PP, 390.
———–David Green. 13 September 1861, Book QQ, 65.
———–William J. Vason. 6 January 1864, Book SS, 228–29.
———–Thomas Pinckney. 6 January 1864, Book SS, 227.
———–Jefferson Thomas. 6 January 1864, Book SS, 229.
Turner Clanton Ex. of—Eliza C. Starr. 22 September 1865, Book VV, 290.
———–William C. Poe. 16 December 1867, Book VV, 586.
Ibid. 27 February 1868, Book VV, 586.
———–Eliza C. Starr. 13 February 1867, Book WW, 382.
———–John P. Eve. 7 October n. d., Book XX, 15.
———–Patrick Armstrong. 11 October 1880, Book KK, 161.
———–Charles Phinizy II. 6 January 1887, Book UU, 767.

Trust Deeds. Richmond County, Georgia
John H. Ruffin, Jr. Court House, Augusta, Georgia
Turner Clanton to Trustees Joseph Thomas, James L. Clanton, Jefferson
    Thomas and Thomas McMillan. 6 January 1854. Book JJ. 212–14.
——— to Trustees William Vason, James L. Clanton et al. 7 November 1859.
    Book NN, 451–53.
——— to Trustees Jonathan Pinckney Thomas, James Jefferson Thomas ,
    James L. Clanton and Nathaniel Holt Clanton. 18 December 1860. Book
    PP, 179–81.

Published Sources
Akers, Samuel Luttrell. *The First Hundred Years of Wesleyan College, 1836–1936.*
    Macon GA: Beehive, 1976.
Anderson, Eugene. *Unchaining the Demons of the Lower World: Petition of Ninety
    Nine Percent Against Suffrage.* Macon: Georgia Association Opposed to

Woman Suffrage. Georgia Division of Archives and History, Morrow, Georgia, n.d.

Andrews, Eliza Frances. *The War-Time Journal of a Georgia Girl, 1864–1865.* Edited by Spencer B. King, Jr. Macon GA: Mercer University Press, 1960.

Andrews, Matthew Page, ed. *The Women of the South in War Times.* Baltimore: The Norman Remington Co., 1920.

Annual Catalogue of Wesleyan Female College and Wesleyan Conservatory of Music. Atlanta: Foote and Davies Co., 1905.

Ansley, Lula Barnes. *History of the Georgia Women's Christian Temperance Union from its Organization, 1883 to 1907.* Columbus GA: Gilbert Printing Co., 1914.

Arnold, Gerald Clifton. "Wealth, Power and Influence in Antebellum Augusta, Georgia 1830–1860." Master's thesis, Georgia State University, 1976.

Atlanta City Directory 1896, 1897 & 1899. Case 290, Boxes 39, 40, 42. Georgia Division of Archives and History, Morrow, Georgia.

Augusta City Directory 1891. Augusta, Georgia: R.L. Polk & Co., 1891.

Baker, Paula. "The Domestication of Politics: Woman and American Political Society, 1780–1920." *The American Historical Review* 89 (June 1984): 620–47.

Ball, Edward. *Slaves in the Family.* New York: Ballantine Books, 1998.

Bardaglio, Peter W. *Reconstructing The Household: Families, Sex and the Law in the Nineteenth Century South.* Chapel Hill: University of North Carolina Press, 1995.

Beard, Mary. *Woman as Force in History: A Study in Traditions and Realities.* New York: MacMillan, 1946.

Blair, Karen. *The Clubwoman as Feminist: True Womanhood Redefined, 1868–1914.* New York: Holmes and Meir, 1981.

Blandin, I.M.E. *History of Higher Education in the South Prior to 1860.* New York: Neal Publishing Co., n.d. [1908]. Reprinted Washington DC: Zinger, 1975.

Blocker, Jack S., Jr. "Separate Paths: Suffragists and the Women's Temperance Crusade." *Signs* 10 (Spring 1985): 460–76.

Boatwright, Eleanor. "The Political and Civil Status of Women in Georgia, 1783–1860." *The Georgia Historical Quarterly* 25 (December 1941): 301–24.

Bordin, Ruth. *Frances Willard: A Biography.* Chapel Hill: University of North Carolina Press, 1986.

———. *Woman and Temperance: The Quest for Power and Liberty, 1873–1900.* Philadelphia: Temple University Press, 1981.

Bremer, Fredrika. *The Homes of the New World: Impressions of America.* Translated by Mary Hewitt. 2 vols. New York: Harper & Brothers, 1853. Reprinted New York: Johnson Reprint Corp., 1968.

Brooke, Ted O., ed. *Georgia Wills 1733–1860: An Index.* Atlanta: Pilgrim Press, 1976.

Bruchey, Stuart, ed. *Cotton and the Growth of the American Economy 1790–1860.* New York: Harcourt Brace & World, 1967.

Butler, John C. *Historical Record of Macon and Central Georgia.* Macon GA: J. W. Burke & Co., Printers and Binders, 1879.

Calvin, Martin V., *Calvin's Augusta and Business Directory for 1865–66.* Augusta GA: The Constitutionalist Job Office, 1865. Special Collections, Reese Library, Georgia Regents University, Augusta, Georgia.

Case, Sarah. "Mildred Lewis Rutherfold (1851–1928): The Redefinition of New South White Womanhood," In *Georgia Women: Their Lives and Times.* Vol. 1. Edited by Ann Short Chirhart and Betty Wood. Athens: University of Georgia Press, 2009.

Casey, Dr. H. R. "Reminiscenses of Columbia County." Compiled by Janette S. Kelley in *Our Heritage: Personalities 1754–1983 Columbia County, Georgia.* Thomson GA: Lucky Printing, 1984. Georgia Division of Archives and History, Morrow, Georgia.

Cashin, Edward J. *The Story of Augusta.* Augusta GA: Richmond County Board of Education, 1980.

Catton, Bruce. *The Civil War.* New York: Houghton Mifflin Co., 2004.

Chesnut, Mary Boykin. *Mary Chesnut's Civil War.* Edited by C. Vann Woodward. New Haven and London: Yale University Press, 1981.

Christian Index 1848. Columbia County, Georgia. Georgia Division of Archives and History, Morrow, Georgia.

Clinton, Catherine. *The Plantation Mistress: Woman's World in the Old South.* New York: Pantheon Books, 1982.

Cohn, David L. *The Life and Times of King Cotton.* New York: Oxford University Press, 1956.

Coleman, Kenneth, ed. "An 1861 View of Wesleyan College, Macon, Georgia." *Georgia Historical Quarterly* (December 1967): 488–91.

———. *A History of Georgia.* Athens: University of Georgia Press, 1977.

———, and Charles Stephen Gurr, eds. *Dictionary of Georgia Biography.* 2 vols. Athens: University of Georgia Press, 1983.

Conrad, A. H., and John R. Meyers. "The Economics of Slavery in the Antebellum South." *Journal of Political Economics* 66 (April 1958): 95–130.

Corley, Florence Fleming. *Confederate City: Augusta, Georgia.* Columbia: University of South Carolina Press, 1960.

————. "Higher Education for Southern Women: Four Church-Related
Women's Colleges in Georgia, Agnes Scott, Shorter, Spelman and
Wesleyan, 1900–1920." PhD diss., Georgia State University, 1985.

Cott, Nancy F. *The Bonds of Womanhood: "Woman's Sphere" in New England,
1780–1835.* New Haven and London: Yale University Press, 1977.

Crowly, Mrs. J. C. *The History of the Woman's Club Movement in America.* New
York: H. G. Allen, 1898.

Curry, Betty L. "Wesleyan College, 1836–1886: The First Half Century of
America's Oldest College for Women." Master's thesis, Emory University,
1962.

Degler, Carl. *At Odds: Women and the Family in America from the Revolution to
the Present.* Oxford: Oxford University Press, 1980.

————. *The Other South: Southern Dissenters in the Nineteenth Century.* New
York: Harper & Row, 1974.

————. *Place Over Time: the Continuity of Southern Distinctiveness.* Baton
Rouge: Louisiana State University Press, 1977.

DuBois, Ellen Carol. *Feminism and Suffrage: The Emergence of an Independent
Women's Movement in America 1848–1869.* Ithaca NY: Cornell University
Press, 1978.

Edwards, Kate F. "A College Girl in Wartime." *Georgia Review* (Summer
1947): 198–206.

Edwards, Laura F. *Gendered Strife and Confusion: The Political Culture of
Reconstruction.* Urbana: University of Illinois Press, 1997.

1805 Georgia Land Lottery. Cambridge: Greenwood Press, 1964.

Faust, Drew Gilpin. *Mothers of Invention: Women of the Slaveholding South in the
American Civil War.* Chapel Hill: University of North Carolina Press, 1996.

Felton, Rebecca Latimer. *Country Life in Georgia in the Days of My Youth.*
Atlanta: Index Printing, 1919.

————. *My Memories of Georgia Politics.* Atlanta: Index Printing Co., 1911.

————. *The Romantic Story of Georgia's Women.* Atlanta: n.p., 1930.

Flexner, Eleanor. *A Century of Struggle: The Woman's Rights Movement in the
United States.* Cambridge: Harvard University Press, 1959. Reprinted New
York: Atheneum, 1975.

The Fourth or 1821 Land Lottery of Georgia. Easley SC: Southern Historical Press,
1986.

Fox-Genovese, Elizabeth. "Scarlett O'Hara: The Southern Lady as New
Woman." *American Quarterly* 33 (Fall 1981): 391–411.

————. *Within the Plantation Household: Black and White Women of the Old South.*
Chapel Hill: University of North Carolina Press, 1988.

Freeman, Douglas Southall. "The War Through Women's Eyes." In *The South to Posterity: An Introduction to the Writings of Confederate History.* New York: Charles Scribner's Sons, 1939.

Friedman, Jean E. *Dictionary of Georgia Biography.* Vol. 2. Edited by Kenneth Coleman and Charles Stephen Gurr. Athens: University of Georgia Press, 1983.

————. *The Enclosed Garden: Women and Community in the Evangelical South 1830–1900.* Chapel Hill: University of North Carolina Press, 1985.

Garrett, Franklin M. *Atlanta and Environs: A Chronicle of Its People and Events.* 3 vols. New York: Lewis Historical Publishing Co., 1954.

Gatti, Stacey Horstmann, "Mary Latimer McLendon (1840–1921): Mother of Suffrage Work in Georgia," In *Georgia Women: Their Lives and Times.* Vol 1. Edited by Ann Short Chirhart and Betty Wood. Athens: University of Georgia Press, 2009.

General Catalogue of Princeton University 1746–1906. Princeton NJ: Princeton University Press, 1908.

Genovese, Eugene D. *Roll, Jordan, Roll: The World The Slaves Made.* New York: Vintage Books, 1976.

Georgia's 1832 Gold Lottery. Danielsville GA: Heritage Papers, 1981.

Ghaemi, Nassir. "Make Them Fear and Dread Us: Sherman." In *A First-rate Madness: Uncovering The Links Between Leadership and Mental Illness.* New York: Penguin Press, 2011.

Gilligan, Carol. *In A Different Voice: Psychological Theory and Women's Development.* Cambridge: Harvard University Press, 1982.

Gillespie, Michelle, "Mary Gay (1829–1918): Sin, Self, and Survival in the Post-Civil War South," In *Georgia Women Their Lives and Times.* Vol. 1. Edited by Ann Short Chirhart and Betty Wood. Athens: University of Georgia Press, 2009.

Greene, Fletcher. "Higher Education of Women in the South Prior to 1860." In *Democracy in the Old South and Other Essays.* Edited by J. Isaac Copeland. Nashville: Vanderbilt University Press, 1969.

Griffin, Richard, W. "Wesleyan College: Its Genesis 1835–1840." *Georgia Historical Quarterly* (March 1966): 54–73.

Griffith, Elizabeth. *In Her Own Right: The Life of Elizabeth Cady Stanton.* New York and Oxford: Oxford University Press, 1984.

Gutman, Herbert G. *The Black Family in Slavery and Freedom 1750–1925.* New York: Pantheon Books, 1776.

Hall, Jacquelyn Dowd. *Revolt Against Chivalry: Jessie Daniel Ames and the Women's Campaign Against Lynching.* New York: Columbia University Press, 1979.

Harris, J. William. *Plain Folk and Gentry in a Slave Society: White Liberty and Black Slavery in Augusta's Hinterlands.* Middletown CT: Wesleyan University Press, 1985.

Harwell, Richard, ed. "Louisiana Burge: The Diary of a Confederate College Girl." *Georgia Historical Quarterly* (June 1952): 144–63.

Hembree, Mike, "Historian's Study Provides Intimate Look at Marriages After Civil War." *The Atlanta Journal and Constitution,* Sunday, 27 April 1986, H 5.

Henning, Margaret, and Anne Jardin. *The Managerial Woman.* Garden City NY: Anchor Press, 1977.

Hilliard, Henry W. "Woman—Her True Sphere." In *Speeches and Addresses.* New York: Harper, 1855.

Hinding, Andrea, and Clarke A. Chambers, eds. *Women's History Sources: A Guide to Archives and Manuscript Collections in the United States.* 2 vols. New York: Bowker, 1979.

History of Woman Suffrage. Edited by Susan B. Anthony, Elizabeth Cady Stanton, and Matilda Joslyn Gage. 6 vols. New York: Arno Press, 1969.

Hooper's Augusta City Directory and Business Register 1874–75. Augusta GA: George W. Hooper & Co., 1875.

Index to the Headright and Bounty Grants of Georgia 1756–1909. Vidalia GA: Georgia Genealogical Reprints, 1970.

Journal of the House of Representatives of the State of Georgia of the General Assembly. Milledgeville GA: Prince and Raglands Printers, 1827 & 1831.

Koch, Mary Levin. "Entertaining the Public: Music and Drama in Antebellum Georgia," *The Georgia Historical Quarterly* 68 (Winter 1984): 516–38.

Kraditor, Aileen S. *The Ideas of the Woman Suffrage Movement, 1890–1920.* New York: Columbia University Press, 1965.

Lebsock, Suzanne. *The Free Women of Petersburg: Status and Culture in a Southern Town 1784–1860.* New York: W. W. Norton & Co., 1984.

Lerner, Gerda. "The Lady and the Mill-Girl: Changes in the Status of Women in the Age of Jackson," *Mid-Continent American Studies Journal* 10 (1969): 5–15.

"Magnolia Cemetery Sexton's Records." *Ancestoring.* Vols 3–5. Augusta GA: Augusta Genealogical Society, 1981, 1982.

Massey, Mary Elizabeth. "The Making of a Feminist." *The Journal of Southern History* 39 (February 1973): 3–22.

McCash, William B. *Thomas R. R. Cobb: The Making of a Southern Nationalist.* Macon GA: Mercer University Press, 1983.

McDowell, John Patrick. *The Social Gospel in the South: The Woman's Home Mission Movement in the Methodist Episcopal Church, South, 1886–1939.*

Baton Rouge: Louisiana State University Press, 1945. Reprinted New York: Arno, 1972.

McMillan, Sally. "Mothers' Sacred Duty: Breast-feeding Patterns Among Middle and Upper-Class Women in the Antebellum South." *The Journal of Southern History* 51 (August 1985): 333–56.

Mesic, Harriet Bey. *Cobb's Legions Cavalry: A History and Roster of the Ninth Georgia Volunteers in the Civil War.* Jefferson NC: McFarland & Company, 2009.

Minutes of the Georgia Woman Suffrage Association 1899. Atlanta: Georgia Woman Suffrage Association, 1899.

Morgan, Sarah. *Sarah Morgan: The Civil War Diary of a Southern Woman.* Edited by Charles East. Athens: University of Georgia Press, 1991.

Morris, Richard B. "Women's Rights in Early American Law." In *Studies in the History of American Law.* New York: Columbia University Press, 1930.

Motz, Marilyn Ferris. *True Sisterhood: Michigan Women and their Kin 1820–1920.* Albany: State University of New York Press, 1983.

Muhlenfeld, Elizabeth. *Mary Boykin Chestnut: A Biography.* Baton Rouge and London: Louisiana State University Press, 1981.

Myers, Robert Manson. *A Georgian at Princeton.* New York: Harcourt Brace Jovanovich, 1976.

Nelson, Virginia Lee, ed. *Loyally, A History of Alpha Pi in 1851 at Wesleyan Female College, Macon, Georgia, through 1964.* Atlanta: Alpha Delta Pi Sorority, 1965.

The New Testament. Philadelphia: National Bible Press, 1952.

Norton, Mary Beth. *Liberty's Daughters: The Revolutionary Experience of American Women, 1750–1800.* Boston: Little, Brown & Co. 1980.

Olson, Christopher J. "Eliza Frances Andrews (1840–1931): 'I Will Have to Say 'Damn!' Yet Before I Am Done with Them,'" In *Georgia Women Their Lives and Time.* Vol. 1. Edited by Ann Short Chirhart and Betty Wood. Athens: University of Georgia Press, 2009.

Orr, Dorothy. *A History of Education in Georgia.* Chapel Hill: University of North Carolina Press, 1950.

Osterwise, Rollin Gustav. *The Myth of the Lost Cause 1865–1900.* Hamden CT: Archon Books, 1973.

Pennebaker, James W. *Opening Up: The Healing Power of Expressing Emotions.* New York: Guilford Press, 1990. Revised 1997.

Phillips, U. B. *A History of Transportation in the Eastern Cotton Belt to 1860.* New York: Columbia University Press, 1908.

Price, Margaret Nell. "The Development of Leadership by Southern Women through Clubs and Organizations." Master's thesis, University of North Carolina, 1945.

Pughe, E.H., *Pughe's Directory for the City of Augusta and its Vicinity.* Augusta GA: E. H. Pughe Printer, 1867. Special Collections, Reese Library, Georgia Regents University, Augusta, Georgia.

Rable, George C. *Civil Wars: Women and the Crisis of Southern Nationalism.* Urbana: University of Illinois Press, 1989.

Rees, Frances. "A History of Wesleyan Female College from 1836 to 1874." Master's thesis, Emory University, 1935.

Reprint of Official Register of Land Lottery of Georgia 1827. Columbus GA: Walton Forbes Co., 1976.

Scott, Anne F. *Making The Invisible Woman Visible.* Chicago: University of Illinois Press, 1984.

———. *The Southern Lady: From Pedestal to Politics 1830–1930.* Chicago: University of Chicago Press, 1970.

Sherwood, Adiel. *A Gazetteer of Georgia.* 4th ed. Atlanta: J. Richards, 1860.

Simkins, Francis, and James W. Patton. *The Women of the Confederacy.* Richmond VA and New York: Garrett and Massie, 1936.

Smith-Rosenberg, Carroll. "The Female World of Love and Ritual: Relations between Women in Nineteenth-Century America." In *A Heritage of Women.* Edited by Nancy F. Cott and Elizabeth H. Pleck. New York: Simon and Schuster, 1979.

Solomon, Barbara Miller. *In the Company of Educated Women: A History of Women and Higher Education in America.* New Haven: Yale University Press, 1985.

Tatum, Noreen Dean. *Crown of Service.* Nashville: Panthenon Press, 1960.

Taylor, A. Elizabeth. "The Last Phase of the Woman Suffrage Movement in Georgia." *Georgia Historical Quarterly* 43 (1959): 11–28.

———. "The Origin of the Woman Suffrage Movement in Georgia." *Georgia Historical Quarterly* 28 (1944): 64–79.

———. "Revival and Development of the Woman Suffrage Movement in Georgia." *Georgia Historical Quarterly* 42 (1958): 339–54.

———. "Woman Suffrage Activities in Atlanta." *Atlanta Historical Society Journal* (Winter 1979): 45–54.

Thomas, Ella Gertrude Clanton. *The Secret Eye: The Journal of Ella Gertrude Clanton Thomas 1848–1889.* Edited by Virginia Ingraham Burr. Chapel Hill: University of North Carolina Press, 1990.

Thomson, Eunice. "Ladies Can Learn." *Georgia Review* (Spring 1947): 189–97.

Welter, Barbara. "The Cult of True Womanhood: 1820–1860." *American Quarterly* 18 (1966): 151–74.

Whites, LeeAnn. *The Civil War as a Crisis in Gender: Augusta, Georgia 1860–1890.* Athens and London: University of Georgia Press, 1995.

———. "Rebecca Latimer Felton (1835–1930): The Problem of Protection in the New South," In *Georgia Women Their Lives and Times.* Vol. 1. Edited by Ann Short Chirhart and Betty Wood. Athens: University of Georgia Press, 2009.

Woodman, Harold D. *King Cotton and His Retainers: Financing and Marketing the Cotton Crop of the South, 1800–1925.* Lexington: University of Kentucky Press, 1968.

Woody, Thomas. *A History of Woman's Education in the United States.* 2 vols. Lancaster PA: New York Science Press, 1929. Reprinted New York: Octagon Press, 1966.

Wyatt-Brown, Bertram. *Southern Honor: Ethics and Behavior in the Old South.* Oxford: Oxford University Press, 1982.

Young, Elizabeth Barber. *A Study of the Curricula of Seven Selected Women's Colleges of the Southern States.* New York: Bureau of Publications, Teachers College, Columbia University, 1932. Reprinted New York: AMS Press, 1972.

Index